YOUR
BEST AGE
—IS—
NOW

EMBRACE AN AGELESS MINDSET,
REENERGIZE YOUR DREAMS,
AND LIVE A SOUL-SATISFYING LIFE

YOUR
BEST AGE
— IS —
NOW

ROBI LUDWIG, Psy.D.

HarperOne
An Imprint of HarperCollinsPublishers

HarperOne

HarperCollins books may be purchased for educational, business, or sales promotional use. For information please e-mail the Special Markets Department at SPsales@harpercollins.com.

HarperCollins website: http://www.harpercollins.com

FIRST EDITION

Designed by Jessica Shatan Heslin / Studio Shatan, Inc.

Library of Congress Cataloging-in-Publication Data

Names: Ludwig, Robi,
Title: Your best age is now : embrace an ageless mindset, reenergize your dreams, and live a soul-satisfying life / Robi Ludwig, PhD.
Description: San Francisco : HarperOne, 2016.
Identifiers: LCCN 2015035870| ISBN 9780062357182 (hardback) | ISBN 9780062357205 (e-book) | ISBN 9780062445667 (audio)
Subjects: LCSH: Self-actualization (Psychology) | Aging. | Women--Health and hygiene. | BISAC: SELF-HELP / Personal Growth / General. | HEALTH & FITNESS / Women's Health. | SELF-HELP / Aging.
Classification: LCC BF637.S4 L838 2016 | DDC 155.6/69--dc23 LC record available at http://lccn.loc.gov/2015035870

---

16 17 18 19 20 RRD(H) 10 9 8 7 6 5 4 3 2 1

To Jason and Jaimie,

My hope for you both is that every phase of your lives is

filled with the possibility of achieving all your heartfelt dreams.

Life can only be understood backwards;
but it must be lived forwards.

—Søren Kierkegaard

CONTENTS

1 • IT'S TIME FOR A NEW MIDLIFE 1

2 • ADOPT THE "BEST PRACTICES" OF YOUTH 19

3 • FIGHTING REGRETS WITH RESILIENCE 33

4 • A MIDLIFE WITHOUT ANXIETY OR STRESS 53

5 • FEELING STRONGER EVERY DAY 87

6 • BEAUTY CAN BE A BEAST 119

7 • FINDING LOVE 146

8 • MAKING A LIVING, MAKING A LIFE 177

9 • A SPIRITUAL OPPORTUNITY 200

10 • DISCOVERING NEW PURPOSE AND MEANING 220

Acknowledgments 231
Recommended Reading 233
Notes 235

ONE

IT'S TIME FOR
A NEW MIDLIFE

It was a snowy New York City winter day, and I was hoping it was the last one of the season. My hair was pulled back in a ponytail, I had no makeup on, and I was wearing my signature Saturday outfit—a sweater, leggings, and boots—as I ran around my neighborhood doing errands. At the cash register at my local wine shop, the young man behind the counter asked to see my ID. He must have been in his twenties. I was pleasantly shocked. I said incredulously, "Really?" but I was smiling to myself, *I could be your mother.* The man looked a little scared by my reaction, and he said softly and almost apologetically, "I'm sorry. I just can't tell how old you are, so I need to see your ID." I handed over my ID and then told him proudly, "Even though I'm only five feet one inch tall, I'm almost fifty years old. You made my day."

I learned a life lesson that day: if I have a youthful mindset, a pair of leggings, and apparently a ponytail, age may be just a number. And my number doesn't seem to carry the same weight it did in the past. Every once in a while, I might even get carded.

This is why when I hear the term "middle-aged" it's hard to know how to respond. Although we've been conditioned to think it's practically a four-letter word, the realities of women in midlife today are far different from what our mothers experienced. The truth is, women in their forties, fifties, and even sixties are living younger, vibrant lives. More important, instead of feeling that the best days of their lives are over, they can fill this unique time with promise and potential, even adventure.

Women in midlife are definitely not experiencing the universal malaise some would call a "midlife crisis." The traditional life shifts or passages we used to associate with middle age are no longer occurring on the same timeline for every woman like they did for our mothers and grandmothers. Not all of us are dealing with the empty-nest syndrome because our kids have left home. Instead, some of us in our forties and fifties are still busy raising toddlers, while others have tweens, teenagers, or even grandchildren. Some are just having their first child, or have chosen not to have children at all. We might be reaching the pinnacle of a long career, or reentering the workforce. And our relationships are all at different stages: married, divorced, dealing with the death of a spouse, caring for aging parents—the list goes on and on. That's why I see this new midlife as a time of challenging transitions as well as fantastic possibilities, and not just a time of crisis.

No matter where we are in checking off the goals of a life well lived, those of us in midlife are now at the age when we can use the wisdom we've secured to rebalance and reinvent: taking stock of what we have accomplished and continuing to dream big about what's in store. Our future is really looking good. So why are we still beating ourselves up, living with anxiety, and, overall, feeling so bad?

THE NEGATIVITY PRESSURE COOKER

Women in midlife feel bad about themselves for a variety of reasons. Ironically, the downer cultural concept of "middle-aged" is actually a relatively new one. Until the term "midlife" was first used in 1807, the chronological period that spanned the middle years of a lifetime was seen as the prime of life. Yet somewhere along the way "middle-aged" became a label loaded with pessimism: "old," "over the hill," "getting up there," "out of it," "not with it," "losing it"—whether "it" was our marbles, our job, our spouse, or our looks. Language has power and can be brutal to our ego. What's more, this perception has been infused in the culture so thoroughly that according to a report from the Centers for Disease Control and Prevention, women between the ages of forty and fifty-nine have the highest rate of depression (12.3 percent) of any group based on age and gender in the United States.

In the past, women talked about midlife in terms of "crisis" or "retirement." We've grown up surrounded by that message and subconsciously adopted those same themes. Many in our parents' generation stopped working in their fifties or sixties and were suddenly left with not much to do. So it's no surprise their version of middle age was a transition from hectic work and overwhelming familial responsibilities to a depressingly slower lifestyle, complete with rocking chairs. This model of midlife was often compared to the changes a woman's body experiences during menopause, which in fact was also treated not as a stage in life but as a disease. Whether these women were contemplating their mental function or their hormonal output, the results typically pointed to one word: "decline"!

Our culture continues to overidealize youth to the exclusion of other life stages. After decades of cultural brainwashing, the pervasive imagery of "youth as perfection" makes it hard for women at any age, but especially at midlife, to find their positive, best self and even harder to find their groove. Worse, we create an internal dialogue of self-criticism based on unrealistic comparisons, which keeps us from seeing ourselves accurately and taking advantage of our strengths. For example, a 2014 study proved how perceptions of age are sometimes more convincing than reality. Researchers from Yale University and University of California, Berkeley, found that people who felt and believed they looked young were more effective during exercise than a similarly aged group who actually had worked out for the previous six months. Imagine, then, what negative thinking is doing to the way you perceive your limitations and your future.

During midlife, many women begin to feel negatively defined by society, through external forces like work, dating sites, or the media—over all of which the typical woman has little control. Midlife is a time in our lives when we begin to rethink the life choices we've made, evaluate our impact on others, and decide what we want to do with the rest of our life's journey. These thoughts often surface because, for many of us, this is the first time we contemplate or confront our own mortality. By this time we've come to understand the finalities of life, and all the anxieties that creep up can collide with our internal timeline.

Society's fascination with youth leaves some women at midlife feeling anxious and out of control. This anxiety is often based on fear—the fear that as we age we won't be relevant in a world geared toward young people; the fear that we won't have options; or the fear that it's simply too late for us to have the life we've always dreamed of. These fears may be triggered by our very natural instinct to fast-forward all the way to old age from the place we are now. When we focus on decline at midlife, we're really worrying about what life will be like when we're eighty, entirely skipping the stage we're in. As a result, too soon we can inadvertently give up on ourselves and our potential for enjoying a great life.

The singular experience of midlife crisis is also a myth. Instead, there are many mini-crises along the timeline of life. Some of them first hit in our teens, more hit in our twenties, and they continue throughout our lifetime. They are part of life and part of growing and changing, period! There's no avoiding them. So when you notice that you're now questioning yourself more about your life, don't be surprised. It's typical and totally normal to have some fear and concern about how other people perceive you and what opportunities are still out there.

Each crisis at other times in your life will have a different focus. In your teens, it might be figuring out who you are and finding your independence. During your twenties and thirties, you're dwelling on whether you'll be able to meet your life goals, personally and professionally. In midlife, the crisis is more holistic: Did you make the right choices, and if you didn't, is it too late to fulfill your desires and dreams? What's more, at this stage fear surrounds the perception of irrelevance—the fear of missing out or of being overlooked entirely.

This fear comes to the surface when we look in the mirror or when we think about our working lives. In the world of work, it's very easy for women to feel old. These days, the younger generation barely out of college are the ones the media promotes as the newly appointed darlings. These young adults can feel uncomfortable supervising people their parents' age, and they are sometimes dismissive of our abilities and what we can offer or contribute. Many younger workers view coworkers in their forties and early fifties as "old people who don't like change." But the truth of the matter is, no one likes change, not even millennials.

THE ONE THING YOU CAN EXPECT IN MIDLIFE IS CHANGE

Many women in midlife worry they will get stuck in one place, or worse, their negative personality traits, which cause them emotional pain, will be impossible to change. This fear is based on the prevailing wisdom that people don't change. For a long time this notion was backed by psychology: it was commonly thought that who we were and what we wanted from life was going to be the same five, ten, and even twenty years from now. Our personalities had been formed by each of five major traits, or characteristics, that were largely set by genetics. Consequently, psychologists believed changes in personality would slow as other functions of physical maturation occurred. In other words, as we got older, our personalities became fixed, or static, in terms of the Big Five Traits:

Openness—an interest in a variety of experiences; an intellectual curiosity; an appreciation for adventure, emotions, unusual ideas, and the arts

Conscientiousness—a tendency to be dependable, to be organized, to ex-hibit self-discipline, and to prefer planned over spontaneous activities

Extroversion—a desire to seek social stimulation and be in the com-pany of others; extroverts are often talkative, outgoing, positive, and energetic

Agreeableness—a tendency to be cooperative, rather than antagonis-tic, toward others, and to be compassionate, easygoing, and trusting in nature

Neuroticism—an inclination to be sensitized to unpleasant emotions, such as anger, vulnerability, and depression

But news flash: this isn't the case at all. Noted Harvard psychology pro-fessor Daniel Gilbert first said in his 2014 TED Talk, "Human beings are works in progress that mistakenly think they're finished." People really do change, and you, my friend, can be one of those people.

The most current research finds that even fixed personality traits can evolve over time. This idea is supported by the study of epigenetics, which outlines how it's possible to alter one's genetic destiny by changing non-genetic factors, such as lifestyle choices. Specific behaviors or envi-ronments can actually cause a person's genes to turn on or off without changing the underlying DNA sequencing. From a psychological perspec-tive, this means that while the basic structure of our personality is con-stant, we make choices every day that either support certain traits or allow them to atrophy. A 2003 study published in the *Journal of Personality and Social Psychology* found that traits including conscientiousness and agreeableness continued to improve or change all the way into our sixties. This means we can always work on how we express our personality. When our personality evolves and grows, not only does our perspective change but so do our goals, hopes, and dreams. It might take some practice and not always feel so comfortable, but it is possible to use our core personality traits to our advantage plus suppress the traits that no longer serve us well. This purposeful reassessment is really what psychotherapy, also known as talk therapy, is all about.

Understanding that we can continue to grow and change throughout our life span positively impacts how we experience ourselves now and in the future. Knowing that we still have time to transform ourselves, we feel more confident exploring the ways in which we can improve. It's not too late for us to become a better, more polished version of ourselves.

For instance, the things we think are important are not necessarily set for all eternity. I once worked with a patient who came from a well-off family. When Robin was in her twenties she was only interested in finding a good-looking, wealthy man to marry. She couldn't imagine herself with anyone outside of this "perfect" type of guy. But as she entered midlife—and was still single—she found her values and priorities had changed. She was able to enjoy a beautiful relationship with a professional man who was neither good-looking nor wealthy. In fact, she described him to me with a sparkle in her eye as "bald and old." Even though he wasn't the package she initially had been searching for, he was loyal and loving, and he helped her to feel secure in a way she had never known. She wouldn't have imagined herself loving a man who was so different from what her younger self thought she needed in order to be happy, yet here she was, glowing about her new relationship.

The mistake we make is assuming who we were at twenty is who we have to be at forty or fifty or sixty. Yet, in reality, we've already changed. The wisdom you've gleaned just from being alive has made you a different person. Your environment and your experiences have influenced your priorities, what you want for yourself, and what you want for your future. And this is good news, because if you are unhappy with the woman you are now, you really can change. For example, if you are a woman who doesn't consider herself good with finances, you can work toward being a self-improved, fiscally savvy version of yourself.

During midlife, there's a desire to say "I want to approach life differently." My patient Shelly was an anxious fifty-two-year-old woman who had been taught by her mother to care what everybody else thought of her and to work to make others like her. This goal was well intentioned but misguided, and it became a life lesson that encouraged Shelly to relinquish her personal power to other people, some of whom were not particularly nice or accepting of her. Her mother's message, combined with her innate tendency to feel anxious, made her an extraordinarily insecure person. Shelly and I worked on modeling her behavior on other women in her life who owned their personal power and didn't let other people define them. Now Shelly is able to nicely say no to unrealistic or thoughtless demands others make of her and to respect her own personal boundaries. She's also gotten much better at identifying difficult people, and she no longer takes their behavior personally or feels emotionally assaulted by them.

However important change is, it often comes slowly, as it did for Shelly. You've already developed habits based on what works for you. Some of these are really good habits because they can speed things up and make life easier. You may be attached to working out Monday mornings and can't imagine giving up this habit. Working out Monday mornings is a good habit to keep. But if you are too inflexible in general, it's going to be hard to get through life in a successful way, regardless of what life phase you're in. Yet the changes you implement can lead to a better life. You have an opportunity to give up the limitations you see as fixed parts of your life and become the person you were always meant to be. In fact, this is the perfect time to change and start feeling youthful, healthy, relevant, sexy, wanted, and unstoppable!

WELCOME TO MY MIDLIFE WORLD

I decided to take on the myth of midlife because, as a Gen Xer, I'm right there with you. Gen Xers begin turning fifty in 2015, and like many of you, all my life I've rejected the status quo. So why should I stop now? This part of my life has allowed me to find the real "me" inside all the different labels I carry: wife, mother, career woman, television personality, and psychotherapist. Once I got past what the culture told me I should do and have, and started to embrace what I wanted to do, I found the kind of happiness I never thought possible.

My midlife journey started a few years ago. As a therapist, I know enough about myself to recognize that no matter what hat I'm wearing, I'm constantly measuring myself against certain goals, and I began to notice I was coming up against more fear about these goals as I approached my midforties. In the television business, casting agents started to ask me how old I was when they were interviewing me for a potential TV pilot or an established show. This question began to bother me—not that I'm self-conscious at all about my age, but I didn't like the fact I was being evaluated or judged in some potentially negative way. I began thinking, *I still haven't hit all my goals in life and now it's probably too late. Is this it? Should I give up on these goals ever happening?*

As I got closer to fifty, this idea of reaching a certain age worried me, even though I feel like I'm in my twenties in terms of my maturity and zest for living (twenty-five, to be exact). Yet I began to incorporate some negativistic stereotypes that didn't seem to fit me, my life, or the people around me. In fact, it made me feel really uncomfortable. I intuitively pushed back: *I don't have to be in this place. Wouldn't it be nice if I didn't have to be? What would it look like if every woman could see her future and not be worried that her opportunities were evaporating?*

At the same time, I was working with midlife patients and dealing with their issues of dissatisfaction, finding purpose, and change. So I started doing some research. And once I dug a little deeper, I found there was no "there" there: there is no biological reason why ageism or a cultural negativity toward midlife should exist.

So let's start with the first of what I know will be many reality checks. It's somewhat ironic that while we cling to old-fashioned notions about midlife, the age at which we consider ourselves middle-aged keeps creeping up. Not long ago, the generally accepted threshold for middle age was considered to be about thirty-five, which matched a life expectancy of seventy years. But now, when the average American woman may well live into her eighties, even forty seems too young to be considered middle-aged. A 2013 survey from the United Kingdom reported that fifty-three was the average age at which people first defined themselves as middle-aged. Surely that's optimistic. Interestingly, the survey found that almost half of the over-fifties interviewed felt they had not yet experienced middle age, and eight in ten thought the term "middle age" was much harder to define than it used to be. In the United States we take a less rosy view: a study out of Florida State University found that the inaugural year of middle age was on average pegged at forty-four. Interestingly, when the same female study participants were interviewed ten years later, they described midlife as ages forty-six to sixty-two. The older the respondents—women in particular—the later they envisioned the debut of middle age.

Think about women in their forties, fifties, and sixties today. Does Meredith Vieira, Ellen DeGeneres, Sarah Jessica Parker, Viola Davis, Roseanne Barr, or Christie Brinkley really seem middle-aged? These extraordinary midlife women are no longer considered "outliers" for looking great as they age. They are part of a growing pack that includes Jennifer Aniston, Jennifer Lopez, Jamie Lee Curtis, and Madonna, all of whom continue to turn heads and stay relevant during midlife.

Now let's compare any of these ladies to your grandmother and the way she used to dress and behave when she was fifty. If not your grandmother, then think about a middle-aged woman portrayed in popular culture twenty or thirty years ago. Think Bea Arthur in *Maude* or *The Golden Girls*. That's not how these Hollywood celebs look in midlife now, or how they dress or act. So if you ask me whether it's possible to be forever attractive, forever appealing, my answer is a firm "Absolutely!!"

Midlife is also a time when women can truly flourish. Midlife gives us the opportunity, even the responsibility, to discover who we really are and what we really want, and to find our true purpose in life. This is a time to pursue dreams, not to quit dreaming. It's a time to discover a kind of joy we couldn't fathom when we were younger, because we're no longer dependent on what everybody else thinks. We may have lived our lives for other people in the past, whether we've catered to others and neglected ourselves or we've looked to others for validation or direction. At midlife, we're inclined to say "Wait a minute—there's no advantage to pleasing someone at the expense of pleasing myself." We are finally allowing ourselves to plug into who we are without making any apologies. There's something really ageless, sexy, and appealing about all this potential. That's why I so strongly believe that wherever you are in midlife, your best age is now!

DON'T JUST TAKE MY WORD FOR IT

Ever since the baby boomers hit their forties, the stereotype of midlife has been slowly falling apart. The same men and women who rallied for peace, love, and happiness created a whole anti-aging movement, and their cry continues to be "Forever young." Boomers never accepted their parents' way of life, and they certainly didn't take kindly to aging, becoming irrelevant, or fading into the background of society. Tireless in their efforts for self-improvement, they rejected what they were told aging had to look like, and they did the hard work to make their dreams a reality. They shaped the science that led to the possibilities of living longer and, by doing so, created a paradigm shift we, the next generation, can not only take advantage of but also enjoy.

The research today is showing our midlife to be vastly different from anything our parents experienced. These findings are often based on a longitudinal study called MIDUS (Midlife Development in the United States), which has been tracking a nationally representative sample of more than seven thousand adults since 1995. For example, the MIDUS data has shown that because people are living longer, there is an increased need to live younger. Among Americans aged fifty and older who currently have jobs, 82 percent expect to work in some form during their post-sixty "retirement years," according to a poll by the Associated Press-NORC Center for Public Affairs Research. This may be due to their need to financially support a longer life span, or simply because they don't feel ready to leave the working world behind.

It also seems like it's taking much longer for people in general to grow up, have children, and settle down. If that's the case, many women might not think of themselves as adults until they hit their thirties, and by forty, they certainly won't consider themselves hitting middle age. This is not bad news. In fact, there are inherent rewards to living this way. Feeling younger longer is the antidote to feeling hopeless, overlooked, or as if the future is filled with dead-end opportunities. We have more time to accomplish goals and become who we're meant to be. A youthful identity also encourages a more appreciative attitude for living in the moment. This delay may help us to feel more hopeful, optimistic, and proactive about our future.

Science has been a willing partner to agelessness, offering unprecedented ways to continue to look and feel good and to maintain a high level of vitality. Many women in their forties and fifties are currently living their best lives, thanks to preventive health approaches, an improved diet, a renewed emphasis on exercise, and affordable lotions and potions that really do work. This ability to look younger and healthier longer has certainly influenced our notions of beauty. Fashion has become more casual and universal, and many women in midlife today are quite good at looking youthful. Considering how we dress, wear makeup, and style our hair, when it comes to the way we want to look, there's not a lot of difference between women in their twenties and women in their fifties. The media has also embraced this notion of agelessness. For example, models and celebrities in their fifties often grace the covers of popular magazines, even those that cater to the young. This is a huge cultural shift and triumph for us.

Most women picture themselves in their mind's eye as their twenty-five-year-old self, give or take a few years. This is why women in midlife can be very critical about their appearance and even become depressed or disappointed when they look in the mirror, because in their head they're still twenty-five. Yet science tells a different story. One poll conducted by the *Daily Mail* in the United Kingdom found that women over fifty felt more confident in their bikinis than women at any other age. These bikini babes reported over the years that they had learned how to dress to flatter their figures, and as they got older, they cared less about what other people thought. Researcher Terri Apter reported in her book *Secret Paths* that most of the women in her survey felt they looked far better at forty and fifty than they had expected, and a full 25 percent believed they were more attractive to men than they had been as young adults.

Besides looking better, we're healthier than ever before. According to Laura Carstensen, director of the Stanford Center on Longevity, scientists are beginning to understand the ways by which aging increases the risk of disease. They are also learning exactly how to slow down and even reverse these processes. The very nature of chronic, degenerative diseases is being revealed, which paves the way for individualized, effective therapies—and possibly even cures—for diseases that would have been impossible to imagine even a generation ago. IVF therapy, along with cryopreservation (the ability to freeze and store human eggs), makes childbirth a possibility for women in their late forties or even fifties, which is a total game changer for women in midlife.

Even the way we perceive the midlife brain is changing. We used to believe we were born with all the brain cells we were ever going to have. While other parts of the body were able to regenerate (skin, for example), the cells of the brain would progressively die off and, once gone, could never come back. This was interpreted to mean midlife signaled the beginning of a precipitous mental decline. However, the latest advances in brain imaging have shown that the brain grows new cells throughout our lives in a process called "neurogenesis." We now know we can continue to learn new things, improve thinking and mood, create new memories, and retain cognition well into old age. Several large-scale longitudinal studies have demonstrated at midlife we not only maintain many of the cognitive abilities of youth but also acquire some new ones. In fact, midlife was noted to be a relatively stable period of cognitive development, during which middle-aged adults performed at a higher level than each of the younger groups with whom they were compared.

According to Suzanne Braun Levine, author of *The Woman's Guide to Second Adulthood,* brain researchers now believe that by the time we reach fifty, new growth is taking place in specific regions of the brain that connect past experiences, empathy, and evaluation of priorities. These neuronal connections foster an important reorganization of thinking: we become better able to integrate data and problem solving and to control our emotions. Some call this new synthesis of information "wisdom." Coupled with a better understanding of how the world works and how we fit into it, women at midlife are poised to employ their enhanced brains in order to make better decisions, increase self-control, and achieve greater self-awareness.

Knowing we can continue to learn and we have a vibrant healthy life ahead of us should be encouraging. Carstensen developed a life-span theory of motivation she calls the Socioemotional Selectivity Theory. According to Carstensen, knowing that our brain and body won't fail us anytime soon can influence us to look and feel younger, and also induces the behavioral patterns of someone more youthful, enabling us to remain productive longer.

Unfortunately, the reverse is also true. A Canadian study from the University of Waterloo, based on MIDUS data, showed that feeling older reliably predicts lower psychological well-being among those with negative attitudes toward aging. This means that if you embrace the fact that you have a long and healthy life ahead of you, midlife will be a piece of cake. But if your outlook is less than rosy, all that science has done to help you cannot change your perception or experience of midlife. However, this time gender is on your side. According to Sue Shellenbarger, author of *The Breaking Point: How Female Midlife Crisis Is Transforming To-*

day's Women, the most profound difference in attitude between men and women going through middle age is that women are twice as likely to be hopeful about the future. New ventures, new skills, new romance, and new levels of happiness not only are possible goals at midlife but can be intrinsic elements of our experience.

Don't get me wrong: whatever you are experiencing at midlife is completely real for you. It could be boredom, stagnation, a feeling of worthlessness, loneliness, a lack of meaning, depression, or anxiety. You may find yourself drinking too much, changing jobs or partners, or obsessively shopping. These feelings could be triggered by a trauma, like divorce, a serious illness, menopause, an empty nest, or the loss of a parent. Signs of aging prompt some women to review their lives and begin to feel dissatisfied with themselves or their bodies. Or the feelings can just occur out of the blue.

ENTER THE MIDLIFE PARADIGM SHIFT

Most books about midlife are based on loss, as in "Once you experience menopause, or your kids are out of the house, you should get used to the fact you're going to feel lonely, unattractive, and useless." Now, that sounds like fun (not!). Here's my thinking: midlife doesn't have to be about loss; it can also be a time of gain and tremendous *growth.* Women today have many more options, compared to previous generations, to seek out their true selves and take on the roles they want. For many women, the party can finally get started.

One of the most important lessons for embracing midlife is to see it as just another stage of development. In actuality, it's a stage that's very similar to adolescence, and there are distinct stages of midlife, just as there are distinct stages of development in adolescence. This means the feelings you have—both physical and emotional—are part of the normal, natural process of maturing and growing into who you are meant to be.

Teens experience a transformation as they move from the familiar place of childhood to the new and somewhat frightening land of adulthood, and along the way, they find deeper levels of self-awareness and new perspectives. Their struggles with identity can be both exciting and challenging. I've discovered that many women feel the same way about midlife. Because we are experiencing the same kind of transition, we can grab on to the psychic energy of our teen counterparts to give us a jolt and fuel some bold moves. This doesn't mean we are reverting back to our high school selves or, worse, making a desperate attempt to hang with our kids. We don't have to relive the traumas and awkwardness of our teen years or replicate bad mistakes or anxious, reckless behavior. Finding that teen energy again is about mirroring normal, positive, healthy adolescent behavior. This time around, we have the advantage of our experience and hard-won wisdom, which allows us to reject the immature and problematic aspects of adolescence that may have tripped us up in the past. Our midlife selves know there are repercussions for our actions; however, this shouldn't stop us from taking chances and living life to the fullest.

There it is: the actual fountain of youth we've all been looking for. If we take valuable cues from our younger selves, or even the youth culture around us, we can borrow attitudes and behaviors that are both healthy and helpful. When we attain—or, rather, reclaim—many of the characteristics that made us bound headlong into the future, ready to take on the world, we'll be able to take on whatever comes our way.

My goal for this book is to help dismantle the faulty mindsets we've adopted regarding midlife and replace them with a whole new paradigm using the lens and the lessons of this adolescent model. Think of it as an inner-life makeover—Botox for your brain, as I like to call it.

I've discovered exciting research that explodes the age-based myths and stereotypes that keep women from feeling great about being middle-aged. You'll have access to my step-by-step strategies based on the same psychotherapeutic techniques I use with my patients. These will help you not only feel better about yourself but also become more resilient so you can embrace the woman you are right now.

I'm hoping this book will be your opportunity to say *It's not too late. I can still up my game.* Your challenge is to dig deeper to refine your identity, pinpoint your most deeply held values, and become your most authentic self. This knowledge can help you radically change your perceptions, rebel against society's so-called rules, and open yourself up to new horizons and paths.

You'll first explore the adolescent model more closely, so you can clearly see the developmental parallels. Then you'll dive deep into self-exploration in an effective, systematic way. You'll look at all the facets of your current life and see how you can rebalance them, beginning with the regrets and disappointments you may be carrying. You might have already spotted the patterns in your life that are holding you back. So in the same way you tweak your food choices for optimal nutrition or review your workout routine to get better results, you can reorient your mindset to optimize your life experience.

You'll identify the reasons for your stress and anxiety that are particular to midlife, and you'll learn new ways of letting go and becoming more resilient. I'll explain why the big three lifestyle fixes of better nutrition, exercise, and sleep are critical for women our age and how you can incorporate best practices to improve both your body and your mind. I'll also explode the myths that disconnect aging from beauty, so you can recognize the beautiful woman you are right now.

You'll uncover the secrets of marriage at midlife and learn new strategies for finding love and creating more intimacy. You'll also learn how to stay relevant in the workplace or find satisfaction by converting hobbies and personal interests into exciting new careers. I'll teach you how to let go of the magical thinking of youth, so you can realistically assess what you have and what you need as you move through midlife. I've found that one of the secrets of happiness at this time is to tap into your spiritual side, too. I'll be stressing, as well, the importance of finding your true purpose, which is the holy grail of midlife.

Throughout the book I'll share my stories and those of some of the women I've helped so you can understand how to clear out the mental clutter, see the huge potential midlife promises, achieve your goals, and, most of all, feel good. You'll hear from a bevy of fabulous women who have found midlife to be a time of exploration, growth, change, wisdom, fulfillment, relevancy, and fun. These women are navigating, or have navigated, midlife with finesse. Among them are *Today* show co-hosts Hoda Kotb and Kathie Lee Gifford; Suzanne Somers; supermodel Emme; financial guru Jean Chatzky; novelist and former *Cosmopolitan* editor in chief Kate White; award-winning journalists and television personalities Joan Lunden, Deborah Norville, Tamsen Fadal, and Sunny Hostin; and many more.

LET'S GET STARTED

As a therapist who has been in practice for over twenty years, I know once you get past the myths, stereotypes, and narratives that limit you, you can embrace this period as a launching pad for a truly fabulous time of life. I also know nobody likes to think too much about their troubles. I want to feel like I'm happy with myself and fulfilled more often than not, and I bet you do, too. I've learned over the years that sometimes even the smallest fix can put a person on the right path. It's not always a big leap or a big change. Instead, you can get to the place you want to go or become the woman you want to be by making minor yet important tweaks, which could be life changing. You can improve incrementally to be happy with the woman you are.

As a therapist, I help patients to challenge their ideas that may not be true and I provide feedback that can allow them to experience themselves differently. I've seen my patients break through their fears, change negative attitudes, become more self-forgiving, and make the most of midlife's gifts. Hopefully this book will give you a daily dose of encouragement and these lessons will be incorporated into your personal goals, so you can walk through this world agelessly and gracefully. There is a future you can look forward to and get excited about; in fact, you may just be coming into the best time of your life.

TWO

ADOPT THE "BEST PRACTICES" OF YOUTH

've always been a walk-to-the-beat-of-my-own-drummer kind of gal. When I was younger, I loved the idea of breaking rules (not laws, just rules), questioning authority, and reaching for the biggest dreams possible. It was fun and liberating for me to not want to please anyone but myself—at least some of the time. But as an adult, I've had to rein in a few of my wilder tendencies, like my impulsiveness, so I could effectively navigate the grown-up world. Over the years, the more responsible, conventional, predictable me has taken over, even though on the inside I feel like, and I sometimes even act like, the rebellious teen I have always been.

Once I hit my midforties, I noticed I had become more humbled by life's inevitable setbacks. The hopeful, magical thinking I loved so much, which had served me so well during my youth, was slowly starting to disappear. It was being replaced by a more "realistic," and sadly pessimistic, point of view. I knew that to get my emotional mojo back, I had to find a way to access my adolescent perspective, so I could reenergize my life and move it forward. I started looking for new ideas to get excited about that made me feel fresh and alive, and this brought out new passions that transferred into both my work and my family life. I began writing more about topics I felt passionate about, topics that challenged and inspired me. I turned my passion for vintage jewelry into a commercial venture: I sold jewelry online and in local New York City and New Jersey boutiques. These creative endeavors reenergized my positive perspective on life and helped me feel an increased sense of hopefulness about my future.

This chapter explores the tools I created—for myself and also for my patients—to tap into my teen spirit. I've found that one of the best ways to navigate midlife is to adopt the "best practices" of youth. The most successful midlifers I know and admire manage to brilliantly blend their adult lives with their adolescent selves.

WELCOME TO YOUR SECOND ADOLESCENCE

Just as adolescents transition into adults by discovering who they want to be, at midlife we find ourselves searching to become a more authentic, better version of ourselves. I'm not alone in thinking this way. As far back as 1976, Gail Sheehy referred to this midlife transition as "middlescence" in her groundbreaking book *Passages*. She recognized that women in midlife experience a time of renewed self-absorption, an introspection akin to the teenage years, but it's influenced by the wisdom of experience. In a 1996 article in the *Daily Mail,* Sheehy wrote, "Imagine the day you turn 45 as the infancy of another life. Instead of declining, men and women who embrace a second adulthood are progressing through entirely new passages into lives of deeper meaning, renewed playfulness and creativity beyond the female and male menopause."

Carl Jung first observed midlife as a transition that spans four unique stages, each of which mirrors the stages of adolescent development. It begins as an unsureness of who you are and ends with a transition into figuring out who you want to be. These stages don't always happen in a straight or sequential way, but they can provide a framework to explain some of the common themes and transitions that take place during mid-life. Recognizing these stages can help you to experience the changes in a more natural way. In each of these stages, I've compared what midlifers are going through to the adolescent experience in order to show how pervasive this developmental link is.

Accommodation

In this phase, you continue to present yourself as different people, called "personae," in different situations. To some extent, whether you're in mid-life or not, aspects of your personality reveal themselves in some situations more than in others. Part of this accommodation is necessary. How you act at work is going to be different from who you are when you're out on the town for a night with your girlfriends. You have to present yourself appropriately and sometimes slightly differently in order to successfully navigate your surroundings.

Adolescents take on different personae in an attempt to figure out who they are: they are trying on different roles for size. But by midlife, you've gotten used to presenting yourself at your best in each particular role, and that effort may feel restrictive or inauthentic. The trick is to not get overly stuck or be overly accommodating, especially when doing so conflicts with your essential needs. You can develop a confidence in your core identity, enough to be willing to stick with that persona, regardless of how you believe others perceive you.

Separation

Remember back when you were a teenager, when you believed to your core that you were always right and everyone else was wrong? You developed this feeling because you wanted to separate from your parents and be different. Separation is the struggle to shed the shell that doesn't quite fit anymore. Teens separate from their parents by rejecting their values in an effort to discover and define themselves.

During midlife, you are also trying to find your true identity, but this time the separation is more about leaving behind expectations rather than individuals. You might have lived in an acquiescent place of *yes* in order to please your parents, spouse, friends, or children, or held a cultural notion of what shoulds you were supposed to be living by (should be married, should have children, should work, etc.). Yet by the time we all reach midlife we can better assess what makes us happy and what doesn't. We are better able to say no to these cultural shoulds and instead say yes to our own needs and desires. There is a strong impulse to listen to one's inner voice and reclaim life as one's own. Midlife women can finally live authentically.

I believe the adolescent sense of inner moxie can serve every woman. Now is the time to stop following the rules that have led to stagnation or, worse, to taking on roles you may have never wanted. To transition into an emotionally healthy midlife, there needs to be a rejection of your doing things exclusively for everyone else, especially when those things are at odds with who you are now. A new and wiser self is ready to be born and heard! Give yourself the space and time to ask yourself, *Who do I want to be now? What do I really want? Am I okay if other people don't like my choices?*

Separation from your old self will not be a smooth transition. It will take focus and self-reflection, which is why analyzing yourself is a necessary step. In the same way teens take two developmental steps forward and one back, women in midlife experience separation with a bit of regression. Teens worry that others are judging them. Adolescents can become self-centered and appear preoccupied with their own needs. Young girls are often fixated on their image—constantly checking themselves in the mirror and flipping through magazines, obsessed with fashion. At midlife, it's quite common for unresolved issues to reappear. You can become self-absorbed and overly concerned with your appearance: *Will others still think I'm attractive? Will they think I'm getting too old?* In this state of uncertainty and flux, you might make more of an effort to present a rosy picture to the world, which may or may not match your internal experience. You might be inclined to present your life how you think it should look, not how it really is. However, once you get through the separation phase, you will find yourself choosing to live more authentically.

Reintegration

In this phase you begin to feel more certain of who you are and adopt a more appropriate persona. You know you've entered this stage when you've figured out what you want and take the first step toward creating change. For teens, this can be when they discover a passion, which then leads them to visualize a future based on their talents and what they like. This might occur when a teen aligns herself with a charity she feels connected to, or when she chooses a college or a vocational school. Midlifers emerge from this phase knowing themselves and their goals in a new and impassioned way. For example, a woman who worked in a structured corporate setting may want to honor her more creative side, turning a favorite hobby into a business.

Midlife is a turning point, pivoting you toward new opportunities, but these changes can come with a little anxiety. Reintegration is a process of moving between ideas and execution, from setting new goals to achieving them. This period can include a direct confrontation with the anxiety surrounding change and is resolved when desires turn into actions.

Teens often turn to role models to help them figure out who they want to become, and you can do this, too. Hopefully you'll find some of the women I've interviewed in this book to be worthy role models. You can also turn to people who can help you along your journey, including good friends, family, and even therapists. Plus, your younger self can be a role model in many ways—as can the adolescents in your life, or simply the nature of adolescence itself. Choose two or three youthful role models (people in the public eye or teens you know personally) and find several ways in which they inspire you.

Individuation

In this last phase, you recognize and integrate the conflicts that exist within you and achieve a balance between them. During adolescence, individuation occurs when the young adult no longer sees their choices as a result of anyone telling them what to think but as a free choice based on their own newly emerged value system and desires. Midlife individuation is an internalized recognition and integration of the conflicts that exist within you. It is more about questioning the authority of others than taking charge of your own life. During the process, you ask yourself if who you present to the outer world is in harmony with who you really are. You also begin looking at whether you are meeting the demands others place on you yet not meeting your own needs. And finally, you acknowledge and accept your personal limitations or flaws, especially when you measure them against an idealized image of who you think you should be.

Let's say you always wanted to make an income as an artist, but your artwork hasn't produced those results quite yet. Sometimes the idealized scripts in your head don't exactly play out the way you imagined (and, really, how many internalized scripts actually do?); but this doesn't mean your life is a failure. Far from it! It's important to be able to forgive yourself for not meeting these exact goals while continuing to enjoy your creative expression.

THE PARALLEL EXPERIENCES OF TEENS AND MIDLIFERS

A number of interesting parallels exist between what happens to our bodies, and our brains, during our teens and again during midlife:

The Changing Body

A teenager's happiness is based on how good they look and feel moment by moment. They are in a constant state of physical change, encompassing growth spurts, puberty, and general awkwardness. Internally, their brain is growing and changing at a rapid pace. Women in midlife notice biological changes as well, and some can be just as upsetting or surprising as the changes that occur during the teen years. Ironically, much of our focus is on the same issues we had as teens: our skin, our hair, our teeth, and our weight.

Fluctuating Hormones

The most obvious connection between adolescence and midlife is the hormonal one. For adolescent girls, coming into womanhood and getting comfortable with their bodies is an enormous change. The same is true for women at midlife, but instead of experiencing a surge in hormones, we feel a precipitous drop. Our hormonal decline affects our body and our thinking. Both can lead us to question our femininity, our sexual appeal, and how we feel about ourselves.

In his book *Brainstorm: The Power and Purpose of the Teenage Brain,* psychiatrist Dr. Daniel Siegel took down one of the most powerful myths surrounding adolescence: the idea that raging hormones cause teenagers to "go mad." While hormonal output increases during this period, these chemical messengers are not entirely responsible for teenage behaviors, such as impulsiveness and risk taking. Instead, changes that occur in their brains at this time are largely responsible.

The same can be said for midlife women. The hormonal shift that often occurs during the midlife transition is not entirely responsible for the thoughts and feelings we experience. Feeling discontent with our life or lifestyle, experiencing boredom with aspects of our life that at one point were a source of great joy, and questioning the meaning of life and the decisions we made in the past may all occur regardless of menopause. Hormones alone can't explain all the emotional vicissitudes happening during this time.

The Emotional Roller Coaster

According to Suzanne Braun Levine, the only other time in our lifecycle that the brain consolidates and changes as much as it does at midlife is during adolescence. For teens, the brain changes and reorganization lead to four distinct characteristics of typical teen behavior. It's quite possible that much of the angst and introspection teens are well known for stem from changes that are also occurring in the midlife brain. Let's look at what we know teens experience and how you may be going through something similar:

Novelty Seeking

The developing reward center of the teen brain creates an increased drive for taking risks. Some parents see thrill seeking as impulsiveness, but I prefer to see it as an invitation to be more open to change and try new things. In fact, part of being a successful adult and remaining youthful is this same ability; openness and spontaneity are what keep us engaged in life.

Adolescents are good at novelty seeking because culturally they're allowed to make mistakes and think outside the box. Midlifers also have a strong desire to seek excitement, yet they often inhibit their new desires for spontaneity, fearing that anything uncontrolled or unpredictable is dangerous. It's important to be able to mix things up and experiment. Bestselling author Brené Brown offered advice during a 2010 TED Talk that focused on vulnerability. She suggested that whenever we're hesitant to try something new, "do it anyway. Because when we avoid risk to save our emotions, we numb joy, we numb gratitude, we numb happiness."

That said, the key is always to do this in a thoughtful, intelligent, and nondestructive way, by using the wisdom you've learned. Is this possible? Absolutely! Try on the new you, one step at a time. A new, outside-the-box experience doesn't have to be a dangerous one. It should simply be a step in a new direction, opening up a world of possibilities and horizons.

Social Engagement

Adolescents typically turn to peers to try to feel better about themselves. During midlife, your relationship with girlfriends may take on a new importance as you strive to connect with others who are going through the same experience. You can also turn to your family, therapists, and anyone else you trust who has the ability to see you accurately and to reflect your thoughts back to you in a gentle way. This input can help you feel better about where you are in the world and remove your limited thinking.

Increased Emotional Intensity

Teens can run the gamut of emotions from laughing to crying in a matter of minutes. These emotions are felt very strongly, and moods are intense. Midlifers, like their adolescent counterparts, also experience intense emotions. Feelings can be very complex, and emotions can be contradictory and confusing. Some feelings can even mask other feelings, disguising themselves until we're ready to deal with them. Strong emotions are scary to come to terms with and sometimes even scarier to express.

There's a lot to be said for developing emotional intelligence and understanding your inner emotional landscape. Emotions provide you with valuable insights and information. Your feelings are more primal, honest, and raw than your thoughts. That's why they can provide you with truthful feedback about your internal state. Understanding your feelings can help you to learn what you want more of or less of in your life. Any type of emotional discomfort forces you to reexamine your life. For example, feeling bored could be an indication you've gotten too comfortable in an aspect of your life and need to mix things up a bit. Feelings can also give you a road map to discover the changes you need to make. For instance, if you are envious of a friend's marriage, this feeling could be an indicator that having a successful intimate relationship has become an important priority in order for you to feel satisfied with your life.

Creative Exploration

Adolescence is about curiosity, creativity, and passion. Teens who have it together view themselves as cool, hip, and in touch with what life is all about. They make their own opportunities, and they rebel against the norm. Midlifers who have it together have a similar creative desire: they want to change up the rules they've been following, but they see change as a way to improve their lives. They are exploring new ways to feel better about themselves and the lives they've created.

Exploration is the ability to give yourself new challenges so you can find the right direction for the rest of your life. Being curious makes you a more interesting person. Staying open not only makes life more fun but also has a number of surprising benefits:

Curiosity about people and the world can make your social life richer. You add more people to your inner circle, and you become more interesting to them.

Curiosity decreases anxiety. Your curiosity and ability to get to know new people might push your anxieties into the background.

Curiosity correlates with happiness. Some believe we develop a "happiness set point" at an early age. We exist at this baseline happiness level most of the time, and the level goes up or down depending on life events. Staying curious can kick your set point up a few notches as you open yourself up to new ideas, people, and events.

I know many women who wouldn't want to repeat adolescence, but we can learn from our past in order to guide us into our future. In the same way we successfully bridged from childhood to adulthood, we can do it again as we seek to become more relevant and better in every way. If we can approach midlife in this new context of taking risks, connecting with friends, becoming more in touch with our feelings, and creatively exploring our options, it just may force us into a whole new world of possibilities.

BORROW THE TEENAGE MINDSET

We know from the multitude of twin studies that lifestyle and life experiences can not only affect genetic expression but also physically age us and our outlook. When identical twins leave home, their lifestyle choices affect both the way they look and how they perceive themselves. According to Brandeis University professor Margie Lachman, people who consider themselves younger are overall happier. This research shows that we have the power of choice. If we choose to live more aligned with our adolescent selves, we can make choices that work for us that will then positively influence our life. When we remove ourselves from the adolescent way of thinking, life runs the risk of becoming boring, isolating, dull, and routinized. Could this distancing be another reason behind the stereotypical midlife crisis? It's very possible. Just at the moment when we are finally "all grown up," we let go of our adolescent energy, and we mourn that loss.

Losing our adolescent oomph makes us feel stuck and bleak about the future, which is such a depressing outlook. Who wants to experience this feeling, especially when we don't have to? No one! We all want to feel joyful, excited, recognized, and alive. If feeling grown up forces us to view our lives so harshly, maybe we need to turn this unflattering light off and try a new approach.

Now, you may be thinking, *Great idea, but when I see my friends acting and dressing like teenagers I'm appalled.* Maybe your friends have taken things too far, but if you ask me, there's some kind of hidden brilliance in their actions, even though it has taken a slightly misguided turn. You want to borrow from the energy and enthusiasm of adolescence, as long as you can also accept that your best age is now, not back when you were eighteen. The goal is to be in sync with your adolescent energy without making poor, short-sighted, or immature decisions about your life.

I was once asked by the producers at *Entertainment Tonight* if there was a psychological reason celebrities acted immature as compared to their real age. Celebrities are inherently creative individuals who choose to present an image that feels eternally fresh and new. They often look young because they probably feel youthful. The fact that they can achieve this ageless state gives the rest of us the license to follow suit and shoot for our own eternal youthfulness. This doesn't mean you're allowed to go all "actors gone crazy," but you can get in touch with your inner artist, which creatively encourages you to be more and do more. In fact, a longitudinal study published in the journal *Developmental Psychology* in 2015 found that the behavior of rebellious, rule-breaking teens was the greatest predictor of those kids growing up to earn more than their peers. It's interesting that a characteristic typically considered negative for teens has been found to have a positive outcome. Perhaps it is a greater willingness to stand up for themselves and reject the status quo that leads to a more financially favorable outcome.

The study suggested that this type of youthful, defiant behavior could benefit both teens and adults in the right contexts. You can trigger your teen spirit any time you have a midlife moment—whether you're facing an obstacle, gearing up to meet a goal, or plotting your evolution. These tools allow you to be more mindful of your intentions rather than just live in a constant state of reaction.

Adopt a Teenage Perspective

Today's adolescents are noticeably delaying their entry into adulthood. They are taking life slower and being more thoughtful. After all, what's the rush? They've figured out they have many more years to accomplish their goals. If we are going to mirror the healthy aspects of adolescence, can we take midlife more slowly? As I've explained in the previous chapter, we already do. That's why we're all at different stages in our lives, even if we are the same chronological age.

Think about your options with a teenage perspective, and use a teenager's powers of curiosity, tenacity, and spontaneity to increase your own:

- The power to speak up, question authority, and shake things up a bit
- The power to try new things and ask for help if you need it
- The power to adopt a sense of possibility and optimism
- The power of relying on your peers
- The power to stay current
- The power to say no
- The power to be a little naughty and rebellious

Cue the Music

When we were teenagers, many of us were very attached to music. Songs that were popular when we experienced key moments of our adolescence often left a lasting impression. The romance, symbolism, and mythology of music speak to us when we're emotional, creative, or looking for answers.

You can create a playlist of your favorite songs from your high school years to get in touch with your inner teen. Pick songs that make you move or bring a smile to your face. Think about the personality you would like to have or the attitudes you would like to adopt. Consider the qualities and attitudes of your younger self that you liked, or ones you wish you'd always had. Choose songs that symbolize these qualities or make you feel them.

Create the time and space to listen to this music regularly. See what new insights and feelings come up for you. Think about how this music influences the way you think about yourself, your emotions, and your goals. Then switch up your playlist to reflect your evolving sensibility.

Tap into Your Past

Instead of the time-honored question "What wisdom would I share with my younger self?" turn the tables and ask "What could my younger self teach my older self?" There's so much we can learn about ourselves in midlife by revisiting our teen years.

Your younger self might remind you about your original goals and dreams. She might encourage you to be true to yourself and your journey, and to fight for what you want until you make it happen. She might remind you to believe in yourself and your future because you're worth it. She would definitely teach you to fight for your yeses and not take no for an answer, to live in the moment and follow your fun, even if you have to rebel and break some rules. She just might help you find your path to feeling happy, fulfilled, and successful again.

• • • • • • • • • • • •

In the rest of the book we'll explore some of the common themes of midlife and how adopting this new, more youthful approach can help us get through them. Here's my challenge: if age is a mindset, what if you embrace life with the same kind of excitement and optimism you had when you were starting out and thought the world was your oyster? Let's change the negative midlife storyline and get unstuck! Let's do it together.

Leverage your adolescent self—or an even better version, the adolescent you always wanted to be—as you take on midlife. In this way, you can discover who you really are and pursue what you want. The first step is to determine exactly what's holding you back.

THREE

FIGHTING REGRETS
WITH RESILIENCE

When I was in my early twenties and wildly ambitious, I remember making a bold statement to my analytic training supervisor: "I don't want to live my life having regrets." I was trying to say I wanted to make choices that wouldn't limit or hurt me and would allow me to explore my full potential. I had seen both family members and friends make poor choices they later regretted that derailed their lives and created real problems for them. I wanted to avoid these unfortunate and frightening outcomes.

My supervisor was a woman in midlife, and she nonchalantly responded, "Robi, it's impossible to go through life without having any regrets."

At first I was a little shocked by her remark. But once I gave it some thought, her words loudly resonated with me. She was absolutely right. We always have to choose one option over another, and each choice always has an impact. Even when we are faced with the most optimal or the easiest choices (chicken or fish; the black shoes or the brown ones), some of our decisions will invariably lead us down a path of regret.

Now that I know more, at midlife, I understand I will have regrets, but I try not to get stuck in them for too long. I've learned through my teachers, my patients, and the wisdom of getting older that it's not so much the regrets that hold us back but how we handle them. We don't have to let regrets pull us down or stop us from achieving our dreams. In this chapter I'm going to show you exactly how you can both acknowledge your regrets and use them to your advantage, so you can not only move past them but move joyously forward.

THE REGRETS OF MIDLIFE

Psychologist Margie Lachman believes that midlife is typical of any experience we're in the middle of: it's a time when we naturally look back to see what has come before, and then we look ahead to determine what comes next. For some women, the view they encounter when looking back from midlife is tainted by regrets. While regrets can surface at any age, midlife can be a time for confronting aching disappointments: *I didn't meet my goals. Is there still time left to accomplish my dreams, or am I fooling myself? Should I embrace my present reality even if I'm not satisfied?*

Our midlife regrets can be very different from those our mothers battled with. Remember, we're coming into midlife at different points on the timeline of life experiences. What's most interesting about midlife today is that regardless of the specific nature of our regrets (family, career, money, love, appearance—the list goes on), women tend to regret the things they didn't pursue rather than the decisions they made. For us, it's easy to see on our self-prescribed timeline the dreams that have gone unfulfilled, and these can range from the mundane to the big-ticket items of life: a family, a loving relationship, a career, or an adventure. We see a long future ahead of us and recognize that there is still time to achieve our goals and dreams if only we can get ourselves unstuck from the parts of our lives—or ourselves—that aren't working. This is when regrets lead to "counterfactual thinking"—the ability to imagine alternatives to our past that never took place. When we only focus on what we could have been or done, we miss the happiness in the moments taking place right now. What's more, the goals we haven't pursued become idealized when compared to our reality. For instance, one of the most wrenching counterfactual regrets my midlife patients express is not having had children when they were younger.

A second type of regret at midlife is ending up in a place we didn't expect to be. This regret also addresses the multiple paths we could have, should have, would have taken as well as the choices we actually made that didn't turn out so well. Some women regret their inability to achieve the perfect version of whatever they were looking for, and they link their regret with guilt. We blame ourselves for not making the right choices or choosing the one right path, which at least in theory would have led to greater success. This type of regret causes us to distrust ourselves and our ability to choose wisely in the future, which can be terribly paralyzing and consequently keeps us stuck, because if we don't believe we can make good decisions, there are no other options than our present reality. Psychoanalysts Mildred Newman, Bernard Berkowitz, and Jean Owen noted in their classic book *How to Be Your Own Best Friend* that the most unsettling experience for people is to acknowledge they were wrong. Yet part of learning to trust yourself again begins with learning from the choices you made that didn't work out so well.

Bronnie Ware, a palliative nurse in Australia who became a bestselling author, was privy to expressions of regret by dozens of her patients in their last weeks of life. She wrote in her book *The Top Five Regrets of the Dying* that many of her patients shared the same regrets: they wished that they'd lived a life true to themselves rather than the life others had expected of them; that they hadn't worked so hard; that they'd had the courage to express their feelings; that they'd stayed in touch with friends; and that they'd let themselves be happier. Each of these regrets is connected to the same theme: we often get caught up in living life the way we think it should be lived, even if it is not in sync with who we really are.

REGRETS LINGER WHERE OPPORTUNITY KNOCKS

While you may have your fair share of regrets, you can use them to move forward and create a positive change. Regrets should not be viewed as insurmountable roadblocks. Instead, I believe regret is often a valid reaction when you are reflecting on your life, and you should be proud that you have been able to identify these sometimes painful feelings.

The key is to use your regrets to your advantage. They can be a real wake-up call to inject energy and meaning into your life. During midlife, regrets can create new opportunities and shifting points because you are finally ready to be in the world on your own terms. Your regrets force you to look at what doesn't work for you and, if used properly, can also force you to make those much-needed changes while you still have time.

Regrets can be very helpful because they get you to ask specific questions, to analyze yourself against your true potential, and to think about other alternatives to achieving your goals. As psychologist Roger Gould describes it, the midlife woman sees her regrets in the context of "Now I'm ready to own myself. I'm ready to acknowledge who I am and who I'm not, and move forward." At midlife, you can finally ask yourself the hard questions: *What do I need to do differently in order to live life with a real sense of fulfillment? Am I pushing myself hard enough? Am I using my talents and skills, and doing what I'm meant to do in the world?*

I love Gail Sheehy's perspective on regrets and failure, which I heard her describe recently during an interview for her new memoir, *Daring*. Sheehy insightfully said, "Life's about failing up." I couldn't agree with her more. We are all going to fail, so let's make sure that we can learn from it. Failure can lead us to a better place if we let it. But we may need to remind ourselves of this powerful idea first. This is why we constantly need to tell ourselves, *If I'm going to fail, let me fail up.*

Recognizing a problem is the first step toward finding a solution, and when your happiness is at stake, there's no better time than now to take a good, hard look at your regrets. Happiness is a choice available to everyone. In order to use regrets in the most positive way, you need to see the connection between the choices you make, why you make them, and where these choices will lead you. If you don't like where you are landing in life, then it's up to you to learn from the experience and make it better. Staying stuck in old patterns and habits, preferring the "comfort" of familiarity, or fearing change can encourage you to pretend you are content. But if you can't pretend any longer, it's important to ask yourself, *How did I end up in this place? Why is this choice not good for me? What can I do about it? While I can't change the past, what can I do to correct it or make my life more right for myself now?*

Regrets are very painful. Once you've identified your regrets, the next step is to acknowledge the feelings they bring up, so you can fully confront the past and get out of your own way. The more you can accept your feelings, the easier it will be for you to release the shame and debilitating power they have over you. Then you can be kinder to yourself, which is the next step in becoming completely free from what's holding you back from creating real and lasting change.

SITTING WITH THE EMOTIONS OF REGRET

Feelings are not facts, but they can sure fool us into thinking they are. We believe what we feel. If we feel hopeless, we think things may always be hopeless. If we feel anxious, we think there is something to be worried about. But in reality, our feelings can be unreliable, because they are based on our perceptions, which are only sometimes accurate. We look at every situation from only our vantage point, and sometimes this perspective is influenced by our past experiences rather than what's happening in the present. This can lead to intense reactionary emotions, which can interfere with our ability to see other possible interpretations of our life. What's more, feelings are changeable from one moment to the next. This is why it's important to respect and acknowledge your regretful feelings, but not to believe they are predictors of your future.

Feelings of regret are characterized as "negative distortions," convincing you that you're a victim of life instead of a co-creator. Negative distortions occur when you view your life from the prism of "the glass half-empty." Feeling sorry for yourself and making yourself into a victim is terribly disempowering. It's far better to distort life in terms of seeing things from an overly optimistic vantage point, because that inspires you and helps you to continue moving forward.

In the extreme, women in midlife can experience regret as feelings of either hopelessness, depression, or paralysis. These intense feelings limit your ability to see a positive outcome for any particular situation. These thoughts are so dark, you may try very hard to control or suppress your regrets and the emotions surrounding them. Unfortunately, keeping these feelings locked inside, or refusing to acknowledge them, only gives them more power over you, leaving you to feel even more oppressed.

Envy and jealousy are two close cousins of regret. Feelings of anger, bitterness, and resentment can develop when you believe other people have figured life out and have it better than you do. When you're envious of people who have more or have it better, you're going to feel some degree of regret about your life, even if it's wholly unwarranted. The truth is, there are always going to be people who have more than you do, no matter how much or how little you have. If you use envy as a way to understand what you want to strive for, great. But living your life focused on all the things you don't have leads to unhappiness. You miss out on enjoying life because you're spending too much mental energy on what you don't have instead of on what you do have.

All these negative emotions can be difficult to tolerate. Most of us don't want to sit with feelings of defeat, and who could blame us? We often don't know how or where to express our emotions, or because we have so much guilt about them, admitting these feelings can be painful or make us feel bad about ourselves. Bronnie Ware wrote in her book that many people suppress their feelings in order to keep the peace with others. As a result, they settle for a lackluster existence because they never take their own feelings into consideration.

In order to get past your regrets, you must first validate your emotions and then use them in a healthy way. The key is to put your feelings into perspective, learn from them, and use them as launching pads to propel you forward. Sit quietly with yourself and your thoughts. Accept your feelings as valid reflections that should be considered normal under the circumstances. Let go of the self-victimizing, "Woe is me" attitude and understand that feeling powerless is actually a signal you're sending yourself that something is wrong. Have the feelings; don't deny them. Feel them fully until they pass, because they will pass. And when they do, you'll realize you survived them and the feelings themselves were not what was holding you back. Instead, you allowed the feelings to impact your behavior. For example, if your regrets made you feel envious of others, it wasn't the feeling of envy that held you back, but how you chose to deal with your envy.

Next, you have to allow yourself a period of grieving, because grieving is not just for when you've lost a loved one. You can also grieve for your regrets and disappointments, the parts of your life that didn't work out as planned, especially if they stem from a relationship that ended or a career that didn't quite work out. Then stop beating yourself up. Punishing or shaming yourself will only keep you frozen with your regrets in an uncomfortable place. Instead, start changing your self-talk, your inner dialogue, to something more positive. Replace *Woe is me; things will never change* with *I know I want something different. I can have something different. I just need to figure out how to do it and who can help me.*

The last phase is forgiveness. Make your apologies to yourself and others who may be party to your regrets. Acknowledge the role you played in your shortcomings. Give yourself a time limit and say, *Okay, I've punished myself enough.* And then it's time to move on.

One powerful strategy that synthesizes this experience and puts your emotional reactions in perspective is to rewrite key aspects of your regrets from a more balanced, empathetic place. Be the heroine or the fabulous biographer of your life.

My patient Cynthia was really angry that her excessive drinking was robbing her of the life she had always wanted to live. At forty-five, she regretted not being more successful in her personal and professional life, and she was horribly envious of her brother, who had been able to achieve many of the accomplishments that seemed to have passed her by. When we worked on rewriting the story of her life, she was able to find the ways in which she was in fact the heroine. She was willing to manage her addictive drinking through attending therapy and joining AA, and she was starting to see results. I taught her to say to herself, *I know I have to work on my drinking, but there are areas in my life that I handle well and will continue to handle well even while I'm getting better. I can trust myself to make better decisions from now on.* She used this mantra every time she started to get angry, and she found that it helped her to feel better about herself. I was also able to focus her attention on her personal strengths: Cynthia had a great sense of humor, and people were naturally drawn to her vibrant personality. We worked together to think about new career opportunities in which she could thrive based on her ability to interact well with others. It wasn't long before we realized that she was a natural for sales, and she got a job as a luxury travel agent.

Once Cynthia saw there were positive aspects of her life and recognized the areas in which she experienced herself to be special, her angry edges began to fade away. Redefining her story by focusing on her strengths allowed her to let go and grieve her regrets and, in doing so, feel more hopeful about her future. Coming to terms with her regrets increased her self-esteem, helped put her past into the proper perspective, and gave her the confidence to effectively beat her addiction.

USING YOUR REGRETS FOR A BETTER FUTURE

If regrets or disappointments are holding you back from fully experiencing the life you desire, you need to shift yourself to a different vantage point. You need to reframe regrets as lessons and opportunities waiting to happen. You can do this by leveraging the power of hindsight.

At midlife, our regrets allow us to recognize exactly how we are responsible for the decisions we've made and how these decisions may not suit the women we've become. Yet we rarely stop to consider the impact these choices had at the time they were first made. No matter what part of your life they affected, your choices may have been exactly right for you then and served you beautifully for years. There is no way you could have foreseen how different your needs and desires would be someday. You went with whatever decision felt good or you thought was okay enough at the time. The problem is, you've changed.

Hindsight first gives you the opportunity to put your life into perspective, which can neutralize regrets. It allows you to see where you need to take responsibility for your actions and when things were completely out of your control. You're not the cause and effect of everything that happens in your life; there are other forces—the economy, someone else's behavior, or world events—that can influence your story. Once you fully understand how these forces and your actions played into the situation you find yourself in, you can relinquish the role of a powerless victim of circumstances. If you're stuck believing *I'm the victim,* it makes it harder for you to trust your ability to make decisions for your future. But if you can own up to the choices you've made, even if they didn't work out, then you're giving yourself the power to make different, better choices.

In order to fully let go of your regrets, use hindsight to reflect on your original decisions, uncover the original legitimacy of your choices, and determine what you've gained from those decisions. Ask yourself the following two questions:

If I had done things differently, would I be in a better or different place right now? For example, if your marriage failed, you can still acknowledge, *If I hadn't gotten married, then I wouldn't be a parent.* Instead of dwelling in regret, focus on what you learned about yourself through the experience, what you may have gained, and what you now need to do to create the future you want.

Why did I make this choice? The answer might surprise you. There are reasons for every decision. You might learn that choosing to marry this person wasn't because you were a bad, dumb person who doesn't know how to take care of herself. It could be something as simple as you were young and had a particular idea of what a happy relationship was about (an attractive spouse, a strong partner, the promise of money). Your decision to marry might have been based on pleasing someone else, such as a parent. Whatever comes up, accept and understand where you were coming from. In the broader scheme of things, you may find that a decision wasn't a failure at all. It was instead a turning point—one of the important life moments we need to have in order to learn and grow.

Another aspect of hindsight is counterfactual thinking—the *What if . . .* and the *If only I had . . .* thoughts that occur when you examine how your life could have turned out differently. While counterfactual thinking can be one of the lenses you use to analyze your regrets, when used in the right way, it is a tool that can help you identify behaviors that did not work. Then you can learn from them and move into the future better equipped to make good choices. By comparing what actually happened with what you now believe you wanted to have happen, you can strategize and actually do things differently in the future.

Researchers have found that through counterfactual reflection, the upsides to reality are identified, a belief in fate emerges—the belief that events happen for a reason—and ultimately more meaning is derived from these life events. For women in midlife, this means that when we compare the what-ifs to what really happened, we can end up feeling at peace. This ability to feel at peace is part of our inner wisdom, our intuitive and knowing voice that guides us and helps to protect us in the future.

• • • • • • • • • • • •

My patient Jerri was a publishing executive who stepped off her career track to raise her children. While at the time she had felt certain it was the right decision, getting back into the game at fifty-one proved harder than she had expected, and whenever we talked she constantly bemoaned her fate, berating herself for putting her career on hold.

Jerri engaged in a lot of counterfactual thinking whenever we got together. For example, she was certain it was too late in her life to reverse her fortunes and get a new job, and she repeatedly said, "If only I had stayed in the workforce, I could have my dream job by now, instead of settling for being a midlevel manager."

I told her we needed to explore the decisions she had made regarding her career in order to move forward. I asked her to use hindsight to find out if her actions at the time had made sense. When she looked at her hiatus from publishing closely, she admitted it was the right decision for her at the time, because her family was her number-one priority. Her years with her children had been invaluable. Unfortunately, she had to deal with the fact her decision had unwelcome consequences: it made it hard for her to simply pop back into the world of publishing, which had changed dramatically during the interim.

While Jerri couldn't go back in time to alter her behavior, she did realize there were steps she could take now to resume her career. Instead of remaining mired in hopelessness, she got back in touch with her former colleagues and contacts, and she took a couple of freelance jobs so she would be in a better position to reignite her career.

As Jerri did, use what you've now learned from hindsight to ask yourself the following:

How have my choices turned out?

What results did I think these choices would produce?

What do I want now?

What do I need to do to change my situation?

If I want to be a different kind of person, what different choices do I need to make?

Do you ever find yourself trying to figure out the *whys* of life? When you're stuck ruminating about your past and your regrets, the kind of questions you may ask yourself can make a huge difference in how well you're able to move forward. Focusing on *why*—why something happened, why you behaved in a particular way, why things turned out the way they did—can sometimes feel like an exercise in futility, a search for answers you'll never be able to find. And *why* questions can sometimes result in judging and blaming yourself, which further incapacitates you.

If the *whys* don't reveal the answers or forgiveness you're looking for, try switching the question to *what*. Focusing instead on the *what* questions, especially if the *why* questions don't get you anywhere, may be more helpful and lead to a clearer vision of the actions that need to be taken now without the judgment of why things turned out as they did. *Why* questions lead to internalizing; *what* questions lead to creating solutions: *What could I do now? What could I learn from this? What was happening at the time that led me to make this kind of decision?*

ADOPTING A "YOU ONLY LIVE ONCE" SPIRIT

As I mentioned earlier, we tend to regret the path not taken more than the path taken. We measure the missed opportunity against the fantasy outcome that never played out. Teens quell this resentment with their living-in-the-moment attitude, and they take advantage of every opportunity that comes their way. Teens are more open to taking chances because they don't think about consequences. The cause-and-effect part of the brain, located in the frontal cortex, is not fully formed yet, so there's more magical thinking going on in teenagers' heads, especially when they say to themselves, *It'll all work out!*

Teenage regrets are usually viewed in the short-term, and the consequences aren't so damaging, as in, *I hurt my friend's feelings* or *I dented the bumper of the car.* Teens have time on their side to fix whatever is broken. They make choices in the here and now most often. Because of this, young people talk freely about living a life without regret. This is embodied in one of their favorite phrases: "You only live once."

"You only live once" is one way of saying yes to life, and in midlife we should be including more yeses in our lives. Whether or not every opportunity presented to you is officially on your bucket list, just try something. It doesn't even have to work out. Maybe you do it just because it's fun. A Columbia University researcher found that people who let opportunities pass them by or chose the virtuous road instead of the iconoclastic one had more regrets in their lives over time. The study participants who said yes to life felt less regret even if they made a decision that didn't work out. They were simply happy to have had the experience.

I cautiously advise saying yes to life, with the caveat that you use your midlife wisdom and developed frontal cortex to be thoughtful about your decisions. Say yes to life, but do it in a way that's exciting, not dangerous. Yet don't be so careful or obsessional that you stop yourself from having an experience that might work out well.

Social media and teens are completely intertwined, and you can participate as well. Facebook, Twitter, and Instagram allow us to share the new experiences we are trying through posts and photos. Seeing how other people respond to them is empowering and adds another layer of excitement to life. I think it helps us to embrace more yeses because we get to show off and we get credit for it. It's definitely an exhibitionistic display, but one that gets us to more objectively see what works for us and what makes our life feel exciting and rewarding.

Embracing a "You only live once" attitude allows us to see all the possibilities out there for every aspect of life. For example, teens explore alternative techniques to reach their goals. They research whatever interest they have and then try to turn it into some kind of business experience. My son uses eBay as a way to research how to earn money buying and selling sneakers on the Internet. Business is a passion of his. He didn't let a fear of failure stop him from exploring his options. He saw his friends earn money and be entrepreneurial in this way and thought, *Why not me? If it doesn't work out, then at least I tried.* I like my son's philosophy. It was very bold and courageous, and ultimately it has been a great learning experience for him, too.

If you regret not following a more fulfilling career path, what creative *yes* could you incorporate into your life? What could be your strategy for living successfully in the moment? Would it be starting a side business based on a hobby you love? Is there a way you can explore your passions to add more zest into your career aspirations or your life?

RESILIENCE WARDS OFF FUTURE REGRETS

The emotionally resilient midlife woman knows how to roll with the vicissitudes of life, including the moments she feels regretful about. She won't let regrets stop her from navigating life purposefully and successfully. When she falters, she has the inner confidence to pick herself back up and move on. She doesn't get stuck in the past or confuse the painful past with what's in store in the future.

Resiliency is the process of adapting well to life's changes, adversities, and stressors. It's having the ability to bounce back from difficult experiences, regroup, and realign yourself with your goals. Resiliency is about practicing self-forgiveness, understanding how you got to a certain place, and using this information to improve your life. It's more of an empowering idea, and it includes a lot of creativity.

A 2014 study led by Concordia University Chicago scholars found that the ability to navigate adversity in a manner that protects well-being can also protect against the negative impact of disability in later life. For women in midlife, this means that the more resilient they can become now, the stronger they will be when facing adversity as they get older.

Resiliency is not a personality trait people have but rather a group of behaviors, thoughts, and actions that can be learned. Coming up with real, concrete strategies you can use in the future can help increase your capacity for resilience. By thinking about your past experiences and identifying sources of personal strength you could have called upon, you can develop new strategies for dealing with difficulties in the future. It's like a mini-metamorphosis during which you learn to shed the choices or mind-sets that haven't worked in the past (e.g., holding on to unresolved regrets or counterfactual thinking), and as a result you're better equipped to face change and difficulties as they arise.

Three traits of resiliency are self-efficacy (standing up for yourself), mastery, and gratitude. Self-efficacy allows you to use either newfound knowledge or your inner wisdom to forge a path and advocate for yourself. Mastery is the confluence of creativity, thinking outside the box, and putting the time in to be good at something. Gratitude is the ability to appreciate your life no matter what; it's a starting point from which to view yourself and your life differently, and with thankfulness instead of regret.

Regrets and gratitude have to be balanced. Gratitude allows you to look at a situation, no matter how awful it is, and find the gift it gave you. The resilient person finds the gift and then moves forward with purpose. One way to increase resiliency as you work through past regrets is to ask yourself, *How could things be worse?* and recognize that while you might not have it all, there are people who have less. Research shows this type of downward social comparison allows us to look at what we have through a new, appreciative, less entitled lens. In this way, we can turn our disappointments into gratitude.

Try this exercise:

Whenever you can be quiet and reflective, write down three things you are grateful for, or three things that went well during the day and that you're happy about. Include in your list at least one reason you're grateful to be the age you are. Perhaps you handled a crisis at work far more smoothly than you could have earlier in your career. Maybe you were able to laugh at something that might have made you mad when you were younger.

Try repeating the exercise daily, reviewing the impact it has on you. Does acknowledging the good in your life bring a fresh perspective to your challenges? Does it make you feel better about yourself and your life?

Incorporate your gratitude about midlife into your day. When you find yourself thinking you're old or wishing you were younger or feeling regretful about the passage of time and the changes in your life, stop and think, *What am I grateful for that relates to my age?* Making an effort not just to be positive but to actively think things through and seek out the positive will help turn around your negative thinking.

TEEN TOOL: BUILD RESILIENCE

Sometimes resilience requires a little boost to support your new perspective. Teens constantly feel judged by their peers, so they often adopt an external "Act as if" bravado as a way to be more resilient. We can also adopt this technique. For example, my patient Jasmine is in her fifties and has never been married. She dates frequently but finds that men judge her single lifestyle. Men have even told her, "I'm not interested in dating somebody who's never been able to commit. You seem all over the place."

I told Jasmine she had to be more creatively resilient when she went out with men, and one way to bolster her self-esteem was to prepare a comeback for when she was faced with a negative comment, just as a teenager would. I suggested she respond to men who question her past single lifestyle with "I wasn't ready to be in a relationship up until this point in my life. I was enjoying myself and now I'm in a different place."

Jasmine loved the idea because it was actually true. At midlife, she was finally able to see her reason for staying single. We all know committed bachelors who are not ready for relationships, but Jasmine had never allowed herself to think she was this kind of woman. Instead of attacking herself and buying into another's negativistic and judgmental image of her, she was able to be more at peace with her choice. She could now use this new language to explain her past in a more positive and accurate light.

Having role models is another tool that can increase your resiliency. It's a technique teens also use all the time: they admire different people and adopt some of their habits, incorporating them into their own personae. Teens pose for photos with their hands on their hips, just as runway models do. Or they mimic a specific sports move in their game. Internalizing the characteristics of their role models helps them along their journey to become who they want to be.

Arianna Huffington is one of my new role models. She hit her stride in midlife, creating a new Internet business model with the *Huffington Post*. I relate to her because she's impassioned and ambitious about her ideas and her mission. She doesn't let age hold her back. She has a full social calendar and is quite glamorous. Whenever I need a little more uplifting motivation, I ask myself, *What would Arianna do?*

Role models make our aspirations more realistic; they give us a road map to follow so we can become more like the person we want to be. It's easier when we can point to someone who has already reached the goals we'd like to accomplish for ourselves. Why reinvent the wheel when you don't have to? Find a role model who has struggled with some of the same issues or regrets you're working through and has made it to the other side. With a little research, you can figure out how they dealt with their difficulties, and see if you can model your behavior on theirs. It's like you're borrowing their bravado, strength, and resilience until you can develop your own.

MIDLIFE MENTOR

Joan Lunden

Joan Lunden is one of the most resilient women I know whose life is completely in the public eye. She was a cohost of *Good Morning America* from 1980 through 1997 and is the author of eight books. Overlapping her professional success were many personal dramas:

she is a cancer survivor, has had two marriages and seven children (including two sets of twins from very public surrogacies), and was a caregiver to her ninety-three-year-old mother. Joan believes that resiliency is the key to navigating the bends in life. She lives her life without regrets because she's been able to recognize the importance of letting go and learning from the past in order to embrace the future.

Joan inspires me because she entered midlife with the expectation that it would be exciting, challenging, and vibrant, and it was. When I asked her, at age sixty-four, how midlife has impacted her, she said with a smile, "When I get there, I'll let you know! It's never too late! I always consider myself to be a work in progress. I'm always trying to improve.

"I grew up thinking fifty was the beginning of the end. Now I consider it's the beginning. I'm far from being on the downslide. I'm headstrong and have no intention of stopping. I feel I'm wiser, healthier, calmer, more daring, and stronger now. I have more confidence and am more willing to try new things. I view the years ahead as exciting. 'Retirement' is not a word I ever plan to use."

She's had to rely on her resilient nature, and she told me, "When you hit some stumbling blocks, you just move forward. My warrior spirit comes from my upbringing. My mother, who we called Glitzy Gladdy, always was a glass-half-full type of person. It's always important to plan something to look forward to. Positive thinking. Each step of the way of my career in TV, my philosophy was 'Go where the angels fear.' Be action oriented toward your dream, and anticipate change. You need to continue to learn how to be more engaged, or else you'll be lagging behind. Today, I run a women's wellness group for about two hundred fifty women at my husband's camp in Maine. The women range from twenty-one to eighty-one. We do yoga, tai chi, and the biggest question I always get during these retreats is 'How do we reinvent ourselves?'"

Joan has faced her challenges and come out on the other side as thankful, grateful, and really strong. She told me that her secret has been to maintain a positive attitude. She said, "I remember when I interviewed Farrah Fawcett after she published her breakout poster in the 1970s, and I asked her what she attributes to her huge success. She said, 'It's my joie de vivre, my love of life.' Every morning at *Good Morning America* I had the challenge to wake everyone up with exuberance for the day. I would look in the mirror and smile to prepare for this. Your attitude is transmitted to other people. Watch what you say to yourself, especially regarding your attitude about your abilities."

Her advice for women experiencing major challenges is to open themselves up to all the opportunities that come their way, which is the "You only live once" attitude I admire. She told me, "I feel stressed and pressured just like anyone else. It's important to refuel emotionally and psychologically. To work hard but then learn how to step away. If you're having trouble, change things up, try something new. Sometimes we just need to look at things with fresh eyes. When I get stressed, I get down on the floor and color with my kids. Do something where you can get lost in what you're doing.

"I also know that successful people in life are the doers. They believe in their mission. I say yes first and then figure out how to do it later. I think the reason why I have succeeded with this way of life is that underneath my spontaneity I have a plan. I don't just experience life as one moment after another. For example, whenever I have a free half hour, I go and buy extra cards and birthday party gifts so I can be prepared for all of the birthday parties my kids have that come up. I'm still the go-to person in the family when anyone is looking for a card to send out."

THE MOST SUCCESSFUL MIDLIFERS

One of the longest-running longitudinal studies of human development, the Grant Study, was engineered by psychologist George Vaillant. Beginning in 1938, Vaillant followed 268 men over a period of 75 years, starting with their time as Harvard undergraduates. He wanted to figure out what makes humans thrive, and he measured all sorts of psychological, anthropological, and physical traits, from the men's IQs to their personality characteristics to the dimensions of their genitals. Now, it's true that this was a study of men, but I think many of the insights Vaillant drew from the study can be applied to women in midlife. He laid out all his conclusions in his 2012 book *Triumphs of Experience*. Here are a few of the insights involving regrets:

> The men with regrets never fully matured, didn't find contentment in work, and never sustained intimacy with a partner.

> The men who described themselves as happy had learned not to obsess about their mistakes or disappointments and to savor the parts of their lives that had gone right.

> Those who successfully dealt with regrets were able to reframe them by focusing on what they had gained.

You can increase your chances of being successful throughout midlife if you learn how to manage your regrets. And once you put your regrets into perspective and become more resilient, you'll find midlife can be a time for you to really hit your stride and pursue the goals you've always wished you could accomplish. By acknowledging your suppressed wishes, trusting your judgment, and engaging your inner wisdom, you'll be able to fully embrace the "You only live once" attitude and get what you want.

The next step is to let go of the stress and anxiety that may be holding you back. In the next chapter you'll learn exactly how these factors affect your physical and mental health, and what you can do to calm yourself down in order to take the next big leap into the future.

FOUR

A MIDLIFE WITHOUT ANXIETY OR STRESS

There are times in my life—sometimes weekly, sometimes daily—when I feel like I'm "losing it." Every once in a while I'll even catch myself taking a really deep breath, seemingly out of nowhere. I always want to do my best and give everything I have to my work and the people I love. My life can get pulled in a thousand different directions, usually at the same time. Wearing several hats isn't easy for anyone, and I admit the pressures of the life I've created can sometimes get the best of me. I feel it most on the days when twenty-four hours is just not enough. A patient is in crisis; my daughter's braces break and I have to take her to an unscheduled appointment; I have an article deadline to meet, bills to pay, dinner to make, and an appearance on a TV show I should probably prepare for. Then there's the internal stress connected to my anxieties and expectations. This typically comes in the middle of the night, when I wake up and say to myself, *My life is falling apart! How am I going to get everything done?*

My reactions to stress are pretty typical. I start chastising myself for not handling my life in a seamless, more graceful manner; then I freeze up, which for me means giving up an important workout I definitely should *not* be giving up; and then I eat too much. Did I mention the part where I feel terribly sorry for myself? Yeah, that happens, too.

The universal truth is that stress is an unavoidable part of every woman's life, especially at midlife. Stress and anxiety can fool us into believing we're powerless and out of control by distorting how we experience ourselves and the influence we believe we have over our lives. These unsettling emotions drive some of us to react impulsively, while others may react to stress physically.

Many of my patients, as well as my friends, report that their anxiety levels go up at midlife. It's no surprise: researchers have found that, no matter where a person lives in the world, happiness reaches its lowest point during midlife. According to the MIDUS research, the stress we experience has a greater impact on our emotions during midlife than at any other age. So if you find yourself snapping at the people you love, breaking into tears watching commercials, constantly worrying about things you can't control, reliving past hurts, or fluctuating between feeling fabulous one day and down in the dumps the next, you're not going crazy; you're just another stressed-out woman in midlife.

The news, however, isn't all bad. Just as the MIDUS research suggests women at midlife are very anxious, other studies show that we can be calmer, less neurotic, and better able to navigate social situations. The truth is, both aspects of mental health can exist, and often side by side. By midlife, our confidence in what we know is good about ourselves has increased, and this point of view can be very gratifying. At the same time we are slaves to an internal, evolutionary "negativity bias"—we tend to focus on the areas in our lives that are not going well. In fact, we are evolutionarily programmed so the bad stuff gets more of our attention than the good—a psychological tool we've been using for survival for hundreds of thousands of years. So while we may have good friends, a good marriage, and a good job, we continue to focus on that one niggling, negative piece in our lives that's worrisome. Maybe it's our health, our weight, or our children. Or it could be any of the big-ticket items that make us feel less than satisfied.

This preoccupation with worry is a very common part of the human condition, particularly at midlife. While it's important to figure out what exactly you're stressed and anxious about, it's even more important to know that you don't have to feel this way. You can let go of your stress and anxiety and create a more balanced life. It just takes a little work.

In this chapter we're going to focus on uncovering some of the feelings that lie beneath your stress, whether the feelings are related to unfair expectations of yourself and others or to your overburdened lifestyle. Once you address these issues, you can return to feeling good about yourself, or maybe feel calm and contented for the very first time. You may even find that you're more motivated and capable of accomplishing your to-do list after you move on from what's stressing you out.

THE MANY FACES OF MIDLIFE STRESS

During midlife, men are more likely to experience the stressors that are focused on them, and women are more likely to take on the stress that is affecting others. This means we not only are anxious about ourselves but also worry about our families, friends, work environments, etc. This reaction may be connected to the mounting responsibilities—at home and/or work—and demands on our time, energy, and money that women in midlife experience. In addition to caring for and about our own well-being, life goals, and aspirations, we are typically responsible for children or grandchildren, spouses or partners, and, increasingly, even parents. According to the National Study of Daily Experiences (NSDE), women provide more emotional support to others at midlife than at any other period. During this time of life, women typically listen to, comfort, and advise others an average of one day a week more than younger and older women do, are twice as likely to emotionally support their parents, and are three times more likely to emotionally support their children.

If you are anything like the superwomen I know, you've been carrying more than your fair share of the load for far too long. The fact is, our lives have not been just about us for quite some time, and this constant level of responsibility can produce chronic stress and worry. Career and family demands can bring us down, so much so that, as a 2008 joint study from the University of Warwick and Dartmouth College concluded, levels of happiness over the life cycle present themselves as a U-shaped curve: well-being is highest in both our younger and older years but at its absolute minimum in our midlife.

Many women feel they not only need to handle everything but must handle all of it well. Adding perfectionism to the mix during midlife can make for even more stress. Faced with mounting responsibilities, the perfectionist may feel like she is not accomplishing anything well and therefore failing, creating even further stress. This particular type of stress can be paralyzing, because the perfection can feel impossible to achieve, making it harder to take those little necessary steps to move out of a stressful situation. What's more, the pursuit of perfection can totally burn us out and wear us down, because we lose the ability to prioritize.

Perfectionism combined with hectic scheduling leaves little time—or room—for having other, more constructive thoughts about how we should purposefully design our lives. Instead, we're constantly thinking about, and reflexively acting on, our list of to-do items. Women can easily be super task-oriented and fill their time with the so-called priorities of daily life. The burdens that seem like priorities become stressful, especially when we focus solely on *I have to* rather than *I want to.* When life becomes dominated by *I have to,* we might feel that we aren't living our lives based on our desires or wishes, which can leave us feeling passionless, purposeless, and increasingly angry, disappointed, and stressed out.

And if we are the hub in the center of a wheel, whether at home or at work, it becomes infinitely harder to think about our needs. One of the reasons stress becomes chronic is that women stop taking care of themselves. It's very easy to stop caring for ourselves, due to lethargy, guilt, or thinking that our time has come and gone. And if we don't have the time or space to think about ourselves at all, we're going to get stressed out or, even worse, depressed.

The flip side of this conundrum is when women purposefully put themselves in a situation where all they're thinking about is busy stuff so they don't have to address the darker feelings they have, which may point to making a change. It's more than a stereotype: women can get themselves into a habit of shelving their disappointments or desires and instead focusing on the doctor's appointment, the school event, or anything else they can use as an excuse. But avoidance doesn't help the psyche reduce stress in the long run. The only way to do this is to address the underlying issues causing this stress and the feelings that surface because of it.

THE STRESS OF REGRETS AND LOST DREAMS

Since middle age is a continually moving target, the challenge for today's midlife woman is less about confronting mortality and more about making the most of her years ahead. One of the most common chronic stressors for women in midlife is the feeling of regret we discussed in the previous chapter, which results in disappointment, insecurity, dissatisfaction, disconnectedness, or unworthiness, often brought up by the nagging confrontation with reality, compared to the myths and expectations we've created in our head. Regrets can cause pervasive, underlying stress that affects us even when we aren't consciously thinking about them. The feeling of regret is a response to something that has or hasn't happened in the past, while stress is experienced right in the moment, though it can be triggered by regret.

For example, my friend Sam was telling me about a new novel he was working on. "It's about a person who during midlife decides he doesn't really like the script he's been handed in life and wants to change everything, give it all up, and move away." I asked him if this was an autobiographical attempt to deal with his own midlife crisis, but he adamantly denied this. Perhaps it was more of an unconscious attempt to deal with some of the strong midlife pulls. At midlife, who doesn't have these same secret feelings sometimes when the entirety of their story is not what they had originally planned for, is out of their control, or is now causing them stress and anxiety? This type of existential anxiety linked to regret is referred to as an "achievement crisis"—the sense that we haven't contributed as much as we thought we would.

If we say to ourselves *When I reach my goal I will finally be satisfied and successful,* we are creating a story, our personal myth of the happily ever after. This story is often accompanied by a timeline: *By the time I'm forty I should* (pick any one or all) *be married, have kids, be financially secure, love my job, be at the top of my game, have a country house, and be able to go on multiple vacations.* These goals are not unrealistic, yet when we miss any of these marks, we go into a self-critical mode, which can make us feel anxious and victimized.

The underlying assumption in our society is that we can be successful if we just work hard enough, and if we miss the mark, we only have ourselves to blame. And in our increasingly linked global lifestyle, "keeping up with the Joneses" is no longer limited to our neighbors; we're forced to compare ourselves on the world stage. However, wanting success is not enough to achieve success. There is always a combination of luck, karma, talent, and being in the right place at the right time involved, too. Although transformational changes can happen, they are more likely to happen when we connect our personal/private dreams to our true potential.

According to a *Harvard Business Review* article, "The Existential Necessity of Midlife Change," without a grounded connection, these dreams are nothing more than idle fantasies that actually waste our energy and become an impediment to change. They also lead to disappointments that can increase our stress level, because we are comparing ourselves to a dream image or images, which encourages us to feel dissatisfied with ourselves or to feel a sense of failure. And with failure comes blame and then shame. I call this the "toxic expectancy effect." Underneath the stress of failure can be a lot of shame—the shame of not feeling the way we think we should feel, or the shame related to Sam's comments: *Wow, I wrote the script and now I'm stuck . . . Maybe I got it all wrong.* These feelings are stressful and depressing because now we are faced with even harder questions: *Where did I go wrong? How can I fix my life when I have so much other stuff to do?*

Sometimes, even when we can check off these accomplishments, we still have a "What's next" feeling or feelings of unhappiness when our reality doesn't match the fantasy version of what we thought achieving our goals would look and feel like. This anxiety connects to the idea that we are creatures programmed to evolve. We're aspirational beings, meaning we are constantly looking and striving for more. Because of this, there's always going to be another goal out there we want to achieve. Deeper still, hitting our marks doesn't necessarily change the way we feel about ourselves. Sometimes our core feelings remain surprisingly unchanged even when we've met success. We may still feel insecure, dissatisfied, disconnected, or unworthy. In the end, these baseline feelings may not be attached to circumstance and may require us to look beneath the surface in order to achieve some degree of resolution.

One of the best things women in midlife can achieve is a shift from aspirational, evolutionary thinking to what I like to call "revolutionary thinking." By the time you've reached your forties, you've already lived through the experimental years of your twenties and the perhaps more settled time of your thirties. Whether your transition is in your marriage, relationships, professional life, or even how you want to look or feel, you are reevaluating where you are and comparing it to where you want to be. That's when you are vulnerable to stressfully attacking yourself with comments like *Why didn't I get what I wanted? What's wrong with me? Did I make choices that were really best for me or someone else?*

Evolutionarily, "What's next" thinking is why we may feel stress and anxiety: once we reach some level of achievement, we can get bored or blind to our success, and then we want to move on and achieve something else. This all-too-common phenomenon occurs not necessarily because we're entitled or spoiled but because we're designed to grow and change. And for many of us change is a very scary proposition.

Answering our evolutionary calling can create a whole new set of choices that require change, which also causes anxiety and stress. Psychologist Barry Schwartz wrote about the choice phenomenon in his book *The Paradox of Choice*. There are so many different paths for women today to choose, yet the ability to choose doesn't seem to always benefit them. In fact, Schwartz found that having choices creates anxiety, depression, and feelings of loneliness. When faced with a choice, we are also faced with a hypothetical loss and a missed opportunity. The reality is, there are many different factors that go into decision making. Our decisions are often not rational; nor are they as rational as we'd like to think they are. In fact, a lot of times they are more unconsciously driven or strongly influenced by what is considered socially desirable or expected of us. All these factors can make it very hard to know if the choices we've made are the "right" ones; there's always a little bit of a leap of faith with any decision.

Famed Danish philosopher Søren Aabye Kierkegaard connected an unhealthy obsession with choice to feelings of anxiety and guilt. He stated, "Anxiety is freedom's actuality as the possibility of possibility." Having the freedom to make choices alters the status quo, which can be scary. When we do make a choice, there is always the potential for the decision to turn out poorly; our mind races to all the possible negative outcomes. Of course, the opposite can also be true. It's just as likely that we'll have a positive outcome, but since our negativity bias forces us to focus on what could not go well, we see only the worst-case scenarios.

Not all of this evolutionary thinking is pointless. When you find yourself thinking *I'm too old,* you are responding to a cultural bias that can easily make you feel stuck. However, if you can use evolutionary thinking to your advantage, you can turn nagging doubts into positive action statements that will propel you forward. The revolution occurs when you let go of the midlife myth and recast your thinking. Instead of feeling angst about your deficiencies, revolutionary thinking allows you to see them as opportunities. Life is an exercise in creative problem solving. Simply looking at your life through a more optimistic lens will prompt you to seek creative solutions so you can get what you want. You'll forget that age is a limiting factor, because you'll see your endless potential and possibilities. And that's not only liberating; it's youthfully exhilarating.

Challenges and change are part of everyone's life. We'd be bored without them. However, we can regain the feeling of being in control by prioritizing our psychological health. By becoming informed and making a few small changes, you can increase your emotional resiliency and raise your self-esteem; both of these factors are essential for combating stress. Psychologist Guy Winch referred to this practice as "emotional hygiene" in his book *Emotional First Aid*. He suggested that we need to take care of our emotional health the way we take care of our physical health, and I couldn't agree with him more. The rest of the chapter will give you the tools you need to make the necessary changes. First, let's identify the many ways stress manifests itself in our lives—and how it affects us.

RECOGNIZING CHRONIC, LOW-LEVEL STRESS— AND ITS DANGEROUS EFFECTS

Stress can come in many forms. Its effects can be felt emotionally, physically, cognitively, and/or behaviorally. One of the ways we can determine whether we're feeling low-level stress, anxiety, or depression is when the people around us reflect back that image. For example, my patient Ann once told me that a friend came up to her and said, "You look much more relaxed today." Even though it was a compliment, Ann realized she must be projecting an appearance of chronic stress that other people were picking up on even though she wasn't aware of it.

Signs and symptoms of chronic, low-level stress and depression include:

- a generally negative outlook

- an overwhelmed, lonely, or isolated feeling

- an inability to relax

- nervous habits (nail biting, pacing)

- procrastination or a neglect of responsibilities

- the use of alcohol, cigarettes, or drugs to relax

It's not uncommon for midlife women to miss signs of chronic stress, depression, or anxiety because they see the telltale signs as part of who they are rather than issues that can easily be treated. I've had many women come to see me who have lived with chronic stress for so long they don't even identify it as such. Instead, they see it as part of their character and in some cases have become attached to it. My patient Nancy once told me, after we had finished working together, that she missed her anxiety because she didn't recognize herself without it. Her anxiety was like a life-long friend.

Even after treating anxiety or low-level depression with behavioral therapy or medication, you may not feel right and may want to return to what's emotionally familiar—even if it is a more anxious version of you. This decision is okay if it works for you. However, if being "yourself" is not working for the people around you, consider how they feel. You have to value what you think and what feels comfortable, but you also live in a world where your success is linked to other people.

Stress can disrupt your sleep–wake cycle and cause cognitive changes, including impaired concentration. It can also trigger mood instability, irritability, and symptoms like those found with depression. The following are the various ways chronic stress can affect your thinking, mood, physical well-being, and behavior.

How Stress Affects Your Thinking

The stereotype of aging, including the loss of mental speed and accuracy, is something close to what Benedict Carey wrote in his *New York Times* blog: "For anyone who is over 50 and, having finally learned to live fully in the moment, discovers it's a senior moment."

Yet, according to the MIDUS research, although it is commonly thought that mental functions decline with age, this may not be the case. Middle-aged adults studied showed little or no decline in mental speed, reasoning, and short-term memory compared to younger adults. Midlife adults performed better than the elderly in the same areas, and even more striking, midlife and elderly adults both outperformed younger adults in vocabulary tests. What's more, we can improve our brain health even as we get older. The brain is constantly evolving, growing, and pruning out unused information and unused habits, and creating new ones. The promise of neurogenesis and neuroplasticity is the ability to make new physical connections in the brain as we age. This is important because the more connections we have, the easier it is to retrieve memories and store new ones.

So why is there such a discrepancy between how we feel about how we think and what science is showing as the reality? The catch is stress: some stress hormones don't know when to quit. Over time, cortisol can chip away at our mental health, injuring and even killing cells in the hippocampus, the area of the brain needed for memory and learning.

How often do you forget a word or blank out on something and say—only half-jokingly—"I hope I don't have dementia"? The good news is you most likely don't. When you're stressed, you can't take in any new information because your brain is already overloaded and overstimulated.

Stress also triggers a second chemical change that makes you either irritable and grumpy or distracted and forgetful. French researchers discovered the reason behind these mood changes is an enzyme triggered by stress that attacks a molecule in the brain responsible for making neural connections. When this happens, you lose your sociability.

Stress reduces the volume of gray matter in brain regions associated with emotions and self-control as well, plus it increases the size and activity of the amygdala, which controls emotional responses and motivation, including fear processing, threat perception, and the fight-or-flight response. Increased activity in this region is interpreted as a constant state of reaction to a perceived threat, which can restrict your ability to take in new information while heightening your emotional reactions. This happens when you become agitated during an anxiety attack. It's also why you're forgetful or sluggish when you're stressed. Worst of all, worrying about how your memory is holding up makes you feel older than you really are.

A lack of sleep can be a stressor in and of itself. I find I think more slowly when I'm tired and sleep deprived, which happens a lot because I'm nocturnal. At 9:00 P.M. I often get a second wind, and all of a sudden my body is ready for some amazing nonexistent party. I could easily stay up until 1:30 A.M. or beyond. I love this time of night, but I typically have to get up at 7:00 A.M., and if I don't get the proper amount of sleep, it can impact my mood and my ability to handle stress. It can also influence my ability to talk coherently, which is something I need to do during early-morning TV appearances.

I hear it from my friends and patients all the time: women in midlife feel stressed and have anxiety about losing their memory and cognitive health. In order to get your mind back on track you have to literally calm your anxiety so you don't feel like a hamster running on a wheel. Once you stabilize your mood, you'll find that your memory returns. For example, at fifty-nine, my patient Evelyn always prided herself on her sharp memory. When she began forgetting little things, she became convinced she'd suffered a drastic loss of cognitive ability. I urged her to get tested, and it turned out her memory was fine. Instead, we worked to find the real sources of her anxieties and developed a strategy for dealing with them.

You can practice a variety of ways to keep your brain sharp and focused on things that are healthy. Ultimately, this will make you feel better about yourself. You can optimize brain health through lifestyle choices: increasing exercise helps, as does a healthy diet. One of the most important things you can do for your brain is to participate in lifelong learning. Pursuits that require intense mental focus, like language learning, actually switch on the control mechanism for neuroplasticity and can enhance memory and learning. Researchers from the University of Santiago de Compostela in Spain found that developing a higher level of vocabulary, as a measure of cognitive reserve, can protect against cognitive impairment. Some women can incorporate lifelong learning at their jobs, which is one of the things I like best about my job. I'm always researching. There's always something new to learn and read. This keeps my mind stimulated and hopefully smarter.

Combining learning with passion and creativity not only improves your thinking but also can help you feel younger. This is one of the reasons why artists and actors stay so youthful. It's not just the Botox and the plastic surgery; they inhabit a creative state of mind. Actors, in particular, continually reenact other personalities and have to learn new aspects about themselves and their characters. This keeps them youthful, engaged in life, and feeling alive.

No one is more creative than adolescents, because they're always in the process of creating and re-creating themselves. They're interested in new ideas. They're stimulated by what's around them. They relate to the world and to one another through the creative process. They make friends with others who like the same music, or they're inspired by what another person wears. They practice with other people's styles to make them their own; they're almost their own art project.

It's really important for us at midlife to adopt this quality. When we're artistic, we're investing in ourselves and what feeds our soul. We're indulging our inner psyche's desire to evolve and create. When we experience ourselves in this way, we're valuing who we are and the beauty we add both to our world and to others around us. This continual sense of creating stimulates our ongoing desire to apply our imagination to who we are and what we want to be. It makes our world an exciting and energetic place.

How Stress Can Lead to Depression

The relationship between stress and depression is a complex one. The negative emotions linked to stress and anxiety can push you toward depression. As I mentioned earlier, chronic stress disrupts the body's biochemistry; the body releases the hormone called cortisol, which is aptly known as the "stress hormone." Stress also causes a reduction of the brain chemical dopamine. When the hormones in your body are working properly, dopamine regulates important biological processes like sleep, appetite, and energy level, which all help to regulate your mood and emotions. In addition, if you suffer from chronic low-level stress, you will often fail to maintain healthy habits. What's more, your coping skills can become compromised, making you vulnerable to depressive symptoms.

It would be so easy to chalk up your frazzled emotional state to the diminishing hormonal output that often accompanies midlife, but it's simply not true. Although levels of estrogen and progesterone become more varied during this time of life, the latest research is showing they aren't directly related to the midlife woman's mood or depression. In one study, researchers compared blood levels of reproductive hormones in women with perimenopausal depression to the hormones of women who weren't depressed and found no differences. This means that no matter where you are on the menopause ladder, your hormones, or lack of them, aren't affecting your thinking as much as we used to believe.

Having said all of this, depression is not always an inappropriate response. We live in a world where we are expected to be happy in order to be living life right. But the truth is, to deal with life's complications, we have to manage and accept lots of emotions and use them as information, even the emotions that are unpleasant. In many cases, they are the exact right feelings to have in any given moment. However, because we don't like to experience the negative, stronger emotions, we reach for the quickest fix to make them go away—medication—or we ignore them entirely and pretend they don't exist. In midlife, we aren't doing ourselves any favors if we respond this way. Instead, we can use our wisdom to synthesize the information we get from feelings and act appropriately on them, even use them to our advantage.

Seemingly out of nowhere—or not—you may experience boredom or discontent with parts of your life that in the past held great interest for you. You may also experience feelings of isolation. We're all in different places at different times, and this can make it hard to determine where we should be or who we can relate to. But believe it or not, there's nothing wrong if you're having these thoughts; this type of thinking is not only to be expected but actually part of your genetic programming.

If these strong emotions interfere with your productivity or affect your physical health, then you need to address them. The truth is, depression can reveal itself in many ways. Women frequently misunderstand depression, thinking it's an illness that interferes with their ability to get out of bed. But you can actually suffer from clinical depression and still go about your day. Mentally, it's a chronic sense of hopelessness and helplessness. Often it is self-isolating, so family and friends may notice you not being as engaged.

Additional signs of depression include the following:

- decreased energy, fatigue, or a "slowed down" feeling
- difficulty concentrating, remembering, or making decisions
- feelings of guilt, worthlessness
- loss of interest or pleasure in activities that were once enjoyable
- persistent sad, anxious, or "empty" moods
- restlessness or irritability
- thoughts of death or suicide, suicide attempts

The epigenetics of stress underscores the differences in the ways we deal with stressors and how stress contributes to our physical state. As you can see, stress manifests in a wide variety of ways, and now scientists believe this is dependent on our genes. For instance, some of my family members have experienced acute anxiety, and some depression. Knowing this, I used to worry that one day I would suffer from depression as well. While I'm vulnerable to feeling anxious or mildly blue sometimes, I grew up in a different home environment and had a much easier life, and this variable might determine which genes get expressed and which ones don't, regardless of my DNA. The environment I grew up in and the environment I currently live in allow me to incorporate and internalize a more resilient mindset.

If you have any of the previously mentioned feelings or symptoms for a day or two, it is not necessarily clinical depression. But if you have them consistently for a period of two weeks or more, or if you notice you're drinking or popping pills to self-medicate, these are signs you may not be handling your emotions in a healthy way.

Don't delay: get evaluated by a professional, starting with your regular physician. You don't need to live in this dark emotional state. Go to your doctor and say, "I noticed a shift." There's no harm in an evaluation, because if you're wrong, so be it. But at least you're taking care of yourself.

If you seek help, keep a few things in mind: Every antidepressant works differently on different people. Just because one drug worked well for your best friend doesn't mean it will work for you. If your medication doesn't seem to be effective, talk to your doctor about changing the dosage or the prescription. Plus, medication takes time to work. It may take up to two weeks before you see an improvement in your mood. Combining estrogen therapy with antidepressants may help medication work better, too (yet estrogen therapy alone cannot treat major depression). Consider talk therapy as well; it is an important part of any treatment for depression. Studies have found that therapy is as effective as medicine for some mild or moderate depression.

How Stress Affects Your Physical Health

Physiologically speaking, the stress response is not just in your head; stress affects your brain and your entire body. When you are faced with a stressful situation, your adrenal glands, which sit on top of your kidneys, release the chemical cortisol. The brain then sends other chemical messengers to quell the cortisol release in an effort to return equilibrium to the body.

An appropriate stress response is actually a healthy and necessary part of life. Another chemical released during stress, norepinephrine, is needed to create new memories and to improve mood once a stressful situation is over. When you're on the other side of stress, problems feel more like challenges, which encourages creative thinking.

However, when you can't recover from stress in a positive way, it can actually lower your quality of life while you're experiencing it and set you up for real health problems later on. Long-term stress suffered by women can ultimately lead to some form of physical complaint, according to a study from the University of Gothenburg in Sweden and published in the *International Journal of General Medicine*. Among the women who reported stress in the study, 40 percent had psychosomatic aches and pain in their muscles and joints, 28 percent suffered from headaches or migraines, and another 28 percent reported gastrointestinal complaints. Stress doesn't just increase your risk of dementia; several studies have shown it can also make you more likely to suffer strokes, heart attacks, and hypertension, not to mention it can affect your sleep and show up on your skin.

As the commercial says, depression hurts. Pain associated with depression and anxiety can range from dull aches to muscle cramps. Depression can also lead to an increased appetite, obesity, or rapid weight loss. Persistent physical symptoms that do not respond to treatment, such as headaches, digestive disorders, and chronic pain, can all be physical signs of stress, anxiety, and depression.

How Stress Can Lead to Substance Abuse

Many women try to fix stress, anxiety, or depression themselves through substance abuse or another type of addictive behavior. This is typically referred to as self-medicating. The bottom line is, everybody wants to feel good. Any behavior we take on is meant to increase the feelings we want to have, or decrease the feelings we don't want to have. While it's normal to have fluctuating feelings, the goal is to find a way to live with the entire range of emotions. Yet many of us are uncomfortable with the darkest emotions, because they're unpleasant and it's hard to believe when we're experiencing them that we'll ever feel better. A momentary fix can self-medicate away the uncomfortable feelings. And when we find an easy way to achieve this, it can be a hard habit to break. It doesn't matter what the self-medicating behavior is, as long as it alters the unwanted mood: it could be having an extramarital affair, overeating, overshopping, over-drinking, or even overexercising.

If you are dealing with your stress or depression in this way, the first step is to recognize it. Most people already know there is an issue on some level, because everybody has a mild tendency to turn toward a specific type of release. I like to call some of these "addiction light." I once had a conversation with a fellow colleague about addictions. I said, "Oh, shopping would probably be my addiction." To which he replied, "Alcohol would be mine." When people talk about their addictions in a light way, they're telling you what actions they take to mitigate unpleasant feelings.

There obviously is something nice about being able to make yourself feel better. The question is, however, is this reasonable? If it's not harming your health, draining you emotionally or financially, putting you in jeopardy with your family or friends, or creating problems in your work life, why not make yourself feel good?

But if you're using these addictions as a way to avoid life or your feelings, the fix is always temporary and often destructive. Addictions stop you from achieving your goals. Any addiction, even a seemingly benign one, can be harmful when taken to an extreme. For any type of addiction, you need to really look at yourself and ask the question, *Is there a better way to deal with these emotions?* Carl Jung's philosophy—what you resist persists—is applicable here. Whatever you find yourself avoiding has to be dealt with in order for you to achieve emotional balance and mental well-being. It may feel unpleasant, but you have to learn how to tolerate discomfort just as much as you embrace happiness and feeling good. It's important to figure out how to manage uncomfortable feelings in a less destructive way, such as talk therapy, medication management, or some type of support group. By doing so, you're less likely to engage in "acting out" or self-destructive behavior.

ADDRESSING MIDLIFE STRESS AND ANXIETY

Research suggests women usually react differently to stress than men, and during midlife, this is no different. While men are prone to reacting with fight-or-flight behavior, meaning they either get angry or turn their attention away from stressors, UCLA researchers have found that during stressful situations women produce the brain chemical oxytocin, the same chemical known as the love hormone because it's released during breast-feeding. This hormone increases bonding and caretaking behavior, which is why a woman's response to stress has been coined "tend and be-friend." This desire to connect may be one of the reasons why we protect and nurture (the "tend" response) and seek out social contact and sup-port from others (the "befriend" response). Interestingly, this is similar to teen behavior: teens also talk issues over with their friends when they're stressed. It's a good idea to make room for this strategy.

Thinking about what you want in life can be useful and positive, but when it turns into relentless ruminating, which spikes anxiety, stress levels, and stress hormones, I say, "Not so much!" Encourage your emo-tional hygiene by taking inventory of what you say to yourself. Everything you say to yourself has power, and in the same way you internally edit what you say to others, you can do this for yourself. It might sound overly simplistic, but telling yourself to "stop right now" is a great place to start.

Since the words you use determine the direction of your life, make your words and the way you talk to yourself inspire you and put you back on the path to success. As we discussed in the previous chapter, reframing your experience and rewriting a kinder narrative goes a long way toward banishing regrets, and the same is true when you want to lessen the anxiety and stress that often accompany them. If you're feeling stressed at work, give yourself credit for being in touch with this feeling and for beginning the process of considering other possibilities. Thank your mind for pointing out your frustrations and then move your thoughts in a direction that helps you develop a different, more capable image of yourself.

It's also important to engage your mind in healthy activities. A challenged mind exercising in healthy pursuits doesn't have the time or space to be as vulnerable to anxiety or stress. A bored mind can be a stressed-out mind, because it's searching for ways to be active; it's just going about it in an unhealthy way. The key is to find an interest that is both stimulating and exciting. For example, if you are passionate about art, going to a museum or even exploring what's available on the Internet is a healthy way to use your mind. If you love writing, jotting down your emotions is a great way to come to terms with your feelings. Once you choose to focus on something and engage your mind with it, your psyche has the opportunity to be in a healthier place and you have a better shot at feeling good about yourself.

Mastering Anxiety Through Mindfulness

"Mindfulness" is the latest psychological buzzword, but it really means working on being more present and less distracted—focusing on the present moment and training yourself not to think about anything that happened in your past or could happen in your future. It's a state of actively paying attention to your thoughts and feelings from a more objective, nonjudgmental standpoint, without labeling a thought or feeling as "good" or "bad," while also accepting those thoughts and feelings, which is very similar to techniques used during psychotherapy (talk therapy). Easier said than done, I know!

If you're distracted and anxious, or you're just going through the motions of life, you may not be aware of what's stressing you out or what your triggers are. But when you're more mindful, more aware, you can look at yourself and your life more objectively. You're able to notice when you're more vulnerable to feeling anxious or stressed, like when you have to pay bills or when your work life is bleeding into your home life.

You can also use mindfulness to assess your response to stress and learn techniques to keep it in check. Some people say aloud, "I'm worried." That's the anxiety part of the stressful experience, but they don't realize, for example, that they're eating or screaming in an attempt to control their stress. You need to develop the ability to observe yourself and understand what sets you off or what's not working in your life so you can change it.

Let's say you're not a morning person. When you become more mindful and knowledgeable about yourself, you realize that if you're asked to do extra things in the morning, it could trigger some irritability and upset. Once you understand this truth about yourself from a less judgmental viewpoint, you can have more control over your emotions and literally calm yourself down or decide not to get as stressed. This self-awareness is hard to accomplish when you're lost in your own head, which can especially happen when you're stressed or depressed.

Once you know your triggers, make a plan of attack. These plans don't have to be deep. Sometimes we think any major change has to be intense or long lasting, but it doesn't have to be. A lot of stress is alleviated by tiny fixes. For example, the next time you get stressed, you could say, *Well, I understand why I'm stressed; I didn't sleep very well, and that always leads to me being more stressed and more depressed. I'm going to deliberately go to bed by ten o'clock tonight, so I'm better rested, and see how that works with my mood.*

Next, create a practical plan for managing stressors and the experience of stress. Setting limits and finding a pragmatic strategy to help yourself out is really the key. If you know that cleaning the house every day is going to throw you over the edge, maybe you say, *I'm going to clean up once a week, and my family is going to help out one day a week, or I'm going to hire somebody to help out.* Remember, it's okay to ask for help. It's okay to reach out and say "I'm stuck" and to rely on your community of friends and family in the same way adolescents would. Too often in midlife we forget that we're not supposed to be a one-woman band.

Mending an Anxious Brain Through Meditation

If you're anxious, you need to take time for yourself, even if you have to establish limits on the time you devote to your loved ones. Trying to find meaning during times of difficulty helps as well. Very often the most trying experiences are also the most valuable ones. Yoga, breathing, and meditation are ways to connect all of these aspects of healing as you learn to focus on yourself, put the outside world aside, and create a space where you can experience your feelings without reacting to or being consumed by them. In the process, you can begin to make peace with yourself and feel more balanced and whole.

According to Richard Carmona, M.D., author of *Canyon Ranch 30 Days to a Better Brain,* scientific research shows that ongoing meditation practice, in particular, can lead to increased development in higher-order cognitive functions, including attention and concentration. Studies of Buddhist monks have shown that a formalized meditation practice has allowed them to develop a profound ability to reduce their sense of pain as well as increase their levels of happiness by activating brain chemistry. Other researchers have found that successful meditators are able to control their stress levels better than non-meditators, reducing anxiety and improving overall mood.

There are many kinds of meditation, each with its own slightly different technique. Some require mental concentration; others activate the imagination. Regardless of the technique, the outcome is the same: a state of profound, deep peace that occurs when the mind is calm and silent yet completely alert. Just like teens retreat into their music to access their emotions, you can find something equally soothing as a basis for your meditation.

When you are ready to start a meditation practice, first decide when you want to meditate each day. Then decide how long you'd like to do it for. Five minutes is a good starting point. Choose a comfortable and quiet space in your house. Decorate your meditation space with candles, photos, or objects of art if you feel it will inspire you. Wear comfortable, nonrestrictive clothing.

Each time you start to meditate, set an intention. Think about why you're meditating and what your purpose is: Are you meditating to increase a feeling of calmness, to feel more centered or more grateful?

Pay attention to your breaths and notice the rhythm of them. Count your breaths on each exhale until you quiet your mind. Counting is an ancient meditation practice designed to help bring you back to the present moment.

Feel the energy in your body. Visualize this energy shining brightly, like the sun, all over your body. Allow this light to bring peace and healing to any emotional issues or stressors you are currently dealing with. Bring awareness to your intentions or any desires you may have.

Acknowledge the emotions that come up. Try to see them objectively and why they may have come up given your current circumstances. Let yourself have this experience without judgment, and then let it go.

Memorize the following affirmation, and when you are finished meditating, say this to yourself: "My life transforms in thrilling and unexpected ways. I accept myself as I am and trust in the natural flow of life. And so it is."

Take four deep breaths to bring you back to the present moment and relax.

If you create the mental space for a stress disruptor in your regular routine—a five-minute period in the middle of every day for you to do absolutely nothing—you could reduce stress significantly. You can even meditate in your office as effectively as if you were sitting in the lotus posture on the top of a mountain. The point is not to be attached to what's happening on the outside but to focus on the inside.

REMOVING STRESSORS ONE AT A TIME

True stressors can't easily be waved away. However, you can prioritize them, in the same way you are so good at getting the rest of your responsibilities in order. The truth is, anxiety typically stems from worrying about things you can't control, so often the first step in relieving anxiety is identifying which worries you can realistically do something about. Then formulating a strategy can help ease your overall levels of anxiety and stress. You'll find that as soon as you create a plan and make a decision to act, your tension will start to lessen considerably.

Make a list of everything you feel anxious about. It could range from cleaning your closets to making a big career change. If any of your anxieties relate to events that happened in the past, take them off your list and create a personalized ritual to help put that event behind you. This ritual can be anything that reminds you the event causing you anxiety is no longer serving you well. Light a candle, say a symbolic affirmation or prayer, take a few thoughtful deep breaths, and let the action you take symbolize the fact that you're letting it go.

The next step is to determine whether each of the remaining items on your list is something you can act on to resolve or control. You can do anything once you stop trying to do everything. Reappraise your goals and ask yourself what's realistic. And if you can't tackle the scariest thing on your list, do a pretty scary thing instead. Designating a super-scary thing in advance as a decoy can make tackling the pretty scary thing much easier.

For each of these remaining items, write down a plan for addressing it. Tell someone you trust about your plan, and ask them to hold you accountable.

You can't get everything done all at once, so what will move the needle? What will let you end the day feeling like you accomplished something? Decide what matters today: What do I need to get done now, and what do I need to get the task accomplished? *Then start making the small fixes that will ultimately lead to accomplishing that task. For many women, their most productive time is the first hour or two of the day, so use that time to your advantage as you tackle your list.*

Don't aim for perfection! Break down each of your stressors into smaller, manageable parts and then give yourself credit as you tick off items on your list to show you're moving in the right direction.

TEEN TOOL: SET BOUNDARIES

Setting boundaries is a way to love yourself—you don't have to be all things to all people. I'm not recommending you become a selfish person. That's never going to feel good, and it's not going to lead you down the right or healthy path. However, to live a life in which the self is obliterated is not the answer either. There always has to be a piece of your identity, a piece of yourself, you're honoring at any stage of life.

Here are two best practices for setting boundaries that you can learn from teenagers:

Just Say No

The most appropriate way to set boundaries when you feel overwhelmed or overburdened is by saying no. Adolescents are great at automatically, and willfully, saying no. Their developmental goal is figuring out what their identity is and what's important to them. Saying no in order to separate from parents is normal, appropriate, and developmentally on the mark. Their mentality is *I'm saying yes to myself.*

Developmentally, women in midlife start getting better at setting boundaries. This wisdom comes from a combination of knowing yourself, knowing your limits, knowing what works, and, perhaps more important, knowing what doesn't work. You will reach a point where you understand that the world won't end if you say no, and others will understand you're still a good person. Whereas in adolescence it's more instinctual, in midlife, saying no is like rediscovering who you are. In midlife, you may have reached a different understanding: *I've followed the rules for so long and in so many ways, and now I need to recognize my own needs and individuality.* Say it, sista!

In order to take on a more adolescent energy and point of view in terms of reducing stress and anxiety, midlife women need to let go of the guilt associated with saying no to others. The challenge is how to say no gracefully yet forcefully. Part of our female identity is the ability to be a helpful person and take care of others, and we enjoy the appreciation that comes with being so needed. It's uncomfortable to say no to the people we love and care about. We don't want to fail them or offend anyone. It's much more pleasant to feel loved than to knowingly disappoint others. Yet a car can't run on an empty tank of gas, and neither can we. If constantly meeting the needs of others is stressing you out, then you have to learn how to say no and set limits as an effort of self-preservation.

"Attend to Me" Day

To help you get in touch with your needs and desires, it's important every now and again to release stress by having an "Attend to me" day. The following tool can assist you in attending to yourself, for all of the right reasons. Afterward, you can revisit your stress list with a new level of objectivity.

Review your list of stressors. Is there anything on the list that signals you've already taken on too much or that you're enabling others by sacrificing your own needs? If so, start by saying no. Sometimes it feels good to say no directly, but if you need to ease into this, read on.

When you're too busy to lend a hand to someone, let that person know. You can share with them why you're so busy or what you're working on to help them understand your situation better. A simple statement like "Unfortunately I won't be able to help you out because I'm really overloaded" works well. If you get a request for help when you're in the middle of something, let the person know that now is not feasible, but then suggest a different time frame that may work better for you. A simple statement like "I'm in the middle of something right now. How about we reconnect later, around X time?"

One way to let others down easily is to tell them you love their ideas but can't contribute or participate due to prior commitments or a conflict of interest. A statement like "I'd really love to help you, but . . ." would work perfectly here.

If you feel you're being asked to do something that you don't want to do or don't have the right background for, offer up someone who is a better fit. A response like "I am not the best person to help you out. Have you tried person X? I think they'd be perfect for you" is a great way to start.

With all your new free time, you can indulge in an "Attend to me" day. In fact, you might find it's not as hard as you thought it would be. And the upside is, when you create more time for yourself, you'll be able to focus on the things that matter the most to you.

MIDLIFE MENTOR

Hoda Kotb

Hoda Kotb is one of my midlife mentors because she is one of the most honest and resilient women I know. As one of the cohosts, with Kathie Lee Gifford, of the *Today* show, Hoda's job is to appear stress-free all the time. But as we know, life isn't that way.

I asked Hoda how dealing with stress has changed for her at midlife. She told me, "When you're younger, you haven't lived enough to know what to stress about. During midlife, you've been through more. I know that if I'm late for a meeting or miss an interview it's not going to be the end of the world. I'm better able to put things in perspective, and consequently, there are fewer things to get stressed out about. Getting cancer, in a weird way, was a huge de-stressor for me. Your life kind of snaps back into focus after an experience like this, and afterwards I was able to peel away what wasn't important.

"I get stressed out less often now because I feel I can deal with situations better. When I used to play basketball, I would run around all over the place. I didn't know what to do or how to play the game right. Then I learned how to conserve my energy. Same for midlife: I'm able to prioritize better now, and I know how to pick my moments to stress about and conserve my energy.

"Today, I have fewer work stresses, because I love what I do. But when I think about a future in which my job went away, I picture my life with lots of adventures and fewer of the anxious what-ifs, what-ifs. I also was able to end a marriage that was bad and was adding stress to my life. Making the decision to leave was the right one for me.

"At midlife, once your life starts to snap into focus, it's such a clear path. You get rid of all the things that have been harming you and are not working for you, and your life opens up in ways you never imagined. It's like you're on the side of the angels. It's like you're riding a wave instead of fighting against that wave. Then one day your life just feels effortless, and you can say to yourself, 'Ah, this is what life is supposed to be like. This is supposed to be how I'm living. This is what it's supposed to feel like.' Every day shouldn't feel like a fight. Sometimes you have to unload what's holding you back in order to get to this place."

Hoda has a very realistic, pragmatic way about her. She believes, as I do, that stress is always going to be a part of our lives; how we manage it and how we look at the world is really what will change the way it affects us. She told me, "You can walk out the door and feel this huge weight of the world on your shoulders, or you can change the equation. I can always wake up every morning and say, 'Ugh,' and list ten things that are wrong before I even start my day. I could start stressing even before leaving the house and say to myself, 'I have so much to do and I'll never get it done. I can't make it work today.' But for a lot of the time, I choose not to go that way.

"Instead, I've gotten better at prioritizing and eliminating things I don't have control over from my list of things I worry about. Ninety percent of what you worry about never happens, and then what happens to you can be things you've never even thought would happen to you, and then you're never prepared for that stuff anyway.

"On any given day I try to do some things to lighten the load. I always exercise; I don't do a lot, but it always helps me out every time I do it. Every morning I start my day by writing a gratitude list, jot down three small things I can be grateful for. Then I write one extraordinary thing, the one thing that happened to me in the last twenty-four hours that was an awesome experience. I look for this amazing experience instead of looking for what's wrong. I look for the tiny things that make me happy. Like on our show, we had on some adorable girls who had illness but were going to this special prom. I loved them! I started thinking about what a ray of sunshine they were. I do this in the morning because it helps me to view the world in a more optimistic way. I say, front-load the day with good thoughts."

When I asked her what is most stressful about her life, Hoda told me that her worries are usually about her family or her health. "Whenever something goes wrong with my brother, sister, or my mom, I feel like I should try to fix it. I guess I'm the family peacemaker, or at least I try to be. I also worry about my health. Ever since the cancer, when I start to lose weight in a weird way or start to feel funny, I find myself saying, 'I hope I'm not getting sick again. I hope it's not cancer.' I don't think about it a lot, but it does happen. It's a thought that does sneak into my mind every once in a while even though I've been cancer-free for seven years."

When I asked what advice she would share with other women in midlife about letting go of their anxieties, she focused on staying in the present. She told me, "I really believe how we spend our day is how we spend our lives. And I think that people think it's so hard to make changes, but we can change if we start with one day at a time. I love the phrase and try to live by it, even though I'm not successful at it all of the time, 'Be here now.' I want to be thinking about where I am now. We're living in the right here and right now, so be here in the right here right now. If you can master that, you've sort of figured it all out.

"Another thing that works for me whenever I feel stressed, horrible, or down, is I remind myself that there's someone out there who is happier with less than what I have, or has worse problems than I have. You feel less irritable, less worried, and less stressed when you can get out of yourself and take the focus away from your problems. The truth is, the world's not all about you.

"I also count on my friends, and I know they can count on me. For the people who are close to me, I'm their 2:00 A.M. phone call and they're mine. One thing I do better than anything else is I pick good friends. I look for people who are lit from the inside, are selfless and humble. The people I surround myself with are better people than me. When I'm really stressed out—and who isn't sometimes—I have the people I can call at 2:00 A.M. on speed dial, and this gives me such peace of mind to know there is someone there to help me work it all out and that they'll take care of me."

GETTING BETTER AT KEEPING IT TOGETHER

At midlife, you have more power than ever to manage stress. The answer may be not reducing stressors but instead figuring out how to manage them better. In order to release stress in a healthy way, start identifying the myths and assumptions that may be triggering your unnecessary self-judgments and reactions. Simply understanding these are myths can be a tremendous relief, because these ideals set the bar too high. It's far healthier to acknowledge your goals but base them in reality. For instance, if you want to have a successful relationship, use the people around you as inspiration instead of hanging your hopes on a television sitcom relationship. If you like the way a couple you know treats each other, you can incorporate their behaviors into your own life.

Next, challenge the cultural stereotypes or faulty societal expectations that have permeated your thinking. For example, even if you do get your dream job, dream partner, or dream house, once it becomes a reality, you're going to have both positive and negative feelings about it. Not only is this normal; it's to be expected. You don't have to feel bad about yourself because you don't always feel the way you thought you'd feel about your life. This doesn't mean you're failing; it just means you're experiencing life.

Try to find the positives in all the great things you've created. Even if something didn't turn out the way you wanted, so what! Once you rewrite your story, you can experience yourself differently and allow yourself to follow a different path.

Once you get a handle on dealing with stress and do the work to control your anxiety, then you can be more reflective and have the honest appraisal that midlife women seem to enjoy. According to University of Michigan and Cornell University researchers, people in their forties and fifties have learned how to take more responsibility for their actions and the consequences of these actions. They are more reflective, introspective, and interested in changing themselves. They are also more likely to have realized they need to let go of the past. Your ability to use wisdom to banish stress and anxiety is another reason why midlife means your best age is now.

....

My patient Maggie learned a great deal about herself when she went through a stressful time during midlife. When she first started working with me, when she was in her early forties, she admitted that although she was a busy accountant, wife, and mother of three young children, she didn't quite feel like a grown-up. Her life had all the hallmarks of success, yet she didn't feel good about herself or her ability to be the right kind of mother to her kids.

Maggie's life reached a tipping point following the unexpected loss of her mother and other close elderly family members. The financial burdens of living in New York City were weighing on her, and she felt pressured to move to a less expensive place, yet she didn't really want to leave and didn't know where she would go. She was also debating where to send her oldest child to school, who had some physical disabilities. Her maternity leave was coming to an end, and she had to make a decision about whether or not to return to work. She loved being a full-time, stay-at-home mom and didn't really love her job anymore. But she was feeling stressed and pressured by her fiscal responsibilities to continue contributing to the household financially. She also felt guilty about not having spent enough time with her mother before her sudden death, and now she felt an added pressure to make sure her dad was managing well after this shocking loss.

Maggie had never really been good at making decisions, even under the best of circumstances. She was obsessional and perfectionistic by nature, which made every decision feel even more stressful, torturous, and burdensome to her. On top of this, whenever she compared her life to her friends' lives, she felt she came out the loser. She had status stress. Everyone around her seemed to have fewer family problems than she did. They were more financially secure than she was, too, which made her feel even more frazzled and depressed about her situation.

I reminded Maggie about a personal truth she seemed to have forgotten during the past few months of tumultuous midlife moments. I pointed out how bright she was, and although she had always found making choices challenging, she had a long track record of making really good life decisions. I also reminded her how thorough she was in her research efforts, and I underscored that I knew she would do whatever it took to make sure she got the correct information she needed in order to move forward in a smart and appropriate way.

After Maggie heard me out, I noticed that her demeanor and stressful emotional state began to lift. By focusing on her areas of strength, she realized she could in fact trust herself to make healthy decisions for herself and her family. Her inner wisdom and confidence was activated. We decided to break down all the decisions she needed to make and put them on a timeline. We talked through the immediate choices in her life, and she gave herself time to figure out the long-term decisions. While she couldn't eliminate all the stressors midlife would bring, she could figure out how to attack some of them, one at a time, in a way she could feel good about. Now in this empowered psychological place, she could address her stress from a position of confidence and strength.

Just like Maggie, you already have the resources to work with. Ask yourself these questions and see how well you already manage your midlife stress:

What have been the most stressful events in my life and how have they affected me?

How did I get through those difficult periods?

Did I learn anything from those experiences?

Was I able to come to terms with what I could control and what I couldn't?

What was the key to overcoming those difficult periods in my life?

Make a mental picture of the ability you demonstrated to get through hardship and periods of extreme stress. Are you just as capable now? Perhaps even more capable? What techniques are you able to identify from your past experiences that you can use now, and going forward? When you analyze your answers, you might realize you've already been more resilient through your life than you thought.

FIVE

FEELING STRONGER EVERY DAY

Knock on wood, I've never had to be overly preoccupied about my health. I definitely miss the metabolism I enjoyed in my twenties and thirties, but besides a few aches here and there, fortunately nothing has caused me much worry. Until I realized that my troublesome shoulder problem wasn't going away. I knew I had to do something about it, so off to the specialist I went, expecting to hear a diagnosis of a pulled muscle. I never imagined the doctor would find anything that a great massage couldn't cure.

Yet the x-rays revealed something more: I had arthritis of the neck. My initial reaction was . . . WHAAAAAT?!? I couldn't believe what I was hearing. Arthritis is something *old* people get. There was such a disconnect between how I experienced myself and what I was hearing that I literally had to sit down, because I almost fainted in his office. My sense of invincibility was pierced. I was sure that the doctor was a quack and had made a horrible mistake, and once I regained my composure, I couldn't get away from his office fast enough.

Later that day I spoke to my regular internist, whom I trust implicitly. He told me that the first doctor was probably correct; arthritis of the neck is very common. In fact, he said, "Robi, everyone has it!" Now you see why I love my internist! He made me feel so much better about my new condition and gave me some easy options for dealing with it, including physical therapy. Once I knew that what I had was common and there were treatment options available for me, I felt so much better about my new diagnosis.

This mini medical drama certainly raised my awareness: as young and strong as I feel in my head, the passage of time will make itself known in small ways. Will this stop me from working on my goal to feel fit, fabulous, and fine? *Absolutely not!* But it was a midlife wake-up call, for sure! It pointed out how important—and easy—it is for me to take care of myself in preventative ways so I can make the most of what's in store for me in the future.

It's not uncommon for me to sit with my friends and talk about some of the life phases and experiences we share, especially when it comes to our health. The topic of menopause comes up frequently now. Some of us have gone through it, others are going through it, and the rest are just listening to all the possibilities they might face. At other times our conversations center on minor physical injuries that either temporarily or not so temporarily interfere with our workout goals and regimens. But regardless of what health topic we land on, some things are very clear: we have an intuitive and objective understanding that our bodies are continually changing; we have a new appreciation for holding on to, maintaining, and, in some cases, reenergizing and improving our overall health; and we have a very strong desire and determination to maintain a physically healthy and eternally youthful approach to life.

According to the MIDUS research, women report more health problems than men during midlife. However, we're also better at taking care of ourselves. The data shows that as we age we are naturally more devoted to improving our health. This may be one of the reasons why, on average, women in midlife today look so good. We're healthier than ever before.

Just as teens project onto an empty canvas their future goals and aspirations, and see a full life ahead of them, at midlife we can take this same long view. Today's healthy women can continue to imagine their lives with a bright future ahead. Our longevity outlook is better than ever, and we can expect to live vibrantly and accomplish our goals not just in the next twenty years but even as far out as the next fifty. We need to tap into the same teen energy of unlimited possibilities, because time is on our side. We can get better as we get older, and this typically starts with our health. If we take care of ourselves and take advantage of the latest medical breakthroughs science has to offer, we can reshape our expectations of the future and be more hopeful.

This doesn't mean we won't age or we won't become ill. Our bodies age from the moment we're born, even if we don't always notice all the small changes right away. However, we don't need to wait until we're in a health crisis before we start taking better care of ourselves. With the right guidance, we can make easy yet significant and effective changes that will turn back the hands of time. By doing so, we'll look and feel younger not only now but well into the future. And when this happens, our overall mood and outlook improve.

MEDICAL ADVANCES FOR LIVING YOUNGER THROUGH MIDLIFE

Our greatest ally in the fight against aging is modern medicine. Science has slowed down the aging process to such an extent, we don't really notice ourselves getting older until something unexpected occurs, such as finding our first gray hairs, or when your doctor tells you it's time to make the first appointment for a mammogram. Advances in medicine have the potential to add ten to twenty years to our life spans, so women in midlife can now look forward to many more years of productive living. Early diagnostics have greatly improved cancer survival rates and general disease prevention. Organ replacement and regeneration as well as stem-cell therapies are becoming more commonplace. We are also finding ways to function as young as we feel through science and technology. With Botox, we can look younger. Safer, more effective birth control gives women far more power over their sex lives. Pharmacologically, antidepressants can help improve mood so we can retain a healthier, positive attitude long into the future.

These factors will undoubtedly further change the face of midlife in the future, but we can reap some of the rewards right now. Doctors are getting better at assessing the body in a more holistic way. Novel approaches, such as bioidentical hormone treatments and nutraceuticals, may hold some of the answers for not only increasing longevity but also allowing us to live younger and healthier during the prime years of our lives.

One of the advances I'm most excited about is the discovery of telomeres, the protective tips found at the ends of our chromosomes. Think of the plastic bits at the ends of shoelaces and you can imagine what they look like. In fact, their role is the same: they protect the end of the chromosome and prevent the loss of genetic information during cell division. It turns out that each time our cells divide our telomeres become shorter. Longer telomeres have been linked to a longer life span, while shorter telomeres have been linked to conditions such as heart disease and dementia. At least one pharmaceutical company is working on an antidote that will increase the length of telomeres, which may be one very real way we can protect our health and prevent disease. Stay tuned!

Meanwhile, medicine is becoming more scientific instead of just observational, and more proactive rather than reactive. J. Craig Venter, a co-mapper of the human genome, believes that in the next two to five years science will be able to provide the context necessary for treatments based on the personalized information in our genes and blood type. Many experts believe this approach is the future of health care. Personalized medicine will move treatment from a one-size-fits-all model to a more proactive, predictive, and preventive approach. Therapies will be completely customized, based on specific information obtained from our genomic sequence or hereditary information. This is going to be a game changer in terms of our ability to live longer and healthier during every stage of our life. In terms of midlife, it might mean we have one less thing to worry about.

THE MIRACLE OF MIDLIFE FERTILITY

Of all the medical advances, the one that has most dramatically changed women's lives is the extension of the ability to conceive. It's no longer uncommon for a woman to put off having children until her late thirties or forties, and science is moving the needle even further, well into midlife. The reasons can be as varied as the women who make this choice: enjoying work, facing professional responsibilities, not finding or being with the right person, having medical issues, or encountering unexpected personal-life changes.

In vitro fertilization combined with cryopreservation (the freezing of one's eggs) used to be an unreliable option for women who wanted to preserve their fertility, but major scientific advances in these areas has extended a woman's biological clock by decades. The oldest documented mother to give birth is currently Omkari Panwar, who had twins in India when she was said to be seventy. And medicine will only continue to move in the direction of offering more rather than fewer options for women when it comes to their fertility.

Cassie's life completely changed when she gave birth to her daughter when she was forty-three. Cassie came from a traditional Catholic family and was one of four kids. While growing up, she was always pretty and popular, a cheerleader who had a good head on her shoulders. She envisioned herself getting married and having lots of kids, living life much like the family she came from.

After high school, she took a job and thoroughly enjoyed the life of a young single girl in a predominantly male profession. Before she knew it, she was in her late thirties, and she realized it was time to get married, settle down, and have kids. At thirty-nine, she got engaged to a man she had been seeing for about a year. He had his flaws, but she thought she could help him change, at least enough to make it work. Plus, she really wanted to get started on having a family.

After the first miscarriage, Cassie and her husband decided to try to get pregnant via in vitro fertilization. The process was sadly unsuccessful, which placed a lot of stress on her marriage. After two years, the couple decided to get a divorce, but Cassie still desperately wanted to have a child, which was one of the reasons why she first came to see me. I told her that, at forty-three, her dream was still possible and science was on her side. I advised her to continue moving forward with trying to figure out how she could have a baby and create the family she wanted.

About a year later, she fell madly in love with a coworker, who was recently divorced and had two grown children. While he loved Cassie, he was not really interested in getting married and starting a family again. However, he agreed to donate his sperm and freeze some embryos with her. This relationship was showing signs of major problems, and when Cassie miscarried again, it was over. Once more, I told Cassie she didn't have to give up on her dream.

She was prepared to become a single parent, with the complete support of her family. On my recommendation, she consulted with her doctor. He advised her to get an egg donor as well as a different sperm donor so this time she might have a better outcome. She researched her options, found an egg donor, flew her to New Jersey, and began the process of getting pregnant on her own at the age of forty-three. Nine months later, she gave birth to Mary.

Cassie had always wanted to be a traditional stay-at-home mother, but her life didn't work out that way. Yet even today, seven years later, she is so grateful for Mary that she isn't bitter at all. In fact, she has a very positive attitude about dating and is clear about what kind of man she is looking for. She wants someone who loves kids and can be part of a mature relationship. She excitedly told me that she had signed up on a dating website called SingleParentMeet.com. Her hopes for marriage and more kids remained strong. And her positive, hopeful attitude paid off. Only four months after our conversation, she connected with a man from her past, who she now considers perfect for her in every way. The two had gone to the same high school, and although they had mutual friends, they hadn't been friendly with each other back then. His face serendipitously kept popping up on her Facebook page. She ended up friending him, and they connected, started dating, and quickly took their relationship to a more serious level. His three kids and her daughter got along like one big happy family almost immediately. I just love happy endings!

WHY MENOPAUSE MATTERS, AND WHY IT DOESN'T

It wouldn't be right to talk about women in midlife without addressing menopause. This biological change is often seen as a clear line of demarcation: before it, you're fertile, young, energetic, and attractive; after it, society labels you less than desirable and noticeably slower. Every woman's experience with menopause is different. For some women, it is a catalyst for change and growth. For others, it is virtually uneventful, while still others find it a rough passage.

The interesting thing is that the further you get from the onset of menopause, also known as perimenopause, the better you're likely to feel about it. In retrospect, maybe it wasn't as bad as you remember. And if you're on the cusp, maybe it won't be as bad as you fear.

So much has been written about menopause that to some extent I think it has become an excuse for women to dwell in midlife. Just because you're in menopause doesn't mean you're old, past your prime, lack options, or have to relinquish your sex life. The truth is, you don't have to buy into the cultural message that menopause must mean decline. Historically, menopause was described as both the death of the womb and a cause of hysteria. Your challenge is to reject the stereotype. Menopause might signal discomfort, but at the same time, it might give you a new perspective.

You may have to address your body in different ways or try new strategies when others have failed.

Even if menopausal symptoms are challenging, take a lesson from the teens in your life saying (and sometimes to you) "Please don't tell me what to think or how to live my life." Instead, make the best of your situation. Perhaps it won't be as difficult as you have been led to believe. You may find that some of what you've been taught is simply wrong. For example, if you believe the symptoms of menopause can affect a woman's sense of well-being, that's not exactly the truth. Perimenopause—the decade or so before menstruation stops—is really the culprit. It's what most women think of when they gripe about menopause, and it's when the majority of symptoms occur. Once you've gone a full year without having a period, then you've entered menopause, when symptoms are likely to continue. Perimenopause can start a full ten years before your last period, meaning you might be closer to menopause than you think.

Perimenopausal symptoms can be tough to deal with, especially if they come "out of the blue." However, if you are in tune with your body, you will notice the small and big signs that indicate your body and mind have changed. Some of these changes are biological and others are behavioral. The symptoms vary widely, and there is a big range of what is considered "normal." Some women sail through this transition without many symptoms, while others have a difficult and uncomfortable time.

Perimenopause has nothing to do with diet or exercise; it's a biological fact. It will happen. Here are some of the physical symptoms associated with perimenopause that can occur even if you are still getting your period monthly:

- aching joints
- backache
- bladder infections
- breast tenderness

- cold sweats

- constipation

- diarrhea

- dizzy spells

- dry eyes

- dry nose and mouth

- dry skin

- facial hair growth

- fatigue

- fine lines around the mouth and eyes

- headaches

- hot flashes

- increased gas

- increased incidence of cysts

- infertility

- insomnia

- loss of appetite

- night sweats

- persistent cough

- rapid heartbeat

- shortness of breath

- skin rash or irritation

- sore throat

- swelling

- thinning hair or hair loss

- tingling in the hands and feet

- urinary incontinence, discomfort, or changes in frequency
- vaginal discharge, dryness, or numbness
- weakness
- weight gain

The mental and emotional changes you are experiencing, including increased stress and anxiety, may have nothing to do with menopause. We know this is so because women in midlife aren't having a unified experience. Experiencing physical symptoms can affect your mental health. Poor sleep can really stress you out; so can weight gain, uncomfortable sexual intercourse, etc.

Perimenopause and menopause shouldn't be taken lightly. These stages of your life might be directly connected to how you're feeling and how you feel about yourself. However, they don't have to signal the "end" of any part of your life. Because you experience so many different stages of personal development during midlife, these physical issues really might not be affecting you. It's good to know what they are, but they don't have to rule your life. There are plenty of great resources available that can help you make the symptoms tolerable. If you are experiencing any symptoms, read up on what's absolutely the most current data. Then talk to your doctor and devise a plan together. It may include conventional medicines, hormonal treatments, over-the-counter aids, or even making lifestyle changes.

LET'S TALK ABOUT SEX

Women in midlife do not have to view great sex as a distant, loving memory from the past. They want passion and, perhaps most important, feel they deserve to have a passionate sex life. Modern-day midlifers don't consider the end of the childbearing years to mean the end of their sexual fulfillment.

While growing older is usually associated with a declining sex drive, I've found that many women actually experience more frequent and intense orgasms as they age. After menopause, they find they can enjoy sex in a much more free and fulfilling way because they know what they like and feel more confident in asking for what they want in terms of sexual satisfaction.

However, the reality is that the physical changes of menopause, like vaginal dryness, can cause intercourse to be more painful. Reduced estrogen levels can lead to vaginal dryness and discomfort. Even something as innocuous as the use of antihistamines can be part of the problem, because this type of medication can dry the vagina as it controls your runny nose. The side effects of other prescription medications, including antidepressants and antianxiety medications, can also create sexual problems such as fatigue, reduced desire, and difficulty with achieving arousal or orgasm.

The good news is, many of these changes can be easily treated, making sex just as comfortable as it was prior to menopause. Talk with your physician to see what options are available. Improving your self-image through eating a healthy diet, exercising regularly, getting the proper sleep, and managing your stress levels can have a tremendously positive influence on how you feel about sex during midlife. Pepper Schwartz, Ph.D., a professor of sociology at the University of Washington, told me that while sexual problems are natural as we age, there are many aids that can restore a great deal of comfort to sexual activity. Investigate over-the-counter lubricants (look for ones that don't contain petroleum, which can break down the latex in condoms). Sometimes another form of medication or a lower dosage may alleviate these particular side effects. Your doctor can also suggest vaginal estrogen to combat dryness.

Other personal factors can impact your sexuality during midlife. Depression, stress, and anxiety can wreak havoc on your sex life, especially if you have issues with body image or performance anxiety:

Self-perception. Changes in weight, appearance, and fitness can affect your mood and your self-talk, and make you feel less desirable and less interested in sex.

Sexual desire. Your emotional state may influence how much you desire sexual contact, especially if you are going through perimenopause or menopause.

Sexual response. Women sometimes complain of having a slower arousal time and, in certain cases, difficulty reaching orgasm altogether.

Midlife may actually be the best time to nurture and improve your sex life, because it's when you are reevaluating your life in general. This makes it the perfect time to explore and reawaken your sexual identity in the most rewarding way. Changing up your sexual foreplay and exploring proven medications that can increase libido may keep your sexual life alive.

Talking with your partner about your sexual needs and how you both might be changing can bring a new intimacy level to your relationship. Now is a great time to experiment either alone or with your partner to see what feels pleasurable.

IT'S NEVER TOO LATE TO START TAKING CARE OF YOURSELF

I'm amazed at how young so many women look for their age these days. Women in their forties, fifties, even sixties, are able to achieve a much more youthful, ageless appearance now than ever before. This is in part due to the power of a healthier diet and working out, both of which help us to look younger.

When you adopt a healthy lifestyle, you can protect your body's healing system and encourage optimum health as you age. Maintaining—or even enhancing—your physical health now is crucial because you're laying the groundwork for your aging experience. While we are all likely to live longer than our parents and grandparents (based solely on the medical breakthroughs that have occurred in our lifetimes), how we are going to live those extra years is completely dependent on how well we take care of ourselves now.

The lifestyle changes we'll discuss in the rest of the chapter are not new, but the evidence that they work is tremendously exciting. According to longevity expert Dean Ornish, M.D., there is mounting scientific evidence that lifestyle changes can work not only as preventative medicine but also as actual treatment for some chronic diseases—either in combination with medications and surgery or by themselves. In randomized controlled studies through the Preventive Medicine Research Institute, Ornish's group has found these lifestyle changes alone can often reverse the progression of severe coronary heart disease, type 2 diabetes, and some forms of cancer. What better motivation do you need to follow this simple prescription of a whole-foods diet combined with the stress management techniques outlined in chapter 4, plus moderate exercise and good sleep? Sexy midlifer Cameron Diaz was quoted as saying in a recent *Vogue* article, "Getting older is a blessing, and not everyone gets to do it. It's not a given. It's a privilege." I couldn't agree with her more!

While midlife women can easily reap the health benefits of lifestyle medicine, SoulCycle trainer Stacey Griffith advises her Spindarellas (the name she's given to women who do indoor cycling regularly) to stop worrying so much about their current size and instead focus on being healthy, strong, and toned. Focusing on your health rather than your waistline will help take the pressure off so you can actually enjoy an exercise program instead of worrying that you're not yet "perfect." When her midlife clients complain that they can't get into their skinny jeans anymore, she advises them to "trade up" and, if necessary, get bigger jeans. So what, if you can't get your skinny jeans on? Who's going to know? Instead, focus on being happy and healthy, and learn to love where you're at.

THE DIET THAT MAKES YOU FEEL YOUNGER

Diet and nutrition can have a profound effect on women during midlife. Two of the biggest health complaints women experience during this time are weight creep, especially around the midsection, and declining energy. Both of these are directly related to the foods we eat, and by making better choices, we can control them.

Even if you had great success managing your weight in your twenties and thirties, you may find you're slowly gaining weight—just a few pounds a year—without making major changes to your habits. This weight gain can be both frustrating and frightening. You are certainly not alone: the MIDUS research clearly shows that as age increases, so do the waist-to-hip ratio and the percentage of women who are overweight in midlife.

However, midlife weight gain does not have to be a fact of life. Metabolic changes affect weight gain, but they can be dealt with. From age thirty onward, a woman's metabolism drops around 10 percent every decade. Translated into calories, we must trim approximately 100 daily calories for each decade just to maintain our current body weight—without any change in exercise. This means a typical caloric intake of 1,800 to 2,000, which may have worked for you in your twenties and thirties, needs to be reduced to 1,700 to 1,900 in your forties and 1,600 to 1,800 in your fifties.

Nutritionist Keri Glassman says it's important to become good at listening to your body. So many of us overconsume when we let ourselves become ravenous, or deprive ourselves and in so doing, or mindlessly eat whatever is on the plate in front of us without recognizing the signals of satiety. It's much easier to train ourselves to eat less when we eat more mindfully.

Glassman believes that weight creep can also be partly a self-fulfilling prophecy. You might believe midlife weight gain is so inevitable that you become less diligent when it comes to your diet or you stop caring about your weight altogether. The problem here is, it's a scientific fact that carrying extra, unnecessary weight can cause heart disease, high cholesterol, type 2 diabetes, hypertension, stroke, gallbladder disease, sleep apnea, breast cancer, colon cancer, osteoarthritis, fatty liver disease, and all the various symptoms that accompany these illnesses. Worse, if weight is an issue you stress about, you're unknowingly making the situation worse. Stress in and of itself can also create weight gain. Cortisol, the hormone released when you're stressed, not only causes you to gain weight around the midsection but also makes it harder to metabolize body fat.

In order to enjoy midlife and beyond, we really need to pay attention to our weight. We can start by accepting where we are and then creating a plan to make small, incremental changes. We don't have to be supermodel thin, but at the same time we don't have to set ourselves up for a less than perfect later life. Even a lack of weight gain—known as defending our weight—is a giant positive response. For many women, it takes just as much work to not gain weight as it takes to lose those extra pounds, but it's worth it!

As we enter midlife, our goals change as to what looks "good"—and how hard we're willing to work to achieve that look. For many women, gaining 10 pounds—one dress size—won't rock their world. For others, midlife is when they finally have the extra time to address their weight. My sister Ramy never had a weight problem, but she really stepped up her game during midlife. Today, her body has never looked better or more toned. Her social network has definitely been an influential, contributing factor to her healthier and trimmer look. Her friends all work out religiously. In fact, that's their time to socialize together. Ramy's posse created a culture in which looking youthful, fit, and fabulous has become their mantra. They have not only encouraged Ramy to be more fit but also served as her muses: she started a clothing company during midlife called Ramy Brook. Her sexy clothes are designed for fit women who want to look and feel glamorous—whether they are in their teens, twenties, thirties, forties, fifties, or beyond.

Regardless of their motivation or desire to lose weight, all women need to change their diet to one that supports their health as they enter midlife. According to Richard Carmona, M.D., former surgeon general of the United States and author of *Canyon Ranch 30 Days to a Better Brain,* experts agree that the same diet that is good for heart, digestive, and brain health is good for midlife. A high-protein, low-carbohydrate, healthy-fat diet has been clinically proven to be the best prescription. These types of foods are loaded with important vitamins, minerals, and antioxidants that all affect your health for the better, and they help to create long-lasting satiety so you won't feel hungry. They also promote excellent brain chemistry, so you will have an increased sense of well-being and high energy. Foods high in fiber and water, like fruits and vegetables, are considered "high volume": you can eat lots of them and feel full because they take up space in your stomach, yet they are still low in calories. This way of eating is referred to by physicians as a "volumetric diet." Basically, you can eat more and still lose weight because the nutrient-to-calorie ratio is the highest of any diet around.

Foods and Nutrients Midlife Women Especially Need

There are foods that provide more energy and contribute to a more youthful look and healthy feeling. The following are some of the nutrients and foods you need to make sure you're getting every day:

Calcium and vitamin D are required for maintaining and enhancing bone health. They can be found in dairy products (even the low-fat varieties) as well as sardines, almonds, Brazil nuts, spinach, and collard greens.

Colorful fruits and vegetables provide nutrients, antioxidants, and water. Aim for five fruits and vegetables daily. An easy way to increase your fruit and vegetable intake is by eating just one more of each than you eat now, and add to that slowly until you get to a full complement each day.

Lean protein is a key ingredient for increasing muscle mass, which decreases as we age. Ideally, you should have some sort of protein at every meal, such as beans, eggs, fish, poultry, beef, or other meats.

Fiber-rich grains, like oatmeal and brown rice, act as powerful appetite suppressants and help you maintain better intestinal health.

Healthy fats keep you properly fueled and feeling full, and help keep your skin glowing. Cutting out a lot of fat, like many fad diets recommend, can promote ultra-dry skin and hair. Olive oil and nuts are some of the best sources of healthy fats. Other sources are those high in omega-3 fatty acids, which can also improve your mood and your skin. Foods like salmon and walnuts are very high in omega-3s.

Soy-rich foods can help make the perimenopausal transition easier. Soy products contain a very low amount of estrogen. But you'll have to eat more than a handful of soy nuts or edamame: the benefits are seen in daily quantities of 25 grams, or three or more servings. An 8-ounce glass of soy milk is only 4 to 10 grams. Check with your doctor if you have a history of cancer or are estrogen-sensitive for any reason.

Stay hydrated by drinking water all day long. Water flushes your digestive system, removes pollutants from the body, and increases your metabolism. Fruits and vegetables, especially apples, broccoli, cantaloupe, grapes, lettuce, oranges, peaches, pears, strawberries, tomatoes, and watermelon, all contain high levels of water.

Dr. Eric Braverman, author of *Younger (Thinner) You Diet,* believes some of the secret weapons of weight loss for midlife women are teas and spices. They'll not only make your food taste better but also improve your health. Teas and spices have thermogenic properties: they actually boost your metabolism so you burn more of the calories you consume. They also contain important vitamins, minerals, and antioxidants, and they have antibacterial properties to help maintain health. Plus, they can stimulate digestion, cleanse the body, and give you lots of energy. Spices increase your overall feeling of fullness, too, so by using them when you cook, you may end up eating less. One study conducted at Maastricht University in the Netherlands showed that when healthy subjects consumed a small amount of red chili pepper flakes or chili powder before each meal, it decreased their caloric intake by as much as 16 percent. Spicy foods also force you to drink more water, which, as I mentioned, is another key to weight loss.

Your digestive system needs to be able to tolerate more spices, so experiment, adding a bit at a time. Start by adding half a teaspoon until you determine what you can handle. Don't use a tablespoon of cayenne or chili powder or paprika if you're sensitive to spicy foods.

Foods and Nutrients Midlife Women Need to Limit

Excess sugar is particularly bad to consume during midlife because it is highly inflammatory, which not only causes bloating but also makes it harder for injuries to heal. Added sugars found in processed foods can go by the following names and should be avoided: high-fructose corn syrup, fructose, dextrose, and sucralose. While it's best to avoid sweeteners entirely, better choices include agave nectar, honey, and maple syrup. These alternatives contain beneficial vitamins, minerals, and antioxidants. Stevia is another natural sugar substitute, and it comes from a plant, *Stevia rebaudiana,* which is native to Brazil and Paraguay and has been used for thousands of years. It's two to three hundred times sweeter than sugar, so just a tiny amount will do the trick, and it contains zero calories. Stevia can be used for anything you might typically use sugar in, including baked goods.

Simple carbohydrates give you the feeling of increased energy in the short-term but are highly addictive and contain lots of unnecessary calories. Madelyn Fernstrom, professor of psychiatry and epidemiology at the University of Pittsburgh School of Medicine, and a *Today* show health and diet editor, told me that women need to remember that "stressed" is "desserts" spelled backward.

Sadly, some of my favorite treats are not everyday foods:

- breads and other foods made with white flour

- cakes

- chips

- crackers

- full-calorie sodas and fruit juices

- pasta

- pastries

- pies

- processed foods

- puddings

- tapioca

- white rice

Fernstrom also suggests that the one thing midlife women don't need is extra iron. With the cessation of menses, monthly iron loss is gone. Daily vitamins for women fifty and over have no iron. However, she advises to stay on top of vitamin D levels. Vitamin D is known to elevate your mood, improve bone health, and cause weight loss since it contributes to the body's ability to burn fat. We simply cannot get enough vitamin D from the foods we eat. Nature provides this essential vitamin through sunshine; however, with sunscreen use and the limited time we tend to spend outside, many women easily become deficient. See your doctor for a blood test—that's the only way to determine whether you are deficient.

Stress eating is a habit that needs to be nipped in the bud. The best advice from the experts is to "think before you eat," so you give yourself enough time to make a better choice. Some women find great stress relief in crunching on raw vegetables.

Sometimes stress eating goes too far. My patient Melinda initially came to see me to work on her goal to lose weight. She was fifty and had at least 100 pounds to lose. She also told me that her weight had been problematic for most of her life.

I quickly realized that Melinda's desire to lose weight was more of a wish than a goal. She was using food as a way to self-medicate intolerable feelings. When she ate, she didn't think about her mother (who was very sick) or her job (which was becoming more stressful by the day). But her weight was finally affecting her health. The physical problems she was experiencing were scaring her: she had back problems, needed ankle surgery, had sleep apnea, had trouble breathing when walking, and, the final straw, had been diagnosed with diabetes.

Melinda knew her health problems were caused by her obesity, but I strongly warned her that being diabetic was no joke. I asked her how she felt about the possibility of going blind or losing some of her limbs. This confrontation helped her acknowledge how dire her circumstances had become. For the first time, she was motivated enough to start a regimented, healthy eating program. She addressed her food choices one day at a time and joined a support group to keep her focused on her goals. She is now learning to tolerate her feelings without resorting to food, eating healthier, and losing weight.

THE IMPORTANCE OF EXERCISE

Exercise is one of the best things you can do for your health and overall sense of well-being. You may know that exercise is critical for keeping the heart and the rest of your body young, and exciting new evidence is showing how beneficial cardiovascular exercise can be for brain health as well. One of the reasons behind this phenomenon is that exercise is directly linked to neurogenesis. A 2010 study from the Salk Institute for Biological Studies connected exercise to enhancing cell production in the brain and improving memory.

The latest study drives this point home. A groundbreaking 2015 Finnish study published in *Medicine and Science in Sports and Exercise* followed sets of twins from the age of sixteen onward. Researchers found that identical twins who shared the same sports and other physical activities as youngsters but developed different exercise habits as adults had quite different bodies and brains, even though they had eaten the same kinds of foods as both children and adults. The study clearly highlights just how significantly exercise shapes our health, even in people who have identical genes and the same nurturing history. By the time the twins were in their midthirties, their health had already begun to diverge. The sedentary twins had lower endurance capacities, higher body fat percentages, and signs of insulin resistance. The twins' brains had also developed differently: the active twins had more gray matter than the sedentary twins. So even if you are thin, or if you're close to your ideal weight and happy with the way you look on the outside, you still need to engage in daily exercise in order to stay healthy and keep your mind sharp and active. Studies continue to show that cardiovascular—aerobic—exercise is best for maintaining brain health.

The most recent science also shows that exercise doesn't have to be exhausting or painful to be effective. One of the easiest ways to boost metabolism—and it's not food—is a brisk 30-minute walk daily. In terms of longevity, the prescription is slightly different. In a 2015 study from the National Cancer Institute, researchers found that the ideal exercise prescription for people in midlife to increase their life span is to work out moderately for 450 minutes per week, which is about an hour per day. A 2015 study from Australia published in the prestigious *Journal of the American Medical Association* found that the ideal exercise intensity includes at least 20 to 30 minutes of vigorous activity within that mix. Fitness experts recommend investing in a Fitbit or other device that logs the number of steps you take each day. To maintain your weight, take at least 10,000 steps; to lose weight, amp up your activity to 14,000 steps.

If you make exercise a daily habit, your genetics do not have to be your destiny. Even if your family culture didn't include trips to the gym, just by moving your body more now you can substantially improve your health.

Women begin to lose muscle mass at midlife, which is why resistance, or strength, training is so important. It is also an excellent way to help maintain a positive self-image and avoid depression. Hundreds of studies have analyzed the effect of exercise on depression and found that resistance training in particular can boost self-esteem, improve mood, reduce anxiety levels, and increase the ability to handle stress. This type of physical activity may help women better cope with perimenopausal symptoms by improving mood. When you combine cardiovascular and resistance training, the capacity to get into better shape as you age is not only possible but likely.

Best of all, research shows that it's never too late to start. In fact, many women find their athletic selves during midlife. Your best age is now because you have so many different options for exercise that are equally effective, especially at midlife. Take Ernestine Shepherd, for example. She became the world's oldest performing female bodybuilder in her midseventies, but she didn't start until she was fifty-six years old. SoulCycle trainer to the stars Stacey Griffith told me she meets plenty of women who were never athletic in their youth but in midlife had the freedom to find their own rhythm. In her opinion, this is why spinning works so well for women—and men, for that matter—during midlife. They put on their gear, they don't need to remember any steps, and they quickly get in sync with a class that's supporting them. Everyone can go at their own pace. It's really changed the way women exercise.

Most women can exercise at fifty the way they did when they were twenty and, in some cases, can perform better. However, Stacey thinks her midlife women enjoy working out now more than ever before. There are so many other options than going to a gym, which can be an uncomfortable place for some women. Instead, you can work out in smaller ways for shorter periods of time, even in your own home. Also, it's really important to break from your regular workout routine and try something different every once in a while. When you shake things up a bit, your body becomes more alert and you'll achieve better results.

The plethora of options is also important to keep you interested, because exercise needs to become part of your daily lifestyle in order for you to reap its benefits. Dr. Carmona says in his book that no matter how long or how intensely you've been training, your body begins the detraining process just seventy-two hours after your last workout.

When it comes to exercising and staying healthy, Stacey Griffith reminds us that the goal for midlife women is to let go of what's not serving us well. Exercising is one form of therapy for the body that allows us to start new, better habits and get rid of the toxic messages floating in our heads that are holding us back. Exercise provides a time to balance, focus, and connect with ourselves while we work toward becoming calm and strong.

THE IMPORTANCE OF SLEEP

The easiest anti-aging remedy is sleep. When you are well rested and less anxious, you not only look younger but are able to have a better perspective about yourself and others. A lack of sleep makes it less likely that you'll engage in exercise and more likely that you'll make bad food choices. Yet for many of us, our ability to sleep suffers at midlife. When we don't get enough sleep, we typically feel more irritable, have a harder time focusing, and are a lot less productive. A lack of sleep can also have serious implications for our health. It not only has been linked to weight gain but can also impair judgment and severely affect mood. Inadequate sleep deprives the body of oxygen, elevates blood pressure, and increases the level of stress hormones. It may also weaken the immune system and increase the risk of high blood pressure and heart disease.

It used to be considered macho for both women and men to sleep less. But now we know adults need seven to nine hours of good sleep in one consolidated batch. Some healthy people only need six hours, while another small subset might require as much as ten, but the bottom line is not actually the number. You want to achieve both a sufficient quantity of sleep and an acceptable quality of sleep. If you get up at the same time every morning, without setting an alarm, feeling rested and refreshed, and your energy is pretty decent most of the day, and if it takes you less than ten minutes to fall asleep when you get into bed, you're probably meeting your sleep needs. But if you have to hit the snooze button a few times every morning before you stagger out of bed, and at the end of the day you fall asleep in front of the TV, you are not getting enough sleep.

Why Aren't You Sleeping?

The responsibilities and stress of midlife are enough to keep any woman up at night. Or you may be dealing with any of the following issues that are also common in midlife:

Obstructive sleep apnea. This condition is caused by a blockage or obstruction in the nasal cavities or the throat, or a floppy tongue, which obstructs your airways either partially or completely during the night. It can be caused by an anatomical obstruction or excessive weight gain. The obstruction deprives the brain and the body of oxygen and causes an automatic response, waking you up just enough so you breathe again, although you may not wake to the point of consciousness. Sleep apnea doesn't just affect your ability to get a good night's rest; the latest research shows that it may be linked to developing dementia. At midlife, who needs to worry about that? Get yourself checked out if your partner tells you that you're snoring.

Depression. It is unclear if sleeplessness causes depression or if depression leads to a lack of sleep. Some researchers believe both occur.

Fibromyalgia. This disorder causes widespread pain, fatigue, sleep disturbance, and often problems with cognition, such as brain fog. Fibromyalgia is often diagnosed after blood tests have ruled out other possible diagnoses.

Reflux. This occurs when stomach acid splashes back into the esophagus, often when you are lying down at night. Reflux can cause you to wake up in the middle of the night feeling hoarse or coughing because the acid has traveled into your lungs.

Hormone loss. Estrogen is necessary for maintaining sleep once you fall asleep, and progesterone makes you drowsy. Doctors sometimes prescribe hormone replacement therapies to resolve sleep issues. Low-dose bioidentical hormones may actually help restore your sleep and improve the symptoms related to menopause that prevent sleep from occurring in the first place, including hot flashes and depression.

Medication use. Steroids, decongestants, ADD medications, and beta-blockers can all interfere with sleep. Antidepressants, particularly the selective serotonin reuptake inhibitors (SSRIs), including Prozac, Zoloft, and Lexapro, can also disrupt sleep, especially when you first start them or change the dosage.

What to Do When You Can't Sleep

Get into a good sleep routine so your body trains itself to slow down and go to sleep. It's important to remember that you're not just nurturing yourself; you're reducing your stress hormones, which is essential. I recommend several measures to my patients who want to address sleep issues:

Get out of bed. If you wake up in the middle of the night and you can't go back to sleep, you need to break whatever behavior you've adopted that keeps you up and worrying. Go into another room and do something calming until you feel sleepy again and can come back to bed.

Shut off all lights. Invest in window shades that keep your room dark, or cover your eyes with a sleep mask. Even the smallest amounts of light emitted from an alarm clock, TV, computer, or smartphone can affect sleep.

Limit caffeine all day long. Caffeine can last as long as seven to eight hours in its half-life. This means that for some women the 8:00 A.M. cup of coffee is still affecting their system at 10:00 P.M., as much as fourteen hours later.

Skip the cocktails. Many women find that after they have a couple of drinks they fall right asleep, only to find themselves wide awake a few hours later. This is a typical pattern at midlife, because it takes a couple of hours for your body to process the sugars in alcohol, and once they clear your system, you wake up. For every drink you have, you get one hour of sedation followed by one hour of arousal. Alcohol also relaxes the tissues that hold your airway open, making you more prone to sleep apnea. What's more, alcohol is a notorious hot-flash trigger and bladder irritant—two more reasons why you might not be sleeping well.

Have a small snack before bedtime. A light, complex-carbohydrate meal, like a small bowl of cereal, may actually boost production of the brain chemicals serotonin and melatonin, both of which relax the brain and help you sleep. A glass of milk is a good source of tryptophan, which is one of the building blocks of protein and known to make you feel sleepy. Foods rich in B vitamins, like bananas, sunflower seeds, and avocado, also help the body produce sleep-inducing tryptophan.

Consider a new mattress. If you've been sleeping on the same mattress for more than ten years, it's time to buy a new one. Shop around to find one that is comfortable for you and your partner. Those memory foam beds sound really nice but are known to pack in body heat; this may not be the best choice for women during midlife.

Treat sleep apnea. The standard treatment for sleep apnea is using a continuous positive airway pressure (CPAP) device. A mask covers the nose and mouth and is connected to a machine that supplies a constant flow of air.

Consider sleep aids. These medications are meant to help you relax so you can fall asleep and stay asleep. They provide short-term relief, yet many people stay on them for years. Discuss this option with your doctor, and never take someone else's sleeping pills.

Try to sleep like a teen. Adolescents relish their sleep. They get to sleep, they stay asleep, they're hard to wake, and they actually get more sleep overall than both babies and adults. Instead of setting your goal to sleep like a baby, maybe you'd be better off trying to sleep like a teenager.

TEEN TOOL: COMMIT TO HEALTHY HABITS

I was never athletic as a teenager, and I definitely never wanted to exercise. Going out for lunch and walking up and down in the mall was my idea of the perfect day. Exercise always equaled messy hair, in my book, which was not a good thing. Fortunately, I developed an appreciation for exercise in my late twenties, and it's something that has stuck with me to this day. I still don't like when my hair gets messy, but I prefer messy hair (at least temporarily) to a messy/unhealthy body.

I am so impressed by how teens today take care of their bodies and their health, including my own children. Today's teens have a much better understanding of the importance of eating healthily and working out. I think this is in part because of the emphasis on health they receive at school, perhaps as an effort to combat the epidemic of childhood obesity. Teens have a strong, innate desire to look their best and fit in with the cultural norms, which now highlight a woman who is both fit and trim. I think teens have a more in-depth understanding of why it's important to eat healthily, be healthy, and exercise than we did as kids. Many are hitting the gym, joining sports teams, and working out, and they are often rewarded with the ability to show off their toned, fit bodies.

Make a commitment to yourself to live a healthy, more vibrant lifestyle, as today's teens are experiencing. Do a bit of research and figure out how you would like to move and eat to have the body you want. Choose activities you know you'll enjoy so you're motivated to keep going. Don't be afraid to switch it up as well. Then put together a contract that will help you achieve a younger, healthier you.

Make a promise to address each area you feel needs more attention, and make the necessary changes over the next fourteen days.

- Assess your health, and schedule an appointment with your doctor to discuss exercise and diet options.

- Research the latest diets out there and see which one resonates with you. The healthiest options will always be diets that promote eating all three types of nutrients—proteins, carbohydrates, and healthy fats—not one to the exclusion of the others.

- Research new exercise options. It's always best to combine cardio and resistance training, along with some stretching, into every week. Don't worry that weight lifting will make you big; it will only make you stronger, which you really do need, especially at this time in your life.

- Prioritize getting a good night's sleep. Give yourself permission to make time for sleep and/or to take more naps.

MIDLIFE MENTOR

Sunny Hostin

Sunny Hostin is a lawyer, journalist, columnist, and legal commentator on CNN. Sunny and I have worked together analyzing various cases on television from our respective professional perspectives. I am always impressed with how diligent she is about working out and staying healthy, even with her very full and active life. The bottom line is, she makes me feel like a midlife slacker, so I made her my midlife mentor. I needed some inspiration!

When I asked Sunny how she stays in such great shape, she told me, "I can't say that I've always been a healthy person, but I've had the benefit of skinny genes. Both my parents were thin. I was always active—took a lot of dance classes, played basketball and softball, and I ran marathons in my late twenties and thirties. I was always active because I enjoyed it, not because there were any health benefits, until later in my life. I could eat anything I wanted when I was younger. I grew up eating soul food and Puerto Rican food. My father is African American and from the South, and my mother is Puerto Rican. I gained 70 pounds with my first pregnancy and was on bed rest for six months, and was on a modified bed rest for thirteen weeks and gained 60 pounds with my second child. I was able to lose my pregnancy weight with just diet.

"When I turned forty, I realized I could no longer eat with reckless abandon, and it was a rude awakening. Forty really changed things for me. I had to be a little more careful with what I ate, and I had to exercise to stay in shape.

"I'm an older mother with a hectic schedule. I found exercise gave me more energy. I've always been athletic, but in midlife I found I was more prone to injury. I couldn't run three miles without stretching first. I couldn't take a dance class without stretching. So now I'm better to myself. I drink more water, and I stretch before and after my workouts. I also changed the type of workouts I do. When I run now, my knees hurt, so I changed my cardio to spin. I take yoga and Pilates classes. It's still strenuous but better and less injurious to my body. I have a Fitbit I love, so I can see how active I've been. I have to work out three times a week to see any change or even just to maintain my body.

"In my opinion, 70 percent of looking good is diet. Now that I'm in my forties I'm careful with my diet. I don't eat bread, pasta, or rice. I don't eat meat, which was a hard adjustment for me. I used to love bacon. I mostly eat fish and vegetables. I drink a lot of green, white, and black tea, do a lot of juicing. It's not unusual for me to have a smoothie for breakfast and a kale, watermelon, cucumber, lime juice smoothie for lunch. I limit my intake of soy (studies show it's not great for black women: it may cause fibroids). Breakfast has always been a challenge. I start my day off with hot water with lemon, before I eat anything. I learned this combo from a friend of mine who grew up in Asia. It's supposed to help your metabolism.

"I give myself permission to enjoy the foods I love when I need to, like fried plantains or rice and beans on a Sunday when I spend the day with my family. I know one day off my diet is not going to break me. It's just not a staple in my diet anymore. I want to be around for my kids, and conscious eating is really an important way to do that. I eat real foods, nothing that comes from a package that contains ingredients I can't pronounce. If you're consciously eating, the occasional healthy dessert makes people feel good. I love a good macaroon and red velvet cupcake. I love wine with dinner. I go on wine tasting trips. I would love to be involved in a vineyard one day. I would rather have a glass of wine than dessert. You can't have your cake and eat it, too—literally."

When I asked if it was harder to stay in shape in midlife, Sunny was very honest with her response. She told me, "I'm two babies in and things are not where they used to be on my body. If I want fit legs and a tight tummy, I definitely have to do much more than before to get it. If I only appreciated what I had when I was younger, I would have worn a bikini every day. Then I realized that every day I'm the youngest I'll ever be right now.

"I really work at making my body stronger and not just skinnier. I don't go for thin, thin, thin. Forty thin is not so great looking, anyway. My motto is 'Strong is the new skinny.' I do something physical every single day. Inactivity is the worst offender during midlife. Sitting in an office for multiple hours is not something we're supposed to be doing with our bodies. I'll do fifteen minutes of squats or ten-minute planks if I can't get to the gym. I take the staircase at CNN all the time. If I have appointments a mile away, if the weather is okay, I'll walk to where I need to go.

"My ideal workout day is I'm up at 6:45 A.M., then I meditate for twelve minutes, I drink my hot water and lemon, I speak to my children—they get up at 7:00 A.M. By 7:40, when they are out of the house, I take a yoga class or a circuit class or do Pilates or spinning. I also do sit-ups, planks, push-ups, for forty-five minutes, which is the most time that I have. I also stretch before and after. For breakfast, I have a spoonful of almond butter or a banana or a smoothie, then I shower and go off to work. I have tried to work out in the evening; it just never works out with my schedule. After work, I come home, eat dinner, have my glass of wine. Read before bed, usually the news feed, then it's nighttime meditation with my lavender oil, and bed.

"I stay motivated by saying to myself, *I want to be the healthiest I can be for myself and my family.* Or *I need to be the healthiest I can be for myself and my family.* For me it's still kind of hard. There are days when I have so much on my mind and so much to do, I could do other things with that hour, but because I want to look good and feel good, and I know how important it is, I push myself. But I can't say that it's not hard, because it is."

HEALTHY FRIENDS MAKE A POSITIVE IMPACT

My cousin Cheryl (who's also in midlife) and I decided to try spinning together a few years ago. We had heard so many great things about spinning we figured it would be a fun way to spend time together and to get in a good cardio workout at the same time. It soon became a regular and healthy staple in our lives. We not only kept each other accountable but also motivated each other, especially when our exercise inspiration wavered. Cheryl's in amazing shape, which serves as great motivation for me.

Just as teens are thoroughly influenced by their friends, we can begin to make good decisions about our health by hanging around the people who are making their health a priority. Our social connections influence our physical and emotional health to such an extent that science has even come up with a new term: "sociogenomics." How much we eat, our personal taste, and our emotional state are all influenced by the community we associate with. When this kind of influence takes a turn for the worse, we call it "peer pressure." But we can use this strong influence to our advantage by selectively choosing whom we spend our time with. It turns out exercise and weight loss are just as socially transmittable as tobacco habits, drug use, and alcohol consumption.

It's more than a coincidence that we tend to look like the people we surround ourselves with, and friends have a greater impact on our health than family. Researchers Nicholas Christakis and James Fowler examined the impact the "ripple-effect connection" has on people and its resulting health benefits or costs. Their study tracked more than 12,000 people over the course of 32 years and found that the influence of friendship over health, and especially over obesity, remained even when two friends ended up living hundreds of miles apart.

By working on your health with a friend, both of you will benefit. The lifestyle changes we discussed in this chapter are infinitely easier to make when you're doing them with a friend who will keep you accountable. And you'll find it's a lot more fun.

SIX

BEAUTY CAN
BE A BEAST

Seeing myself on TV can highlight what I think are my "beauty deficits," which, let's face it, aren't always fun to face. A number of years ago I was watching a TV segment I had done for *The Oprah Winfrey Show*. It was taped right after I had given birth to my daughter. I was experiencing some temporary hair loss or thinning after my estrogen levels had plummeted. My hair looked bad. Really bad!

Now, to be completely honest, my hair has never been my best feature. But after seeing myself on-air and how horrible my hair looked, I felt really self-conscious. I missed my thicker, more youthful-looking hair, and I was envious of other women who had plenty of hair. My self-esteem was at an all-time low.

Then I came across a great quote: "You can't control everything, and your hair was put on your head to remind you of that!" Well, I couldn't agree more! But I thought, *I can certainly try to make the best of what I can't control*. Beauty, after all, takes a little work, and you know what? I'm okay with that!

So I went to several doctors and hairdressers to seek their advice. While thirteen years later my hair is still not as thick or as full as it used to be, I have finally figured out the right regimen to get my hair to behave and to achieve the look I want, even if it's a challenge sometimes. I give my hair lots of attention and an exacting combination of products, along with professional primping, straightening, and highlighting. Even though I still have my fair share of bad hair days, I feel good about the way I look.

When I see photographs from my past, I often say to myself, *I like her. I remember that day, but I don't want to go backward.* This is one of the reasons why I never lie about my age. I've earned all my years. They add up to making me who I am. To lie about my age is like dismissing major parts of me and what I've learned. I refuse to do that.

It can be a very powerful exercise to go back and look at old photos of yourself and be able to say, *I look better now.* I've interviewed many midlife women who like the way they look today. They have figured out how to eat more healthily, exercise more, and work with their unique features and body shape. They know what looks best on them, and they are more comfortable in their own skin. And while they are still influenced by cultural messages, they don't feel defined exclusively by them.

Self-image and attractiveness have been hot-button issues for women since the invention of the mirror, so it's no surprise we continue to be preoccupied with our appearance. Fortunately, midlife women today are able to find a plethora of role models who present a sexy, youthful image and seem to enjoy themselves and the way they look. Women like Rene Russo, Juju Chang, Savannah Guthrie, Emma Thompson, Holly Hunter, Michelle Obama, and one of my favorite midlifers, Madonna, are all redefining what this stage of life can look like, and it's having a positive domino effect on the rest of us. In terms of the ease and accessibility we have for tapping into our most attractive selves, this is not your mother's midlife.

THE MEDIA AND THE NEW MIDLIFE

Women our age grew up during the golden years of advertising, when women were considered relevant only when they conformed to a single standard of beauty. In the past, actresses quickly aged out of their leading lady status once they hit forty. Actress Kristin Scott Thomas commented about roles for midlife women at the 2013 Cannes Film Festival, when she was just fifty, "Somehow, you just vanish. It's a cliché, but men grow in gravitas as they get older, while women just disappear."

My friend and colleague, Dr. Jill Muir-Sukenick, is a psychotherapist and former model who has written in the book *Face It* that our youth-oriented culture tends to pathologize aging as if it were a disease. As a result, she has seen many women who experience an identity crisis as they get older. In extreme cases they may resort to inappropriate coping mechanisms such as excessive dieting, alcohol or drug use, sexually acting out, and repeated plastic surgery. Too many of us have internalized this same cultural bias, and we respond by giving up on ourselves prematurely. Just as the women we've come to love on the big screen fade out of sight, we might fear we are going to disappear, become irrelevant, or lose our options and opportunities. This can be especially true for women who have relied on their looks to navigate the world. Our feelings regarding the way we look reinforce our perception of who we are and where we fit into society. So when we look in the mirror and see a sexy woman looking back, we become sexy. When our appearance is not in sync with how we feel we should look, because we look older than we think we should, it can have a negative impact on how we experience ourselves. Then repetitive images driven by the media of the same type of beautiful women can be either upsetting to our psyche or inspiring.

As long as we can keep the message society sends us in perspective and understand the underlying motivation for those images—which is to sell products—there is nothing inherently pathological or irrational about wanting to achieve a culturally valued appearance. In fact, it's very normal. It's rare to find a woman of any age who has not been affected by the messages of our society, resulting in feelings of insecurity and a bad body image. This phenomenon has been defined as "normative discontent," a normal dissatisfaction with one's appearance. During midlife, women can become even more aware of these societal expectations, and when they don't quite measure up, they can become depressed, feel anxious, or have lower self-esteem.

Our challenge is to eliminate the pervasive idea that midlife equates to loss. Over the course of a lifetime, we might lose something or someone we really loved, like a pet or a friend. Aside from this, in midlife we're not really losing anything. We're simply transitioning into something else, but something equally fabulous. A butterfly doesn't age out of being a caterpillar. It just gets better, and we need to adopt this philosophy so we can enjoy our beauty throughout our lives. Once we can accept that even with the changes to our faces and bodies we look as beautiful as we looked when we were younger, it will move the entire cultural conversation in the right direction. Ultimately, our society is going to have to adjust, especially if we are going to meet the needs and reflect the realities of our ever-evolving midlife community.

Naomi Wolf, author of *The Beauty Myth,* talks about her experience as a woman in midlife in a way that closely mirrors my observations. She too originally bought into the culture's narrative that getting older would feel like a loss, but over time, she found this idea to be more myth than reality. Looking at her contemporaries, she sees women her age as "dynamic and magnetic." In fact, she refers to these women as "change agents" who are not buying into the cultural fear of aging and instead are redefining beauty.

Another woman who takes ownership of her appearance is Tony Award–winning actress Viola Davis, who spoke out against being constantly criticized by the media as "less classically beautiful." In a 2015 interview on the television show *The View,* Davis said, "Being a dark-skinned black woman, you heard it from the womb. And 'classically not beautiful' is a fancy term for saying 'ugly.' And denouncing you. And erasing you." While she said these comments had demeaned her self-esteem when she was younger, they don't impact her at midlife. Today, she recognizes her beauty and is proud of the way she looks. In the interview, Davis went on to say, "Because at the end of the day, you define you." This positive attitude certainly translates to her success: in midlife, she continues to be cast on both the big and small screens.

Davis belongs to the cohort of celebrities who are remaining in the spotlight well into midlife. Midlife women on the big screen, like Cameron Diaz, Nicole Kidman, Meryl Streep, and Julianne Moore, continue to succeed in roles other than the asexual and nurturing best friend. And how great do they do midlife! We're also seeing more and more women over forty, and even over fifty, gracing the covers of magazines, promoting products, and on our screens. Companies like L'Oréal continue to use famous actresses, including Diane Keaton, Jane Fonda, and Andie MacDowell, to pitch their products. Lauren Hutton is back modeling for the top designers, and so are Iman and Naomi Campbell.

Emme—the world's most popular curvy model, television personality, author, lecturer, creative director of clothing lines, and globally recognized women's advocate—devotes most of her time and energy to speaking about positive body image and self-esteem. More than twenty years ago she was able to help redefine beauty in the hypercompetitive fashion industry. Her personal goal was to show that a size 14/16 woman could be sexy and desirable day in and day out, without succumbing to the pressure to be thinner. She told me, "The public has spoken out with social media, and companies and art directors are starting to listen. Social media has been a huge game changer. Not only is it redefining what beauty is, the public is now in control and can boycott when advertisers make decisions that offend a larger part of their buying public. But I don't consider major movements happening until models regardless of their age and/or size are used in all the runway shows, projecting an image of strength."

Today, Emme is working with Syracuse University to create change within the global fashion community through a program called Fashion Without Limits (#FWL #SUFWL), where new designers are taught how to visualize, drape, and create patterns for size 4, 6, 8, 16, 20, and 22 dress forms, expanding the fashion conversation to include a much wider population of women than ever before. There is something we could all learn from this!

OUR APPEARANCE IN MIDLIFE IS MORE RELEVANT THAN EVER

At midlife, one of the most valuable lessons we can learn is the futility of looking to others for validation, including validation for how we look. Giving other people the power to tell us that we are good enough is always a dangerous proposition, because we're relinquishing control over our psyche without discounting another's perceptions and judgments. If we define our self-worth exclusively by the responses we get from others, we are coming at life from a weak place that ultimately only serves to make us feel bad about ourselves.

We will have moments in life when we take center stage, and moments when we don't. If aging is your Achilles' heel, then you will be especially aware when you are not the center of attention and blame it on the fact that you're getting older. This is what we call in my business "confirmation bias"—the tendency to assess situations in a way that reinforces our biases about events. This is one of the reasons why celebrity midlifers and other successful women our age are looking better than ever before. Their mindset is already working on their behalf, making them feel and look younger than any previous generation. It's like mental plastic surgery, only better, because there is no recovery time.

Confirmation bias can also work against you, leading to faulty thinking. For example, if you walk into a party and no one comes over to talk to you, and you are sensitive about your age, you may jump to the conclusion that no one is interested in you because you're too old. The reality might be something very different, and even something that has nothing to do with your age.

Your confirmation bias might be contributing to the feeling that you've become invisible. I can assure you, this is just your perception. When I asked Dr. Ellen Langer, professor of psychology at Harvard University, about women feeling invisible when they age, she said, "Most people feel invisible, no matter what their age." It's pretty safe to say that everyone would like to be recognized a bit more than they are. And this has nothing to do with age and everything to do with our innate desire to be recognized, valued, and unconditionally loved. To jump to the conclusion that feeling invisible is linked to getting older is a confirmation bias women in midlife may too quickly adopt and should reconsider.

The reality is, as you get older you don't become less relevant. In fact, in many ways you become more powerful, even in your sex appeal. When you turn yourself into the best version of yourself, authentically owning and liking who you are, it's an extremely seductive and powerful combination. Gail Sheehy tells a great story about Margaret Thatcher, who was prime minister of England when she was in her sixties. At the time, some of the most powerful men in the world found her to be very appealing and seductive. Thatcher owned her power and stayed authentic to herself. According to Sheehy, Thatcher took ionic footbaths that were meant to detoxify, cleanse, and balance the body by drawing out impurities through the feet. Thatcher believed these baths were the key to keeping her youthful, vibrant, and sexy, and who's to say they weren't? Perhaps they did. This little historical tidbit shows us that a powerful woman in her sixties had sexual confidence and a desire to be alluring as she aged.

By midlife, we've unpacked the media myths of youthfulness and seen where they don't hold up. For example, we now know that the beautiful women in magazines aren't flawless but have been Photoshopped to look perfect. On some level it's nice to think perfection is out there somewhere, because it can be a positive for us: It gives us something to work toward. It's comforting, like a modern-day fairy tale.

However, perfection is a demanding role model. In 1985, one in three women interviewed for a *Psychology Today* survey said they were unhappy with their appearance. When asked the same question in 1993, just a few years after Photoshop became a staple tool in the fashion industry, one in two women felt that way. Twenty years later, we are exposed to more digitally altered media than ever. Now we know the tricks, so hopefully we can be a little more forgiving about the way we look. We can still want to look good, but we can also recognize that our imperfections are no different from anyone else's. In fact, imperfections are normal and make us uniquely beautiful, especially if we work with them.

We know, too, that no one rolls out of bed looking gorgeous and ready to face the day, at any age. Looking good requires effort. I recently went to an amazing exhibit called *Beauty Is Power* at the Jewish Museum in New York City, which celebrated the twentieth-century cosmetics industrialist powerhouse Helena Rubinstein. I love what her attitude was about beauty and women. She once said, "Beauty is a matter of developing the right attitude and doing something about it." Say it, Helena!

The women we love to look at probably have a team of professionals at their disposal and work very hard to maintain their appearance. This is not to say it's impossible for the rest of us to look as good. But it's still nice to remind ourselves every now and again of what it really takes to look good. To me, it's worth it.

We need to learn how to gracefully turn the chapters in our lives. You may no longer be the youngest woman in the room, but if you embrace your new role, you can shine just the same. You don't want some external, outdated expiration date stopping you. You can choose to reject these misguided myths, recognize your attractiveness, and radiate your true beauty. But you first have to know that this is true and can happen! I love Madonna's Instagram posts, especially the ones that show off her midlife attitude. Recently she offered, "Shall I tell [my daughter] that she and her friends cannot be fierce when they are 56? Nope! I am raising #rebelhearts. Watch and learn."

There are many ways to combat midlife normative discontent. Finding other women your age to talk with about midlife and the physical changes you're experiencing is perhaps one of the best and most helpful ways. Understanding there is universality in how you are feeling can be tremendously comforting. What's more, you might pick up a trick or two from a friend to keep you looking and feeling younger and better about yourself.

AGELESSNESS IS BEAUTIFUL

Even with all of this progress, it would be naïve to say our culture has completely changed. The truth is, there will always be pressure to stay in shape and take care of ourselves, and as you learned in the previous chapter, some of the reasons for this pressure have nothing to do with beauty or self-worth. Beginning with the baby boomers and continuing into our generation, plenty of us want to look young not only to stay relevant but also because we intuitively know it is healthy for us.

In response, some midlife women have taken on the quest for youthfulness like it's a full-time job. This is a dramatic shift from the past, when mothers and grandmothers begrudgingly accepted a dowdy, matronly appearance. But thanks to the baby boomers, we have options. These women never accepted anything about getting older. Because of medical advances, they were able to see the downside of extended longevity, and they want to age differently.

Suzanne Somers has enjoyed a high profile and a successful multidimensional career for over four decades. The actress, singer, entrepreneur, and author of bestselling books, including *Ageless,* recently told me, "The way I look is the way I look. [Fashion designer] Tom Ford said to me, 'Suzanne, you would look weird if you didn't have wrinkles.' Tom Ford also said, 'I am tired of the cult of youth.' The cultural rejection of old age, the stigmatization of wrinkles, gray hair, of bodies furrowed by the years. I am fascinated by Diana Vreeland, Georgia O'Keeffe, and Louise Bourgeois—women who have let time embrace them without ever cheating. Society today condemns this; me, I celebrate it.'"

Suzanne told me, "I am focused on keeping my organs and glands youthful and healthy, which manifests on my exterior. I refuse to cover

my body with harsh and expensive chemical-laden skin care." Since Suzanne couldn't find products that were chemical-free, she created her own
line of organic hair care, skin care, and cosmetics called SUZANNE Or-
ganics available at SuzanneSomers.com.

Dr. Langer has set out to prove that how we perceive ourselves can
positively affect the way we age. One example is a 2010 study she conducted in a hair salon. She theorized that women who aged faster were
less influenced by their biological makeup and more influenced by the way
they perceived themselves. She approached forty-seven women, ranging in
age from twenty-seven to eighty-three, who were about to have their hair
done, and she took blood-pressure readings. After the subjects' hair was
styled, they filled out a questionnaire about how they felt they looked, and
their blood pressure was taken again. Langer reported that the women
who perceived themselves as looking younger after their hair had been
styled experienced a drop in blood pressure.

The women who can successfully navigate midlife are the ones who
can hold on to a more youthful self-image. Langer told me, "If [we] see
someone who looks young, we assume they are young (even if they're
not); if we see someone who looks old, we assume that they are old
(even if they're not). We find evidence for whatever we seek. If you
look for positive examples of aging, you'll find more numerous examples for what you're looking for. That's why ageist thinking allows us
to give up on ourselves prematurely. We hold lower expectations for
ourselves."

Today, many women in midlife continue to strive to look fit, wrinkle-
free, and fresh, and I don't believe that's a bad thing. There's some power
in taking care of yourself and feeling youthful, and the result is that we're
achieving a sort of agelessness. Women like Rene Russo and Christie
Brinkley, both of whom are in their sixties yet don't look old, and they
certainly don't give you the impression they are old. They present themselves as relevant and energized. Their age is not what walks out first; it's
who they are, what they've done, and what they're offering. When you

adopt this attitude yourself, you're saying *I'm still important, I'm better than I've been before, and I know I have so much to offer.*

You may know better than to compare yourself to any top model, yet at midlife I would bet that more than pining for your younger self, you are pining for a feeling your younger self had: that the future was hopeful and filled with possibilities, and that your body complied with whatever you asked of it. That's normal too, especially if you have occasional aches and pains. But when you can't stand to look at any sign of aging, it's a denial of reality, which doesn't serve you well. It also means you have a negativistic and distorted interpretation of what aging is all about. Women in midlife need to move forward, not look backward. You can't drive your car forward while looking in the rearview mirror. The goal is to feel beautiful in your own skin, not to look like you are twenty or thirty. Enjoy where you are. Forget your age and just have fun!

Being younger doesn't necessarily mean feeling better. One interesting finding of the MIDUS research was that anxiety about attractiveness is higher among women who are younger. We can idealize how we think we felt when we were younger, but the truth is, you might not have felt much different about yourself, or you might have been insecure about different things. This is particularly true for teenagers, who are overly preoccupied with the way they look, an adolescent behavior we don't want to adopt— and at midlife, we really have the wherewithal to avoid it.

REIN IN YOUR INNER DIVA

It's healthy to want to look good, feel good, and present yourself in a certain way, especially if your motivation is as simple as *I want to like myself. I want to feel good when I'm interacting with other people, when I go to work. I want to feel purposeful. I want to be healthy to support the life still ahead of me.*

But if looking good is all you think about, it's not really a healthy way to go. When you are too focused on your looks, it can become an obsession.

Focusing solely on your appearance can actually make you come off as insecure and dull to others. Worse, this preoccupation will increase your self-consciousness, forcing you to compare yourself unfairly to others. A better strategy is to find the right balance: you have to care enough, but not too much.

Your appearance can also suffer when you're very nervous and stressed out about the way you look. One recent study concluded that worrying actually makes you less attractive—and even makes others less attracted to you. Men find a worrier's face less attractive than a non-worrier's face. Perhaps this is partially because of the bloating effect a spiked level of the hormone cortisol has on the skin and on the body in general. As we've discussed, worrying leads to stress, which lowers self-esteem and ruins what could otherwise be an attractive feature: your confidence. What's more, compulsive interest in your appearance clouds your perception of what it really takes to be attractive to others, which is more about an attitude of living in the moment, enjoying yourself, and appreciating the people you're socializing with.

So take a break from focusing too much on your looks. Did you know that staring at yourself in a mirror can do more harm than good? According to researchers at the Institute of Psychiatry, Psychology, and Neuroscience in London, as reported in the journal *Behaviour Research and Therapy,* if we look at our reflection in a mirror for up to ten minutes, we can become increasingly anxious and depressed about our looks, even if we were satisfied with our appearance before looking in the mirror. The study showed that staring at the mirror increased distress among both healthy participants and people who suffer from body dysmorphic disorder, a condition in which sufferers chronically worry about their looks. Although everyone likes to take a quick glance at themselves every now and again, people who look in a mirror less frequently tend to focus on the parts of their body they feel good about. This makes perfect sense: when we stare at ourselves for too long, we tend to focus on our perceived imperfections.

If you want to feel good about yourself or your looks, here's an assignment to help put you on the right track:

For a whole day go without looking in a mirror or thinking about what you look like, and see how that feels. Do you experience a sense of freedom? What did you learn from that situation? Did you notice if others responded to you differently? Did you feel younger, older, or the same?

BODY IMAGE ISSUES DON'T END AT MIDLIFE

As I just touched on, extreme anxiety regarding self-image is referred to as "body dysmorphia." Those who have body dysmorphic disorder are overly preoccupied with an imagined imperfection or physical flaw others can't see. People who suffer from this problem often see themselves as homely, which is used as an excuse either to avoid social situations or to get plastic surgery to improve their appearance. This preoccupation can also lead to engaging in unhealthy ritualistic behaviors, such as constantly picking at themselves or continually looking in a mirror.

Body dysmorphic disorder is similar to an eating disorder, especially for women in midlife. Margo Maine, Ph.D., wrote in her book *The Body Myth,* "When eating disorders or body image conflicts are mentioned, the face we imagine is one of youth. It may be a preteen, an adolescent, or a young adult woman, but we rarely visualize an ageing face in that picture. Yet more and more older women, approaching or beyond midlife, are admitting that they too struggle with their bodies and their eating and are seeking professional help."

Researchers Tamara Pryor, Ph.D., and Kenneth L. Weiner, M.D., reported that women who develop anorexia or bulimia in midlife may have experienced long-term struggles with body image, had an eating disorder during the adolescent years, or developed an eating disorder after a critical illness. The physiological and psychological changes that happen during menopause echo changes at puberty, which may make midlife a high-risk period for the development of new eating disorders or the reemergence of old ones.

Some professionals call the development of eating disorders during midlife the "desperate housewife syndrome," referring to the hit TV series, which featured thin and attractive women in their forties and fifties. Rather than blame eating disorders on pressures from television images, I believe eating disorders during midlife link back to the fear and anxiety of getting older and what we've been led to believe getting older means in terms of staying attractive. This may be coupled with a fear of obesity. Midlife anorexics and bulimics are desperate in another way: they want to take control of some part of their appearance, which triggers unhealthy eating patterns. They believe the right appearance, weight, and diet can mitigate their stress and answer their relentless questions about their worth, to themselves and to others.

Many of the treatment options for addressing eating disorders will depend on the severity of the illness, and they include outpatient, intensive outpatient, partial hospitalization, residential, and inpatient. What's most important is to get professional help. While eating disorders are often challenging to treat, during midlife women can bring their maturity, insights, and life experience with them into the process. They also tend to have an increased awareness of how dangerous eating disorders can be, which is a major motivation to get well. With the proper care and intervention, these very serious disorders can be successfully addressed and overcome.

ATTRACTIVENESS COMES FROM LOOKING INWARD

While we aren't striving to look like our younger selves, we may still want to improve the way we look, dwelling on correcting something that has always bothered us. You might have always wanted thinner arms, bigger (or smaller) breasts, straighter teeth. Or you might obsess about your weight. In today's world, where plastic surgery, orthodontics, and liposuction are just a phone call away, all of these fixes are possible, but they aren't going to make you feel better about yourself. The harder work is taking ownership of *why* you feel the way you do about your looks, *why* you want to look different, and *what* you want to change. Start by asking yourself these questions:

How do I talk to myself about my looks? Does this help me or hurt me? Write down a statement you often say to yourself. If it's hurtful, see if you can replace it with something more positive and truthful about yourself. For example, instead of saying "I hate my thighs," you can say "I'm a work in progress, and exercising more will tone up my body, including my thighs."

Am I using my appearance as a way to isolate myself? Is it a way to not be in the world? Is it a way to deal with my insecurities? If any of this is the case, I want to introduce you to something called the "spotlight effect." This is a real psychological term that refers to those times when we think everyone is homing in on our imperfections (a true teenage reaction if there ever was one). The truth is, people in the world are far too involved with their own imperfections to notice what's wrong with you. So take the pressure off yourself, and keep this reality in mind.

What don't I like about myself? What can I improve? First, you need to figure out the underlying reason why you are unhappy with the way you look. Part of it is holding yourself responsible for your appearance. You may need to give yourself some tough love and do an intervention. Tell yourself, *The buck stops with me. If I want to look and feel better, and be less anxious, I have to trust myself to make the right changes happen.* Then make a realistic plan to work on each of the areas you want to improve.

Action is always the antidote for feeling powerless and paralyzed. Taking the first step in the direction you want to move is more than half the battle. If you are totally committed to making midlife great, choose three new behaviors you can put into action immediately that will change the way you look and feel. The right diet, the right exercise program, and getting better rest, as we discussed in previous chapters are ideal places to start. Fruits and vegetables are full of hydrating water, which will give you a healthier appearance. Adding healthy fats to your diet will not only make your skin supple but also bring back the natural luster to your hair and even your nails.

When you can trust yourself to makes these changes, your anxiety will dissipate. Remember, anxiety is just the feeling of not being in control, and once you prove to yourself that you are in control of your life, by taking these actions, you can start to rebuild your sense of self and your self-esteem.

MAGICAL AGE-DEFYING SKIN TREATMENTS

The lifestyle choices you make show up in your skin. A fascinating 2009 twin study identified the environmental factors that contribute to facial aging. It revealed that a slightly higher body mass index was associated with an older appearance in twins younger than age forty but resulted in a younger appearance, including an increase in hair quantity after age forty, with even better results at age fifty-five (which is one good reason not to obsess too much about your weight, especially if you are within a healthy range). Increased sun exposure as well as the years spent smoking were associated with an older appearance. Women who used hormone replacement therapy had a younger appearance, but those who took antidepressants generally looked older. In addition to the aging effect of depressed people's sadder facial expressions, certain depression-relieving drugs can weaken eye muscles, causing the area to look droopy. Women who didn't drink looked younger than their twins who did. Divorced women were judged to look an average of 1.7 years older than their married or single twin—possibly because of higher levels of stress or depression.

While we can't erase our past actions, we can attempt to reverse the damage. Women have an unprecedented number of options for slowing or modifying the aging process that we've never had before. Science and commerce have joined together to create game-changing options for women who want to look their best. These opportunities are important to explore because you don't have to resign yourself to premature aging. The truth is, when you look your best, you feel your best. There is an undeniable correlation. When you like the way you look, you carry yourself with more confidence and you experience yourself as more beautiful and powerful; these factors influence how you present yourself to the world.

The latest research proves my point. In her book *How the Body Knows Its Mind: The Surprising Power of the Physical Environment to Influence How You Think and Feel,* Sian Beilock stated that while we know the mind influences the body, the body can also have a strong influence on the mind. Our body influences our thoughts by sending messages in real time to the brain about how we are experiencing ourselves in an environment. So if you are happy with the way you look and you are carrying yourself with more confidence, the subtle signal the body sends will reinforce the positive experience.

New Skin Treatments to Explore

There is an incredible range of beauty products that can effectively soften wrinkles, fill in lines, and otherwise change the way we look. One goal for looking healthier is to find ways to help stimulate new collagen, a protective fiber located just below the outermost layer of skin. Collagen has the flexibility and strength to hold tissue and organs together, expand with growth, and repair damaged cells. With age, sunlight, and free-radical exposure, collagen production tapers off, and the quality of collagen is not as good. You'll notice that your skin loses its elasticity. You can replenish collagen through the foods you eat (fruits and veggies high in vitamin C, along with lean proteins) and with various skin care treatments.

When it comes to skin care, prevention is always the best medicine.

A 2013 study published in the *Annals of Internal Medicine* proved that those who used sunscreen every day had noticeably more resilient and smoother skin than those who didn't. Consistent use of sun protection led to fewer wrinkles and better protection against future skin aging. In addition, topical products and skin treatments can restore collagen production. Other studies have shown that salicin, a compound produced from willow bark, may regulate functional "youth gene clusters" to reflect a more youthful gene expression and, when used topically, may reverse the appearance of aged skin.

Most dermatologists can provide laser treatments, fillers, and Botox injections to erase the lines of midlife. The downside of Botox and peels often stems from either treatment not being done well, according to dermatologist Doris Day, M.D. There is no long-term commitment necessary with Botox or a peel; even if you have only one treatment, it's still helpful. Day also advocates for inexpensive skin care products that are just as effective as higher-priced department store brands. She told me that she believes Oil of Olay and Neutrogena are good brands, and she is currently collaborating with Christie Brinkley on a new skin care line called Authentic Skin Care, which will be sold at Kohl's and on HSN.

There are also inexpensive devices that can improve the skin's appearance. Light therapy is an exciting and inexpensive option. Dr. Z. Paul Lorenc is the chief medical and scientific officer of La Lumière LLC and a board-certified aesthetic plastic surgeon. He has created an anti-aging phototherapy mask called illuMask, which sells at Walmart for less than thirty dollars. The technology uses LEDs of specific wavelengths to even out skin tone, reduce the appearance of fine lines, and improve the overall appearance of skin. This light therapy captures the healing power of the sun but filters out the harmful ultraviolet rays. The light stimulates cellular rejuvenation of the skin, making it more supple and noticeably more youthful looking. Dr. Lorenc believes that one day we'll have a more advanced light therapy that can reverse the signs of aging entirely. I'll be signing up for that therapy, for sure.

The most interesting trend came to my attention from a New York City dermatologist, Dr. Macrene Alexiades-Armenakas, who says her typical midlife patient is seeking an improved middle-aged look. These women don't want to look unnaturally younger, just better. Her clients are professional women who believe the right image for them no longer means looking young.

FIND YOUR SEXY SELF

My patient Tanya stormed into my office one day, visibly upset, and said, "My husband and I have been married forever. We work really hard and have three great kids. Now not a day goes by when I'm not tired. I don't feel sexy anymore. I'd be afraid my husband would leave me except for the fact that he's exhausted, too. But I feel like I'm disappointing him, and more important, I'm disappointing myself."

Tanya was expressing how many women in midlife feel. So much of our self-worth is tied to how attractive we feel and how attractive we believe we are to others. Straight or gay, women want to be desired. At midlife, some women worry that men will no longer find them attractive or that only skinny people are in love or able to find love. Single women at midlife might fear that they are competing with women half their age or that no man will want them. When this happens I instruct my patients to look around and take an informal survey. Is it only the most beautiful people who find themselves happy, in love, and in satisfying relationships? The answer I always hear is "No," which is when I remind them that's not the way love works. People of all shapes and sizes are able to find love; it's not reserved for only the young and the beautiful.

The first thing I asked Tanya to focus on was what she thought was sexy about herself. We talked about the last time she had felt sexy and what it would take to re-create those circumstances. Finally, I suggested she find a role model whose look she admired and could incorporate or borrow from. It's almost an exercise in rethinking ourselves. I explained that sexy isn't natural and effortless for anyone. I sent her home with an assignment: to bring back some photos of women she knows whose appearance or style she found sexy.

At our next session Tanya came back with a handful of photos of her friend Alison. I was pleasantly surprised, because even though Alison was a strikingly beautiful and sexy woman, Tanya told me that Alison was actually a good eight years older than she was. We looked at the photos closely, like we were private investigators. Was Tanya responding to her clothes, her makeup, her hairstyle, or her body? I find women choose role models whom they feel similar to in some way. Maybe it's in looks, maybe it's in intellect, or maybe it's in personality. But they identify with them.

I asked Tanya to describe the ways she felt similar to her friend Alison. The underlying question was, how could Tanya become a better version of herself by incorporating Alison's look? Then I explained that if she was going to feel good about herself, she would have to do something, even one small fix. If she really wanted to look just like her friend, she needed to lose some weight, but in the meantime, she could find a similar dress, get her hair blown out, or just buy a new shade of lipstick. Tanya realized that if she put some attention and effort into the way she looked, her sexy self could shine through.

At midlife, women can rebel against the notion that they are only considered attractive if they look a certain age or a certain way. The real goal in midlife is to identify your best self, and accept and embrace your beauty and sexuality. Part of looking attractive is recognizing your strengths, knowing how to play them up, and enjoying yourself and your uniqueness in the world. It starts with acknowledging what you like about yourself. Everybody likes something about themselves. Even the most insecure woman likes one thing about her appearance. If you start with what you like, you can make that incredible and build on your looks with what works now.

Look in the mirror, and see if you can isolate what makes your face unique. It can be something as small as your eyebrows, as long as

*you identify and own it. Tell yourself how much you love this fea-
ture. Then write yourself a love or affirmation note. Put something
positive in it about yourself, such as "I love my _____ and I am
beautiful." You can even use an inspiring quote to keep you on track.
I love this one by Golda Meir: "Trust yourself. Create the kind of self
that you will be happy to live with all of your life." Or use whatever
resonates for you. Put it in a place where you can see it every day,
and read it out loud if you need to. Do it until you can feel like your
own supportive best friend.*

We all have days when we look in the mirror and notice what looks
terrible. When I have one of those days, I focus on that flaw and try to
improve the way I look. It's really important to be able to access, embrace,
and turn up the volume on your inner sense of beauty. And sometimes it's
as easy as taking care of yourself via a very simple beauty routine. Nothing
fancy—just an easy ritual to remind yourself that you're worth investing
time and energy into. Sending your brain the message that you're worth
it can enhance the way you feel about your looks—what I like to call your
"prettiness self-esteem."

I engage in this routine with the intention of feeling more beautiful
and alluring. For me, maybe it starts with something as simple as taking
a shower or washing my hair, because being clean is always a good place
to start, right? If I'm still not happy, I put on something comfortable yet
semi-stylish. Usually something plain so I can rock some bold piece of
vintage jewelry I have. Then I put a little more effort into my makeup routine. First, I focus on my eyes, putting on mascara that makes my lashes
look as long as possible, and then I put on my favorite neutral lipstick. If
I'm really feeling ambitious, I wear a pair of high heels. Since I'm short, I
always think I look better when I'm a little bit taller.

When my patients are down about the way they look, I encourage them
to take a second look at their wardrobe and their hair and makeup, and
mix it up a bit.

Dress for the Life You Want

Author Tess Whitehurst encourages women in midlife, in her book *Magical Fashionista,* to use clothing and fashion as a tool for self-empowerment. She advocates that we should not miss out on a day of feeling good, even if we have nowhere special to go. Dressing up doesn't have to be left for only special occasions. She also suggests we dress for the life we want and use fashion as a way to express our inner desires, whether they involve getting a new job, finding a new love interest, or simply having a great day. She believes, as I do, that clothing choices are a powerful way to get our inner and outer realities in sync.

When we feel better, Whitehurst reminds us, we make better choices, exude more confidence, and elicit a greater degree of respect from others. One of the first steps is to get rid of the clothes that no longer suit you. Throw out everything that doesn't fit, looks shabby, or brings you down for one reason or another. Without you even wearing them, these clothes are holding you back. Fashion is accessible to every woman and at every budget. Take the time to find clothes that highlight your best features, your inner radiance, and your agelessness. Have fun with your choices, and make sure you're always dressing for the person you want to be. What you wear not only speaks to other people; it speaks to you, too.

Adolescents are willing to stay fresh and current and try new things. They take chances to find their style and are aware of trends in a way that keeps their spirit youthful and creative. Karen Pine said in her book *Mind What You Wear,* "We really can enrich our lives when we experiment with different outfits, learning to be more playful with our wardrobe choices, trying things we may never have tried before, even getting something the opposite of what we might normally wear can break us out of our myopic rut. As much as your brain likes routines, it also likes novelty. The reward centers of the brain are stimulated when we try something new and unfamiliar, it gives us a sense of pleasure." At midlife, you may have a certain style you like; you may be drawn to certain colors or patterns. But if you're willing to stay current and fresh, you'll feel younger, because you're always in that space of willingness to do something new, which keeps your mind-set current and open instead of closed.

"Sexy" is a mind game any woman can play, regardless of her age. Just look at Madonna: at midlife, Madonna is as sexy and racy as ever. If you want to dress sexy, go for it. What you choose to wear is only inappropriate if you think it's inappropriate, if you're not being authentic with yourself, whether you're sixty or forty-five. It is every woman's prerogative to age in the way that's right for her. Those of us who do want to dress to showcase our physical attributes and our sexuality shouldn't be expected to stay home because we're no longer menstruating. What's beautiful about midlife is that we no longer have to care if somebody doesn't like what we wear.

Express Your Personality with an Updated Look

How you look influences how you experience life and think about yourself. It also affects how you experience others. If you continue doing the "same old, same old" forever, especially with your hair, it's going to bring you down. You are not the same person you were in your twenties and thirties, so why should you have the same look? Perhaps it's time to communicate who the new you is, even to yourself. You owe it to yourself to give expression to the various and sometimes unexpressed parts of your personality—and your hair and makeup are great tools with which to do that.

If you can tweak your hairstyle just a little bit and freshen up your look, you'll be happier with the result. And this doesn't have to be an expensive endeavor at all. Actress Juliette Lewis shared her midlife beauty secrets in the *New York Times,* and they were refreshingly simple and attainable. She shops at Whole Foods for all her beauty products, prefers a natural cosmetics line by Raw Beauty, and uses coconut oil for everything, including on her hair and body. Now, that's one-stop shopping!

Be your own art project. Experiment with different looks, different ways to wear makeup, and different hairstyles. The conventional wisdom used to be that if you're past a certain age, you cut your hair short. That thinking has been thrown out the window, so go ahead, let it grow. Try on that smoky eye look. What's the big deal? Nobody's going to die if you try something new and it doesn't work. Be willing to consider what's fresh, what's current. This is a time when you don't need to ask others for permission to change up your appearance or try something different.

Whatever you decide is right for you is the right decision. Beauty is all about saying yes to yourself. At midlife, we get too used to saying *No, I can't do this. No, I can't do that. I shouldn't wear this. That's too tight. I can't say yes to that; I don't have time. I shouldn't buy this; I should be spending my money on other things.* If you're always in a place of *no,* you're shutting your life down. Is there a place for *no*? Of course. But there's also a place for *yes.*

TEEN TOOL: FIND YOUR INSPIRATION

Teens look to others for inspiration. They create collages, posters, and Pinterest pages of people and things they find compelling and beautiful. It inspires their fashion and beauty sense and allows them to creatively discover who they want to be. You can literally take a page from their book. It can be a virtual page, like Pinterest, or as low-tech as a notebook or a folder. Collect magazine clippings or photos from the Internet that inspire or appeal to you. Keep your eye out for images of beautiful women, and notice how close they are to your age. Then analyze what you see. Notice what you're drawn to—all the looks you like, etc. This technique can help you not only discover your sense of style and beauty but also find a new and improved look. Now assess if what you surround yourself with in your life resembles what's in your collected images. This can inspire you to try some different ideas and freshen up your look, and help you to discover the new you.

Then think of a woman who is comfortable in her body and exudes confidence. Don't just choose someone who has the face, hair, and body you've always wanted to have. Think of someone who appears to feel confident, sexy, relevant, and good. What do you notice about her?

What is her posture like? Her expression? How does she carry her body? What does she do when she meets or chats with others? Now close your eyes and let your body relax into her posture. Imagine yourself walking and talking the way she does. What does it feel like? What clothes are you wearing? Are you smiling? Now imagine you living your life as that confident person. Would you do things differently? How would living like this person affect your responses to people on a day-to-day basis? Would you feel emboldened in some areas of your life?

My Mom

My mother, Helene, has always had a huge impact on my life. I suppose one of the reasons for this is because she continues to be an amazing source of insight and wisdom, especially when it comes to the topic of beauty. Youth does not always equal beauty. As my beauty mentor, my mother taught me that getting older can mean becoming more beautiful. Midlife in my childhood home was not portrayed or feared as a time when you lose your looks. It was considered just another phase in which to be beautiful, fabulous, and sexy.

Helene was always a bit of a fashionista. At age seventy-five, she still believes that her best age is now, and she shows it by continuing to wear the latest fashions. When I was a kid, I was always mesmerized when she'd put on her makeup and fix her hair. Before leaving the house, she was always so well put together. The false eyelashes and her long black hair made her stand out in a crowd. During my youth, she looked like a combination of Audrey Hepburn (especially in her wedding photos) and Marlo Thomas (during the *That Girl* days).

But what I particularly love about my mother's beauty philosophy is her approach to aging. She has never had an issue with it. I never once heard my mother say "Now I'm over the hill" or "Wow, I'm old." She seems to appreciate, feel pretty at, and enjoy every age she entered. God bless her! My mother admires good looks whether she is looking at a fifteen-year-old or a sixty-year-old. And she is always the first to point out when someone is getting prettier with age. I feel lucky Helene passed on to me this ability to see beauty at any age.

I recently asked my mother if she had ever felt invisible. She said maybe sometimes, around strangers, who might at first assume she had nothing important to say or contribute. But she said she never felt invisible around the people who mattered most to her, including her children, her family, and her friends. My mother knows how to live life with exuberance. She enjoys every moment, especially when she's around the people she loves. Her attitude is infectious, ageless, and always beautiful, both inside and out!

VALIDATION FROM THE OTHER SIDE OF THE MIRROR

While how we feel about our appearance does influence how we experience ourselves, we also need to find other ways to validate ourselves besides the way we look. Nothing is more attractive than confidence. A woman with confidence can shine as much as the most beautiful woman in the room. Confidence affects the way we express and carry ourselves. It creates an inner glow and a "wow factor" that radiate outward.

I know it may sound paradoxical, but finding fulfillment really has more to do with whether your life vision is in sync with your values than what you look like. Are you doing what you want to do in life? Do you have intimate relationships and supportive people around you? Do you have a purpose? Having meaning in your life and a community that allows you to discuss your feelings can make it much easier to come to terms with the normal changes taking place in your face and body, and in your life. Women who believe they are where they need to be in their lives are less affected by the tyranny of external beauty.

As Diane von Fürstenberg wrote in her own book *The Woman I Wanted to Be,* "In my older face I see my life. . . . My face reflects the wind and sun and rain and dust from the trips I've taken. My face carries all my memories. Why should I erase them?" This idea is an incredibly empowering one. Diane von Fürstenberg is certainly a role model for aging gracefully and naturally. Getting older can make us better, wiser, and, *yes,* more attractive. Every year you've lived has made you, you. You may look different from the way you looked in previous decades, but who's to say that difference means you're getting worse rather than better? You can internalize the idea that as you get older you continue to move into your true greatness and beauty.

I love the question Suzanne Somers posed when I interviewed her for this book. She said, "If you didn't know how old you are, how old would you be?" At sixty-nine and looking amazing, Suzanne doesn't get caught up in thinking that getting older means anything negative, and neither should you.

SEVEN

FINDING LOVE

My patient Brad was one of those guys who had always had a way with the ladies. They love him, and it isn't hard to see why. He's a good-looking man in his late forties who is smart and successful—the total package. When he finally got married, he never imagined he'd be back in the dating world seven years and two kids later.

Brad came to see me when his marriage fell apart. Even though he was angry about the divorce, he was ready to start dating right away. We talked about the kind of woman he was looking for this time, and he was really clear: there was no question he was looking for a woman his own age. When I asked him why he felt so strongly, he said, "Younger women are looking for a knight in shining armor. Their expectations are too high and too unrealistic. Women my age have a better sense about what a real relationship looks like and what it takes to make it work. They are more realistic, more mature, and just as sexy."

I told Brad he was smart to stick with his instincts. He eventually met a forty-five-year-old single mother of two kids around the same age as his, and now they live very happily together as a large blended family.

The most recent studies show that Brad's choice is not so uncommon for men in midlife. While men looking for short-term relationships may prefer younger women, according to Andrew Smiler, Ph.D., author of *Challenging Casanova,* 95 percent of men are looking for long-term mates, and these men prefer peers with similar intellectual and cultural preferences. They want a partner, an ally. But more important, they are looking for the traits only women in midlife have in spades: experience, confidence, and wisdom. And men also feel the sex will be better. Christian Rudder, author of *Dataclysm,* found when studying women's stated preferences on the dating website OkCupid. com, midlifers have more sex-positive attitudes compared with younger women. This is good news for any midlife woman, straight or gay, because having a satisfying sex life is one of the most important ways we can continue to feel young.

Brad and other men like him are proof that love is not the sole province of the young. Great love can happen at any point on the timeline of a person's life, either within a relationship or by finding a new relationship. Yet too many women have bought into the conventional wisdom that at midlife it's too late for love. Many have sought my help navigating difficulties in their marriages, breaking unhealthy relationship patterns, or seeking out life companions. Often these women feel locked in, or locked out, and don't believe things can change.

When I meet with these women, I'm quickly able to reduce their anxiety with facts. The truth is, an increasing number of women are creating their own midlife love story, whether they are rekindling their marriage or finding new love. They are discovering they are just as sensual, sexual, and loving as they age. In this chapter we'll uncover why midlife just might be the exact right time for you to reawaken your love life and find the happiness in your relationship that you deserve.

MIDLIFE IN LOVE

As women's roles in society continue to change, our ideals of romance and marriage change, too. The old mindset about relationships was attached to a pretty fixed timeline and structure. You had to be married in order to have a legitimate family; you had to be young in order to have children; and the only valid marriages were between a man and a woman. Today, we know that none of these so-called defining features of marriage still hold. What's more, in the past women might have been satisfied with a mate who matched their temperament, could take care of them financially, and would allow them to stick to their traditional roles of housewife and mother.

Our generation came up with a different love story narrative. Tara Parker-Pope, *New York Times* columnist and author of *For Better: The Science of a Good Marriage,* found that, beginning with Generation X, couples now have far higher expectations from the institution of marriage. Instead of marrying a good provider, women in our generation have sought the perfect life partner. Both women and men want their partners to be a soul mate—someone who will be there for them when they need them and validate their feelings and desires. They want a pleasing, fulfilling experience that includes an element of personal satisfaction, i.e., *I should be happy in my relationship.* This desire for a greater emotional connection arrived just as women had increased financial freedom and independence.

Midlife is the natural time for women to question what they really want in life. It's a wake-up call to address who they want to be. Their changing roles along with their changing views of themselves can shift their priorities; what they want from a relationship now might be different from their earlier desires. Every woman has goals for her relationship that look a little bit like a checklist, and they can change as she gets older. *I regret marrying him* and *Did I make the right choice?* are thoughts women in midlife can often have.

Similar role changes are happening for men as well. While they might be biologically attracted to women who can provide offspring, they are also interested in women with earning power. I've noticed a clear shift in the relationship dynamic among men our age who realize they don't have to be the only one carrying the financial pressure. I've met plenty of midlife men, whether they are dating or married, who want life partners who bring financial value to the table. What's more, they want to understand a woman's spending habits as well as her earning potential before they commit.

Some psychologists believe women of all ages want levels of emotional connection from men that, unfortunately, most men were not raised to deliver. The gap between what's desired and reality can create intense feelings of disappointment for women, and by midlife they are ready to share exactly how they feel. With the prospect of a longer life span ahead of them, some women begin to think, *This is not what I bargained for. I still have a long life ahead of me and I want something different. Where has the love gone in my relationship?* Men, on the other hand, are often confused by these complaints and feel that their wives demand too much, that their efforts are taken for granted, or their wives have unrealistic or unfair expectations of them. While it's true we place our highest expectations on the people we love, these expectations can cause real strife in a marriage during midlife.

However, there is plenty of good news. Our generation succeeded in extending youth, and because of this we typically married later in life. These marriages are succeeding more frequently as a result, which means women in midlife are working out their issues with their spouses. Research featured in the *Journal of Family Psychology* indicates that risk for divorce drops significantly when couples wait to wed until after the age of twenty-five. And according to Tara Parker-Pope, delaying marriage means many of the weakest relationships end before the actual wedding occurs.

Midlife women who divorce or were never married are finding love in their forties and fifties and beyond. In fact, more people are marrying during midlife than ever before. These relationships tend to be better, because we know ourselves and what we're looking for. And best of all, what we're looking for are the qualities that make up healthy relationships, like who can be a good partner, friend, and father, instead of qualities associated with over-romanticizing a relationship, such as the perfect partner who will save and take care of us.

While being in a relationship is not the only way to achieve happiness, a good relationship can have many positive effects. First, a solid, loving relationship can help you become a better version of yourself, or the person you are meant to be, by supporting and encouraging your interests and goals. It can also help you to see the world from a different point of view, one that provides a clearer and healthier perspective: for example, viewing yourself less as a powerless victim and more as a valuable person with viable choices and options.

At midlife, I know you can find what you want in love. The wisdom you've gained about yourself puts you in a great position to enhance your relationship, or find a new one that speaks to your deepest truths and desires. The key is to keep the fears, distortions, and myths about midlife from holding you back. Then you can take a good hard look at yourself and see how you can modify your ideas and behaviors to have the loving relationship you've always wanted.

THE HARD WORK OF RELATIONSHIPS BEGINS WITH YOU

When Diane first came to see me she was forty-eight, hopeless, angry, and frustrated. She was picking up the pieces of her life after a long-term relationship with the man she believed was the love of her life had ended abruptly. After dating for ten years, he broke up with Diane and instead chose to be in a committed relationship with someone else. Diane truly believed she was destined to remain lonely, depressed, and single for the rest of her life. She was devastated and felt hopeless about ever being happy or in love again.

I helped Diane mourn her relationship and then began to correct her distorted thinking about herself and her future possibilities. Together we pierced her negativistic attitude about finding love during midlife by challenging her rigid mindset. She expressed an extreme fear of rejection and held unrealistic expectations of the people in her life. These factors, along with her negativity, were holding her back from accepting the truth: we can fall madly in love at any time of life. We talked about some of the people she knew in her life who had found love successfully during midlife. She agreed that in many ways they were no different than she was. In fact, when she thought about it more during our session, she felt she had even more to offer than some of the women she knew who had been successful in finding love later in life. As she considered this new perspective, she began to view herself in a much more positive and confident light. It made a huge difference in how she experienced herself and her prospects.

Next, we explored some of her strengths. She told me, "I can be very funny, and at work men really do like me." As her list grew, and she was reminded of how often she had been successful with men, she started to carry herself in a very different way. Although she was not always hopeful about how her story would end, I told her not to act on her fears. I instructed her to follow her plan, not her feelings. She decided to take my advice and act on her goal of finding true love. She signed up for an Internet dating service called OurTime.com and wasn't on the site long before she found a man who was everything she'd always wanted but never thought she'd find. The two started dating, and within a few months she was able to obtain a level of commitment she'd never had before.

Every woman experiences Diane's pain and frustration at some point during midlife. Relationships never seem to quite measure up. It's hard enough to have a good relationship with yourself and want to be around yourself all the time, let alone another person. What makes us think our partner will be someone we're going to want to always be around?

Seemingly dysfunctional relationships are often created out of personal unhappiness. Even if it looks like your relationship is the problem, the solution might be to first do the work on yourself. Your personal baggage may interfere with feeling satisfied with your relationship. It can influence everything from who you choose and who you feel you deserve to how you experience even the best relationship. And, of course, a dissatisfying relationship can certainly interfere with you feeling personally and emotionally fulfilled.

When I'm working with a woman in midlife who is unhappy in her marriage or looking for a new love, we start by asking questions. Often the answers reveal exactly how she feels about herself. The following questions to ask yourself are equally useful if you're single or in a relationship and want more from it. Just because you're in a committed relationship doesn't mean you stop having goals for what you want your partnership to look like.

> *What kind of relationship am I looking for?*
>
> *What didn't work in the past?*
>
> *What do I want a relationship to do for me?*
>
> *What do I really like about myself that other people don't know, and how can I get other people to know this part of me?*

These questions can help you parse out exactly what you want from a relationship, including your deepest needs and desires.

THE REALITIES OF MIDLIFE MARRIAGE

Marriage at midlife can be comfortable and familiar. It can also be dependent, dysfunctional, and, at times, monotonous. Some women in long-term relationships may long for more: more romance, more financial stability, more compassion, more excitement. Marriages suffer when we've developed a tendency to take one another for granted, we live parallel lives, or there is a noticeable shift in dynamics once children are either the sole focus or no longer living at home. Where we are as parents in midlife greatly affects the marriage. Women who had children when they were young are in a different space when their kids go off to college compared to midlifers who are still raising their children.

Marriage burnout often occurs at midlife. It is a state of physical, emotional, and mental exhaustion that occurs when couples finally realize, despite all their efforts, their marriage does not meet their emotional needs. Periods of discontent become more and more frequent, and what were once mild feelings of dissatisfaction grow. Some believe marriage burnout, or marital dissatisfaction in general, is related to menopause, but Pepper Schwartz, Ph.D., does not put a lot of stock in this correlation. She told me, "If there is a huge emotional upheaval, it's usually indicative of there being a problem prior to menopause, like an issue with depression or a marital problem. The main reason for a problem in the marriage during menopause tends not to mirror a drop in estrogen."

Earning potential and shifting roles at home have also changed what midlife marriage looks like. Dr. Schwartz believes navigating these changes is a critical factor for a successful marriage. Can a wife come to terms with her husband earning less? Can a husband come to terms with his position or the fact that his wife earns more? Can they work together given this new dynamic? If the wife realizes she's married to a great guy, even if he earns less than she does, she may decide it's better to redefine her priorities than to divorce.

For example, my client Rebecca loves her new job as a college professor and doesn't feel it's an issue that she earns more money than her husband. She told me that her husband had worked for most of their married life, which had given her the opportunity to be the stay-at-home mom she had always wanted to be. Now that she earns more than he does, she realizes this shift is not a deal breaker for their relationship but a way for them to finance a more enjoyable life together.

Dr. Schwartz sees marriage during midlife as different for those who are in their second or third marriage. These marriages are marked by either increased points of conflict or more understanding in general. The personal problems that didn't get worked out in an earlier marriage return in subsequent marriages. Different lifestyles can also be a source of tension in remarriages during midlife. However, because midlife women can be more forgiving, by the second marriage they may overlook the things that don't matter. Socks on the floor or extreme neatness are not deal breakers and they get filed away in the bigger picture of life. Women in second marriages know that all partners are imperfect. At midlife, they can review the landscape around them and then look at their own relationship and say, *I think I'll keep what I have. I'm not going to let little complaints get in the way of my happiness. I'm appreciative of having a loving partner and being in a committed relationship.*

Being in a "good marriage" at midlife means you're getting several characteristics you can work with. You are still irritated by the things that always irritate you, have irritated you for twenty-four years, and will probably irritate you for twenty-four more. However, the underlying belief is that you tolerate these irritations because they are overbalanced by the good stuff.

Judith S. Wallerstein, Ph.D., coauthor of *The Good Marriage: How and Why Love Lasts,* came up with this helpful list about what marriage is really like. I think it perfectly applies to marriage at midlife.

Marriage is not a 24-hour repair shop. Your partner is not supposed to meet your every need. Some of those needs you may have to take care of yourself.

Marriage is when you can separate emotionally from the family you grew up in; not to the point of estrangement, but enough so that your identity is separate from that of your parents and siblings.

Marriage is based on a shared intimacy and identity, while at the same time maintains boundaries to protect each partner's autonomy.

Marriage is often embracing the daunting roles of parenthood. Learn to continue the work of protecting the privacy of you and your spouse as a couple. Remember, after the kids leave, it's just going to be you and your partner.

Marriage is when you can confront and master the inevitable crises of life together as a team.

Marriage is a safe haven in which partners are able to express their differences, anger, and conflict.

Marriage is the early romantic, idealized images of falling in love while facing the sober realities of the changes wrought by time.

THE DISAPPOINTMENTS OF MIDLIFE MARITAL LOVE

A typical midlife marital challenge is a reflection on life in general: disappointments are going to happen. What do we do with the anger or regret in a marriage? People in successful marriages are able to put anger and regrets into proper perspective and maintain a realistic and adaptable mindset. If your love story isn't satisfying, you need to examine your beliefs, challenge them, dig deep, and uncover what your unfounded assumptions are based on.

For example, love and relationships are fraught with stories we tell ourselves that just aren't true. One of these false beliefs is that the right relationship always feels good and is easy and stress-free. This fantasy is culturally reinforced: the myth of the perfect connection. We unconsciously carry an image of the perfect partner. From fairy tales like Cinderella to the modern-day *Fifty Shades of Grey*, we've been taught to confuse lust and attraction for true love. Movies and books portray relationships as passionate and exciting all the time. I like the term used to describe this phenomenon: "emotional porn." Just as visual pornography creates unrealistic expectations for sex, our fanciful stories of love wire our brain to expect a daily epic moment of dramatic love. When life doesn't look like this, it's easy to think something is wrong, and it's not uncommon for women in midlife to feel like the love is gone so it may be time to move on. How can realistic love compete with emotional porn when it's filled with the daily drudgery of taking out the garbage, paying bills, and cleaning up after everyone?

A regressed fantasy of love usually reflects the powerful wish that another person should be close to perfect and meet all our needs: a sexy, idealized parental figure. We're inclined to choose a partner who is familiar to us, based on what we experienced in childhood, which is why people believe we either marry our mother or father, or choose a partnership that reenacts our parents' relationship. This idealized image is also based on the cultural messages we have received about love from movies, stories, and TV. We then compile and internalize these images, and the partner who closely matches these images is most likely to give us the feeling of being in love. And when this fails to happen, it can create resentment and upset.

The fact that we think there should be no problems in the right relationship in part causes the problem. We want our romantic partner to be a mirror image of ourselves so we can feel perfectly in sync. When our partner doesn't live up to our expectations, our first thought is not that our expectations may be too high but that we may be with the wrong person. It's not uncommon to jump to this conclusion, especially if we're not experiencing our personal happily-ever-after love story. It's also not uncommon to jump to the conclusion that someone else might be a better match.

The truth about marriage is that marriage just makes you married. Every union is based on two different people who each have distinctive needs. Sometimes these needs are met, and sometimes they are not, which means partners will intermittently disappoint each other, and that's totally normal. We're flawed people, and we end up with other flawed people, which is why there are always challenges in relationships. Once we understand that real life is a lot messier than any idealized image, we can be much more forgiving of ourselves as well as the other people who share our lives.

I tell my patients all the time, "It's normal to fantasize about getting rid of your husband every now and then." Anger and frustration are typical impulses because you're dealing with the behaviors and needs or demands of another person. But once you understand the reality of relationships, and recognize that the fantasy version never really exists, then you can buckle down and try to do the best you can to meet each other's needs. This is a much better mindset to have and a more realistic way to live. Your relationship isn't meant to be perfect; it is meant to help you grow and become a better person.

Women also hope the person who can take away their pain and take care of them in the perfect way will be their partner. We choose that partner because we believe on some level they will be able to meet our needs in a way even our parents couldn't. Our romantic relationships give us another opportunity to get the kind of attention we seek to make us feel unconditionally loved and whole. This sometimes unconscious expectation is overly high and can place a relationship in jeopardy, because it's an expectation that can't be met and is therefore bound to lead to disappointment. While it's understandable that you may want someone in this role, especially at midlife, no one person is capable of taking away all your pain. Once you come to terms with this, you'll find that you're less disappointed with your partner and can stop placing unrealistic burdens on him or her.

GETTING A MIDLIFE MARRIAGE BACK ON TRACK

Like it or not, we live in a culture that caters to couples. There is something about having someone in our lives who cares about us that is very comforting. What's more, according to a 2013 study featured in *Time* magazine, having a partner in middle age can be one of the secrets of longevity. Researchers believe having strong social connections of any sort is one of the secrets of healthy aging. Marriage or any type of long-term, intimate relationship—straight or gay—has been shown to increase longevity because it provides ongoing emotional and physical support.

If you're willing to do the work on your marriage, you will reap the rewards. The benefits of marital friendship are most vivid during middle age, when people tend to experience a dip in life satisfaction. Those who are married have much shallower dips along the U-shaped curve. The National Bureau of Economic Research concluded that being married makes people happier and more satisfied with their lives than remaining single—particularly during the most stressful periods, like midlife crises. Those whose lives are difficult could benefit most from marriage, according to John Helliwell of the Vancouver School of Economics and Shawn Grover of the Canadian Department of Finance. Their study also found that those who consider their spouse or partner to be their best friend get twice as much life satisfaction from marriage.

When you're first married and deep into the promise of the love part of your relationship, marriage doesn't seem like hard work. Every marriage has peaks and valleys, but at the beginning, it's all peak. Yet over the long haul, and especially in midlife, marriage becomes hard work, because you're no longer on your best behavior. In fact, you're often on your worst behavior, because there's a safe feeling you only get from being married. I found this out when I was writing my last book, *Till Death Do Us Part: Love, Marriage, and the Mind of the Killer Spouse,* which chronicles the scandalous ends of marriages. Most people don't get to this horrific place, but many married couples live as if their motto is "You're stuck with me. Now you have to deal with the real me, warts and all." While it's okay to present yourself authentically, it's not okay to present only your worst self and expect someone to accept it, even if it's your spouse.

Successful couples in midlife marriages find ways to embrace their everyday life and take pride in the shared history they have built together. Brain research reveals the most primitive response center in the brain, the amygdala, helps us during midlife to see our lives through a more optimistic lens. Our brain becomes more responsive to our likes versus our dislikes. The dislikes are filtered out to the point where they hardly register at all. This may be why during midlife there is a general acceptance of the vicissitudes of life as well as the flaws and limitations that exist in all relationships.

If you are going to embrace reinventing every aspect of yourself at midlife, how can you keep your relationship not only alive but fresh? One of the most reliable pieces of marital advice is to find activities you can do together in which you learn or experience something new. This does not have to be an extravagant or expensive endeavor, just as long as it is out of your typical routine. Introducing something new to look forward to creates a sense of excitement and intimacy.

This advice is especially true in the bedroom. According to a 2010 study conducted by the AARP, nearly six in ten adults over the age of forty-five believe that sexual activity is critical to a good relationship, and fewer than one in twenty believe sex is only for younger people. Sex is one of the most important aspects in a healthy relationship, and finding your sexy self adds to the feeling that you're with the right person. Sex is about liberation, vitality, and vigor, and you will become most comfortable with that liberated part of yourself as you pass through midlife. If you have been in a long-term, committed relationship, you've had sex with the same partner thousands of times. So mix it up sexually. Get creative!

A lesson we can learn from adolescents is to utilize the power of touch. Teens are much more physical than adults, and they respond positively to touch, especially when it's not sexual. Have you ever seen a bunch of teenagers watching television and lounging in close proximity? Instinctually, they know to seek the benefits of touch. Through touch, they are comforting one another, enjoying one another, and in their own way saying yes to life and to each other. Adults, on the other hand, behave much differently when they are with friends. Sadly, men and women in midlife almost shy away from touch, even during intimate situations. They've repressed this type of social connection. I don't know why this is exactly; maybe it's stress or just our ability to connect and communicate verbally as opposed to physically. But the result is that we're saying no to ourselves more often or putting limits on ourselves. In marriage, touch can be truly transformative, even when it's not sexual!

Lastly, partners in successful midlife marriages have learned to be more appreciative. Research supports the fact that gratitude and being appreciative increase relationship satisfaction and our sense of feeling or being connected. They also improve our personal happiness, our overall health, and our sexiness factor. Couples who are able to focus on the good aspects of each other and find ways to experience each other in an ideal way, instead of a devaluing way, have a more loving and enjoyable marital relationship (which makes complete sense when you think about it). However, being appreciative is actually easier said than done. Let's not forget our negativity bias: it's natural for us to dwell, even ruminate, on the negative because we're hardwired to focus on the bad parts of our lives and to worry, feel pessimistic, and experience our frustrations more intensely than our joys.

In order to change your relationship for the better you have to deliberately shift your perspective to appreciate the good things going on. The key is to make sure these changes are noticeable and sustainable. Start with a list: *What are the things I like about my partner? How is my life better because of him or her? What am I thankful for in this relationship?* Re-read your list whenever you're angry or upset. Then try to point out your partner's strengths on a regular basis.

This appreciation filters down into other components of a successful marriage. Midlife couples who are committed to each other also make a commitment to grow together. They know how to respect and value their partner even when they are angry with them. They find ways to combat feelings of overall negativity toward their partner so they can maintain a sense of respect for each other. And, finally, they have good coping skills, which include the ability to find humor in a situation, to ask for what they want, and to negotiate frustrations in a way that's acceptable to both of them.

Every relationship needs to be reenergized, especially if two people have been together for a very long time. The following strategies are designed to reboot your relationship so it feels as rewarding and fulfilling as you want and need it to be. They offer ways for you to better interact with your partner as well as set new expectations for your own role within the relationship.

Rewrite Your Love Story

Sometimes we get so caught up in our own perspective and feelings of disappointment that we internalize our love story in the most negativistic way. For example, Ellie could only focus on how angry she was with her husband, John, for always taking his mother's side in a family argument. She began to question what type of weak and unsupportive man she had married.

A negative inner dialogue takes a toll and makes you feel bad about yourself and your situation. One of the ways to break this cycle is to reframe your narrative by literally writing down a new one. This exercise allows you to be the author of your own life, and in this case, you're going to write a new love story. Research suggests writing true emotions can help in terms of professing feelings. You may find writing in this objectifying way changes your perception, because it brings to light some inner truths you may have forgotten or taken for granted. It can help you to get out of a victim mindset and, at the same time, have a little fun.

Whether you're single or in a long-term marriage, this activity is invaluable during midlife, because you've reached a point where you're no longer relying on a fantasy of perfection for your future; you're fully aware of reality. There's a lot of power in objectifying your story in a positive light. When you write your new love story, you can see your hopes and dreams concretized. You make yourself the heroine and highlight the positive aspects of your relationship in more of a loving way, which can help you see the relationship from a different viewpoint.

For example, Ellie decided to rewrite her marital story by writing down what she felt was positive about her husband and her relationship. Instead of demonizing her husband for not standing up to his mother, she could now focus on her list that covered what a good husband and father he usually is, the fun and fulfilling life they've shared together, filled with friends, the lovely home they have, and the jobs they both enjoy. She knows her husband is an honest, hard-working man any woman would be proud to call her own. In this new version, Ellie's mother-in-law problems come up rarely, and when they do, Ellie and her husband are able to conceive some type of solution as a couple, even if it's only temporary.

Speak Nicely to Each Other

Honest, nonthreatening communication is essential for working out problems in any relationship, but it is particularly true at midlife. The same women who are finding their voice and expressing what they want, especially those who are doing this for the first time, often end up hurting their partners. Sometimes we treat the people we love the worst because we feel the most comfortable with them. For example, my patient Samantha and her husband met when they were both twenty-one, and they have been married for twenty-three years. Samantha told me that she thinks she has a really good marriage, although sometimes she and her husband treat each other more like siblings. That closeness, that familiarity, periodically hinders them from being nicer to each other.

I've found that the most successful marriages are created by people who realize that *how* they talk about a problem is just as important as talking about a problem in the first place. When we talk in a way that rips our partner apart or hits below the belt, we make it that much harder to address the underlying difficulties. While there is no perfect set of rules to manage conflicts for every relationship, it usually comes down to communicating positively and effectively so that what you say is actually heard.

Timing is everything. If something is upsetting you, make sure you find the right time to talk about it. By midlife, you probably know when it's a good time to talk to your partner and when it's not. It's usually best to avoid having an intense discussion in public, right before going to sleep or having sex, or when you are stressed out or actively engaged in something important.

Don't address the issue during the heat of the moment. Wait a day or so. Partners aren't mind readers (which may be a good thing during midlife!). Mention what you're upset about to your partner, but don't bring up past problems or issues even if they are relevant. Break problems down into manageable parts. And remember that after you get an apology, be willing to let go of your anger.

Don't Attack

Marriage is not the place for criticism or abuse. Even when we don't mean to, it's easy when we're upset to come off as confrontational. Making your partner feel defensive almost always leads to a zero-sum game. Using the words "I" or "we" over "you" can really change a conversation and make it feel less aggressive. For example, look at the difference in tone between the following statements: "I want you to be a more involved parent" rather than "Your selfishness leaves little time to spend with the kids." Acknowledging your imperfections and apologizing when necessary go a long way toward making your partner feel less defensive. Be sure your body language is communicating that you're open to what's being said, that you really do care and are listening to your partner. Make eye contact, and keep your face kind and empathic. Really listen to what your partner is telling you. Give nods of acknowledgment with an open and relaxed body stance.

MIDLIFE DIVORCE BY THE NUMBERS

Midlife divorce is on the rise. For the first time, more Americans fifty and older are divorced than widowed, and the numbers are growing as we live longer. Our life expectancies decrease the likelihood that marriages will end through death and increase the risk of divorce. Today, the majority of all divorces take place when the husband and wife are between the ages of forty-five and fifty-four. Sociologists call them "gray divorces."

Stephanie Coontz, Ph.D., and others detect an increase in divorce among midlife couples who have been married twenty-five years or more. In one interview, Coontz told me, "Staying together until death do us part is a bigger challenge than it used to be, because we expect so much more of marriage than we did in the past, and we have so many more options when a marriage doesn't live up to those expectations. Women have long been more sensitive to—or less tolerant of—a mediocre relationship than men, and with their increased work experience and greater sense of their own possibilities, they are less willing to just 'wait it out.' What's more, we expect to find equality, intimacy, friendship, fun, and even passion right into what people used to see as the twilight years."

We used to believe a midlife crisis hit only men, who would then leave their wives for younger women, but this is no longer true. While women are sometimes the victims of spousal infidelity, more often than not it's the woman today who is initiating a divorce. According to Abby Rodman, author of *Should You Marry Him?*, 70 percent of divorced women in midlife are the party responsible for dissolving their marriage. Most of these women complain they were victims of either psychological or emotional abuse. A wife's negative perception of marriage occurs when she sees that it's hopeless, and this predicts her ending the marriage. The same does not hold true for a husband, who is more willing to stay in an unhappy marriage.

Midlife divorce appears to have long-term financial consequences, especially in regard to wealth accumulation for women. However, Pepper Schwartz, Ph.D., shared that 80 percent of divorced, middle-aged women do not regret their decision. Schwartz believes one of the possible reasons for this is the realization by women that midlife is the last period when they can get out and still have time to build a relationship with someone else. By midlife, women have recognized that after the kids have left the house, they still have something to offer in the dating market.

It is interesting to note that life satisfaction does not necessarily increase after a divorce. Divorced individuals who remain unmarried do not appear to experience a considerable difference in overall happiness compared to individuals who are unhappily married. However, divorced people who do remarry have higher levels of overall happiness.

The decision whether or not to stay in a marriage is based on a complex set of feelings that vary as much as the people who make this decision. If your emotional needs or your expectations of marriage are not being met, you may start to think, *I can do better* or *I want something different.* At the same time, you've become better at saying, *This part of my relationship works for me, but this part doesn't. I can create my own rules and feel okay about that.*

Asking the following questions can be helpful in terms of making a sound and emotionally healthy choice:

Is my partner supportive of me?

Is my partner helping me to be who I want to be?

Is my partner supportive of the things that matter to our family?

Has my partner been there or showed up for me during the challenges in my life?

Am I my best self when I'm with my partner?

WHEN LOVE IS ELUSIVE

Jena came to see me as a new patient. She said, "I'm forty-seven and recently divorced. My action plan was to get out of my marriage, but now that I'm out, I don't know how to start dating again. How do I get back in the game? I'm still not sure men are going to want me."

I told Jena that I meet with lots of women like her. I helped her understand that her thinking was wrong and fear based, and then we focused on what made her unique and special. When she was able to get in touch with her strengths, instead of coming across as damaged, she began to shift and therefore became more attractive to men.

A second problem I find when I'm working with women who are single in midlife, because they either have been divorced or never married, is the pervasive frustration and hopelessness they feel when they're not finding the relationship they want. They may feel *There are no good men out there* or *No one's looking for somebody my age*. Single women aged forty to sixty who are still looking for love may feel like they've somehow missed the boat and they're left thinking *How did I get here?* or *Did I miss out somehow on the youthful, good years?* Some begin to wonder if they are no longer attractive to others or if they'll ever be in a relationship at all.

I really believe that your best age to find love is now, because at midlife, you've never been more secure in knowing yourself, what you want, and how to go about getting it. I see it every day: people in midlife finding each other and being incredibly happy. In fact, I suspect they are happier than if they had made a choice earlier on that wouldn't have been right. Not everyone is ready to get into a committed relationship in their twenties. People are getting married later in life for a whole host of reasons, including their job commitments, their finances, or they're just enjoying the single life. Some people are not yet ready for intimacy, but this doesn't mean intimacy is not going to happen for them. Not at all! For instance, one of my patients got married when she and her partner were fifty. It was the first marriage for both of them. It just took them a while to find each other.

Connecting with another person, no matter what our age, is challenging. Plus, let's face it: there are only a handful of people we would really want to be with and who can fulfill our emotional needs. When women in midlife incorporate a negativistic attitude, it makes it difficult for them to feel good about themselves while they search for a life partner. What's more, these women seem to have forgotten that it was equally difficult to find a love connection when they were younger. Now they can use their age as an excuse, but the reality is, the same complaints exist at every stage of their lives.

CREATING A DATING PLAN

I'm not a matchmaker, but I do know women in midlife are in the best possible position to meet men and create a lasting relationship. Many women in midlife have an idea of the type of relationship they want yet haven't identified the specifics. Focusing in on what you want in a relationship is an important step toward getting what you want. In this section, you'll explore some core relationship aspects and come up with a nonnegotiables list.

The most common problem I see regarding dating during midlife is that women have a very long list of nonnegotiables. If you're too rigid, you're creating a fantasy relationship that will never allow you to fulfill your desire for a true relationship. Now, letting go of some of that rigidity is different from lowering your standards or having no standards at all, which is certainly not what I'm recommending. If you are choosing partners who aren't aligned with your nonnegotiables, then you are lowering your standards. Let's say it's really important to you to date someone who is a college graduate, has the same spiritual beliefs, and lives nearby. If you meet someone who didn't finish college but is smart and supportive of you, satisfies the other two criteria, and is interested in doing the same things in life, though it's just not exactly what you imagined, it still could work. It's close enough. At the end of the day, you are not marrying a résumé. You have to be able to see the bigger picture and then be able to make a smart decision for yourself.

View your nonnegotiables list as an opportunity for personal growth. Enjoy learning more about yourself and what you want in a partner by answering the following questions:

What must I absolutely have? These are your core values.

What do I absolutely refuse to put up with? These are behaviors you cannot live with.

What might be negotiable? These are choices, behaviors, and personality traits you could accept.

What am I willing to do? These are changes you would be willing to make.

Things I must absolutely have.	Things I absolutely refuse to put up with.	Things that might be negotiable.	Things I am willing to do.

Using the chart, write down at least two answers in each column. Think very hard before apportioning anything to columns A, B, and C. What truly matters to you? Are you being realistic? Consider what you could put into column C. Compromise is important in every successful relationship. What could you live with if the core aspects of the relationship (columns A and B) were satisfactory?

Next, for every item you've listed in columns A, B, and C, ask yourself, *What am I willing to do to have what I want?* What are you willing to give to a relationship? What are you willing to give up? How can you be the kind of person who attracts someone who lines up perfectly in your A and B columns? Put those answers in column D.

Now that you've sketched out a representation of your ideal relationship and have a strategy for seeking it out, plant a vision of it in your head. Remind yourself that you are deserving of having great things in your life. Visualize yourself in a functioning, satisfying relationship. Allow yourself to be excited by the possibility. End your visualization session with the statement "I will enjoy the present and have trust in my future."

GET OUT THERE AND HAVE FUN!

Some people looking for love assume it's going to appear magically in their lives. I don't recommend you wait around for it. Wanting a relationship without dating is like leaving your retirement planning to a unicorn: it just won't happen. Instead, plot an action plan for increasing your chances of getting the love you want. Where are you likely to meet this person? What interests might you share? Might friends or colleagues know someone? Focus on steps you can take to improve your "luck" and resolve to take them.

The next step is to just put yourself out there until something clicks. Go out and attend events or take a class. Say yes to invitations whenever possible, and you'll quickly see how easily your world opens up to meeting new people. Do something you're passionate about. Check off the items on your bucket list. However, television personality and professional matchmaker Siggy Flicker advises her clients not to go out with other single women. She shared her philosophy with me: "Would you take another person looking for the same job with you to an interview? Go out with a woman who's in a happy relationship and who's rooting for you."

Siggy reminded me that even at midlife, men are hunters, and single women should let them fight for you. "Don't reach out to them first. Don't text them first. And the longer you can put off sex, the better!!" She also recommends that midlife women lead with their assets: their personal combination of life experience, self-awareness, sexual maturity, intelligence, compassion, patience, and understanding. These inner qualities will always set midlife women apart from younger ones.

No matter your age, dating makes everyone feel like a teenager. The excitement, and anxiety, never goes away (but that's part of the fun of it, right?!). It automatically lifts your spirits: you can never feel depressed and flirt at the same time. This is because you're enjoying each other's sexuality, and there's a charge that happens when you're in that place of having fun with sexuality.

Flirting doesn't come naturally to everyone, but it's something that certainly gets better the more you practice it. It always helps to come from a place of confidence and lighthearted fun. Practice makes perfect, so flirt away whenever and wherever it feels appropriate, using these tips:

Make eye contact—this is where communication always starts.

Smiling makes you seem approachable and interested in connecting. Just signaling you're interested is half the battle of getting someone's attention.

Let your body do some talking. Show you're interested with your body language, but do it in a subtle way. Lean toward the other person. Mirror their body language. Wear an outfit that shows off your assets, but in a classy way. Wear an interesting necklace or another piece of jewelry that serves as a focal point and conversation piece. Think *sexy,* not *seedy.*

Be a bit mysterious. Always leave them wanting more. And asking for your number.

Siggy also feels that every date should be fun. She says, "Don't go out on dates thinking that particular man is going to be your next husband. Just go out and have fun. The date could end up introducing you to another man you'll be with for the rest of your life. Enjoy yourself. You never know who will be your next love."

TEEN TOOL: SET UP A DATING PROFILE

I'm a big supporter of lots of dating, to have the experience of going out, meeting interesting people, hearing about their lives, and getting back into the game. This is one of the reasons why I love the new technology piece of dating. The truth of the matter is, we only have access to a certain number of people every day, so with technology we have access to a larger group, and with particular interests.

This means working your online profile—really think through the type of image you want to convey of yourself and the message you want to send about what you're looking for. Some of the most active cohorts in online dating are middle-aged men and women. My patients have introduced me to OurTime.com, the dating site for the fifty-plus crowd. AARP has a partnership with other sites that cater to midlifers, which include HowAboutWe.com and Stitch.net.

I've helped many of my patients create their online profiles to make sure they come off as appealing and seductive as they feel and are. Your profile is in effect a marketing tool; it showcases how you want to be seen and what's important to you. One of the first recommendations I make is to get a great photo taken. Here are some other useful online dating tips:

Review your nonnegotiables list and work it into your profile. Getting specific can help your profile stand out from the crowd. Use your past experiences to shape your list. Really think about what you've learned over the years and how it affects what you want.

List what makes you unique. Even describing your flaws has been found to have a huge appeal. If you like your laugh lines, emphasize them. Your honesty will convey a midlife confidence and straightforwardness.

Create a catchy screen name, one that represents what you like or what's special about you. If you have a hobby you love or a job you're proud of, create your screen name around this. This is the beauty of midlife: knowing who you are and making it work to your advantage.

Create a headline that is eye-catching and clickable. You may want to study other people's headlines to see which ones stand out and then take a page out of their book.

Be positive. Everyone has a nightmare story, but dating sites are not the place to share it. Show your appreciative side! This is one of the traits that makes midlife women stand out amongst the dating crowd.

Be honest. You don't want any lies to catch up with you in the future. You want someone to love you for who you are, and the age you are, not who you want to be or wish you were.

When you're ready, post, pray, and send it out in good faith. Now it's time to see all the interesting people who come your way.

MIDLIFE MENTOR

Tamsen Fadal

Tamsen Fadal is an award-winning journalist who anchors the New York metropolitan area local news. She has interviewed some of the most exciting newsmakers and celebrities, from U.S. presidents to Hollywood royalty. In 2002, she was embedded with the American troops in Afghanistan. She was awarded an Emmy for Best News Anchor in New York in 2014. She has also received multiple Emmys and other awards for her investigative and creative reporting ventures. Now in midlife, she is divorced and lives in New York City with her Chihuahua, Matsen. She is the author of several books, including her latest, *The New Single: Finding, Fixing, and Falling Back in Love with Yourself After a Breakup or Divorce.*

Tamsen told me she's enjoying midlife because it has been a time for her to explore who she really is. "I think it has become easier to get older. I remember years ago my grandmother refused to tell anyone her age. It was something women were ashamed of. I think it is becoming increasingly easier to talk about it, be honest about it, and even brag about it. I am also no longer worried about the stigma of being single or of divorce, or of the fact I'm in my forties. If you are proud of yourself from the inside out, your self-esteem does not diminish. I am proud of who I am, what I have accomplished, and especially the fact that my divorce didn't destroy me—rather, it gave me the strength to encourage other women who are having a difficult time in a relationship."

When it comes to dating, she told me, "The only way to truly relate to someone else in a potential relationship is to be able to relate to yourself first. It is critical to figure out who you are and make sure you can rely on yourself for your future happiness. For a long time I thought a man was going to 'fix' me. The truth is, you can only fix yourself. Friends, family, and how you set up your life determine who you will date. I have learned if you don't take the time to work on yourself—which isn't always easy—you will end up in the same type of relationship you had before, except with a different person."

Tamsen enjoys meeting new people. She believes there are true advantages to dating during midlife. She told me, "I am dating without an agenda. I go out because I enjoy being with the other person, not because I'm in a race to find a man to run down the aisle. At this time of my life, dating is actually relaxing and more enjoyable. I think my attitude shift makes men appreciate me more, and they want to be around a woman who feels this way, because they don't feel pressured."

Her advice for women who are dating during midlife is to stop trying to get to the end. "Enjoy the moments. Don't look for a man to fix you. Don't dwell on your age. Stop the negative self-talk about your body, and feel what your mind thinks. Take care of yourself inside and out. Appreciate people who are good to you, and remove the people who are the soul suckers in your life."

Tamsen has it exactly right. It's important to like who you are as you experience your journey. Removing agendas of who you should be, how you should be, and how you need to live is a gift more and more women are choosing to give themselves during this amazing time we call midlife.

SINGLE IN MIDLIFE AND LOVING IT

A record number of Americans will stay single for life. The most recent report from the Pew Research Center offers a remarkably important prediction: only 29 percent of divorced adults say they want to remarry, and women are more likely than men to pass on marriage in the future. The old assumption that everyone wants to marry is no longer valid. Being a part of a couple is a culturally constructed idea. When it doesn't serve us well, we can opt to leave it.

I have a friend from my college days whose parents divorced when she was very young. Her mom remarried in her midlife, when my friend was in high school, and almost immediately the new husband passed away. I remember the mother was a very modern woman back in 1987. She once sat us down when we were in our early twenties and said, "You always have to be happy with yourself, because men might not be there for you. As long as you are happy with yourself, you'll always be happy." I have never forgotten her wisdom.

This seems to be the same for my sister Lori's friend Wendy Witt. She doesn't need to define herself in the context of a relationship and doesn't accept the limitation culture often places on us. Wendy married, when she was in her late twenties, a man several years older than her. A few years later, she had two sons. After seven years she realized she was done with her marriage, but it took her a few more years to completely get out of the relationship. She managed to separate in a very friendly manner. She now has a great relationship with her ex and his new wife. She is even the godmother of their two children. Her two sons, her ex, his wife, and their two children all consider themselves to be one big family and are all very important to one another. Instead of feeling jealous, Wendy feels blessed that everyone is so happy in their new lives. In fact, this arrangement helps her feel less guilty that she left her ex-husband.

Wendy had been in many relationships over the years and has even had marriage proposals. At fifty-five, she is more than happy to remain unmarried. She enjoys her work, her kids, her family, and time out with her friends, some of whom are now divorced and single again. Does she sometimes look at certain families and say "I wish I made this happen for myself"? The truthful answer is yes. But at the same time, she feels very content with her life.

When her mother asked her if she was worried about being lovable later on in life, she confidently replied, "No!" She knows there is a man out there for her who will love her when she is ready for it (even if she's "older"). In the meantime, she's having fun, even dating younger men. While she has felt the prejudice of ageism in the dating world, it doesn't change her sense of satisfaction with her life. Her theory about men is, the ones who did not have a happy marriage, especially the widowers, may want to start over with someone younger. The men who were in a happy marriage don't necessarily care about a woman's age; they appreciate the companionship and the connection that comes from dating midlife women.

Wendy believes that if women gave themselves the chance to find out how rewarding being single was, they might actually enjoy it. If they can financially support themselves and develop the confidence to meet their own needs, being single can be an amazing ride. If the right relationship comes her way, great! But she's not seeking it or making it her mission. She is living life on her terms, and it's working very well for her.

Wendy's life is empowering. She understands her fulfillment comes from having the freedom and choice to create the life she wants. She's not listening to the negative self-talk of *I'm too old; I'm aged out* or *I have to be in a relationship in order to be valid or happy.* Her approach is so modern, especially her connection with her ex-husband and his new family. She refuses to believe that once you are past a certain age you are expired. Way to go, Wendy!

EIGHT

MAKING A LIVING, MAKING A LIFE

Sara was in her midfifties when she lost her longtime job as an executive assistant at a law firm. She was sad about having to leave a situation she enjoyed that also paid well, and she worried she wouldn't be able to make the same amount of money in a different job. She was upbeat about her prospects, but one day when she came into my office I noticed she was not her usual cheerful self. She explained that when you sign up for unemployment compensation you have to meet with a counselor before you start receiving benefits. Her counselor, like Sara, was a woman in midlife. Sara told me, "The counselor said I'm old and that I have to be realistic about my expectations. Now I don't know how this job search is going to turn out."

I was incensed that my patient had been spoken to in this way, no less from another woman in midlife. I immediately told Sara that this woman's statement was offensive, untrue, and likely a reflection of how she felt about herself. We then explored all the reasons why Sara was the perfect person for the type of job she was seeking. She had a great personality, was likable, had wonderful experience, and was at a point in her life when she could be relied on to be a stable, available employee—it was unlikely that her personal life would pull her away from the office, which could easily happen with a younger worker. Sara realized the wisdom of my message and began to focus on all the assets she brought to the workplace instead of her age.

Six weeks later, Sara was hired for a position perfectly suited for her skill set. Her new boss appreciated her experience and maturity, and viewed her age as an asset, just as we had discussed. Even though she missed her old job and had never thought about leaving it, she was now excited to try something new.

The stereotypical attitude—"You're old; people won't want you"—can inflict terrible damage on our psyches if we let it. Midlife is often a time of career transitions, whether they are self-imposed or not. There may be unpleasant realities midlife women face, because the job market can seem to favor youth, and there is evidence of outright ageism in some fields, but this doesn't mean that once we've celebrated a certain birthday we've aged out of the workplace, it's too late for finding fulfilling work, or we're too old to reinvent our career entirely. These are simply midlife myths. Our search to find ourselves and our place at midlife is transformative in every aspect of our lives, including both our work identities and our bank accounts. Whether we want a corporate job or a retail position, or we want to explore entrepreneurial options, we can continue to make money by creating new possibilities for fulfillment.

Next to health, having enough money is one of the biggest fears that surfaces during midlife. Because we're living longer, we need to ensure we'll be able to afford our lifestyles into the future. This means we will need to work longer and save more. Midlifers want, and need, to continue working as they age. The percentage of workers fifty-five and older increased from almost 30 percent in 1993 to more than 40 percent in 2011, and that age group will continue to claim an increasing share of the workforce. Midlife marks the middle of not only our life span but also our working years. According to Carlo Strenger and Arie Ruttenberg in a 2008 article for the *Harvard Business Review*, since few people enter the workforce before their twenties, the average midlife woman today has as many years of productivity ahead of her as she has behind her.

Women who have taken time out of the workplace to attend to family issues pay a price, more often than not. Caring for children or aging parents can interfere with these women's value and upward mobility in the workplace. However, as we are all working longer, we do have time to make up for these lost years. Women in midlife need to remember that the end of their working life is probably not going to be at age sixty-five.

This chapter explores both issues: returning to work after taking time out from the workforce and the absolute necessity of planning for a longer life span, including the issues surrounding money, so we can let go of our anxieties and move forward in the most productive and profitable way possible.

MONEY AND THE MIDLIFE WOMAN

Money, and the issues surrounding it, can be a source of anxiety, resentment, fear, and concern during midlife. No other issue at midlife snaps us into reality more than finances, because it affects not only the way we feel about ourselves but also how we plan for our future. The issues are varied and complex, so much so that I believe I'm not alone in fearing not having enough money for retirement more than I even fear death. In death, what are you going to do? Either you're in another dimension or you're not. But if you don't have money in this lifetime, that's going to impact the way you live your final years.

Our generation of women still carries some of Cinderella's DNA. We have been raised to expect men to provide for us, and this means men taking on the lion's share of financial responsibilities. For many women in midlife today, the reality is quite different. A 2013 report from the Pew Research Center showed that four in ten households with children under eighteen include a mother who is either the sole or primary breadwinner for the family. The model of the husband earning money and the wife staying home is now very rare. And even when this model works, women at midlife want to do something else with their lives.

How we handle taking on financial responsibility has a strong correlation to how we feel about ourselves during midlife. Researcher Deborah Carr at the University of Wisconsin found that women who fall short of their career goals suffer from lower levels of psychological well-being and purpose in life and higher levels of depression, and they are significantly less likely to report they are "very successful" in their work lives compared to women who did not have goals or who actually surpassed their goals. I believe this is because our evolutionary brain is always looking for the next new challenge. That's why it is so important to set goals and work toward them, even if your goals shift and change as you accomplish them.

Some couples embrace a dual-household income, or even a complete role reversal, making this financial shift easy. My client Jill's husband wanted to be a restaurateur, but it never worked out. She, meanwhile, had a great job that could keep the family afloat. They needed somebody to take care of the kids, and the husband stepped in. Luckily, he enjoyed his new role. He loved taking care of their children. He loved cooking. He loved doing all the housekeeping, even though he came from a family in which marital roles were very traditionally set. Interestingly, the midlife women I've met have an easier time accepting their new roles compared to younger women in a similar situation. I've seen this scenario become a deal breaker with younger couples. Perhaps the ability for midlife women to take on a nontraditional marital role is due to our greater resiliency. As Patricia Cohen described in her book on midlife, *In Our Prime,* their focus is on achievement, including professional success. Researchers studying both men and women in midlife find their judgment surrounding financial matters has reached an all-time high.

Other women in midlife find carrying any part of the financial responsibility hard to handle. According to a 2013 American Psychological

Association report, women already experience more work-related tension than men and have a greater tendency to internalize this tension. They may feel resentment or feel overburdened, or have a longing for the situation to change. They may be disappointed that the way their life played out didn't fit the model. Or they may be dealing with a partner's disappointments involving his or her failures or bad luck. All of these feelings are valid, but here's the reality check: you can't get to midlife without feeling you failed at something. Everyone has scars, and it's tempting to admit defeat. Instead of beating yourself up, remember that midlife is the developmentally appropriate time to manage the inevitable disappointments of life by acknowledging the good, the bad, and the ugly. The key to overcoming these disappointments is not to let your past setbacks stop you from moving forward creatively and authentically. What's more, if your partner's frustration is weighing you down, encourage and support them as they work on resolving their frustration. In midlife, you can loan your partner your strength, but the strength and determination for lifting their load must come from them, not from you.

Regardless of whether they are the sole breadwinner, the co-breadwinner, or not responsible for bringing in the money at all, women at midlife want to rely on and trust themselves financially. By this point we've weeded through our desires for material things and we can hopefully recognize what we no longer need to pine for in order to live happily. We also have a better understanding of what we can do with our money. We're more in touch with reality so we've realized how valuable money is and learned not to be haphazard with it. However, because we know that it's likely we'll live longer and earn less than the men in our lives, we may have anxiety about how long our money will last. Michelle Matson, author of *Rich Chick,* said, "While men may be motivated by the thrill and challenge of investing, women are more concerned with the long-term results."

Women in midlife have to be aware of what money means to them, and understanding this isn't something that happens automatically. We might be just beginning to think about the life we want to lead in the future and what we can live with, and what we can live without. We recognize there will not be a bottomless pit of money or a parental god who will provide whatever we need. I have some midlife patients who have seen what has happened with their own parents, who did not save enough for retirement and are now living on practically nothing. Witnessing this frightening scenario definitely serves as a wake-up call.

Many women—even those who are affluent and tremendously successful at midlife—harbor a secret fear of ending up destitute. A 2013 study by Allianz Life Insurance, quoted in a *Forbes* magazine article, found that 49 percent of all women feared ending up broke and homeless. This fear has been popularly referred to as the "bag lady" syndrome. According to Andrew Shatte, Ph.D., who was quoted in the same article, this fear is part of our evolutionary stress response. It taps into our deeply rooted concern that our future is threatened and we are in danger of losing resources and being left behind. Although we may be hardwired to have this fear, it's important not to let it scare us to the point of paralysis. While not all misfortunes can be predicted, the key to creating a secure, safe, and productive life is to build our resilience. And one of the best ways to do this is to educate ourselves and make informed choices about how we spend money.

When these anxieties or other issues surrounding money come up with my midlife patients, I try to find out whether they are coming from a real place or are fear based. Once we can resolve the psychological part, I always recommend that they begin to work with professionals who can advise them on how to manage their finances so they can take control and, consequently, become less anxious. Whatever the case, I always compliment them for considering this area at all, because women can be tempted to stick their head in the sand and say to themselves, *I don't want to think about money. It's too painful.*

I certainly understand where this desire to avoid dealing with finances comes from. When I reached midlife, I forced myself to grow up regarding my relationship with money. My work life was on a fantastic roll in my early forties. I was hosting my own television show, had written my first book, and was regularly appearing on some of the top-rated national television shows. I had hit a lot of my personal and professional goals and, on one level, was feeling really good about these achievements. However, my financial maturity was way out of sync with my professional and personal maturity. I distinctly remember the sinking feeling that accompanied calls from a few credit card companies saying I was late for a payment. I would say to myself privately, *I don't want to be irresponsible about money anymore.*

I operated like a child when it came to money and finances. I was impulsive and had almost a delusional idea about how debts would get paid. But avoiding reality just created more chaos and anxiety. I didn't like myself in this area of my life, so I made a decision to get smarter about money, one step at a time, a goal that was long overdue. I enlisted some help in getting my finances in order, and I worked on becoming more diligent and responsible about paying my bills on time. I have to say, it's still an ongoing process, even a struggle for me, but one I'm glad I've committed to. It certainly makes me feel mature, and perhaps best of all, I feel smart. It has also helped to raise my financial self-esteem by leaps and bounds.

GETTING YOUR FINANCIAL LIFE IN ORDER

Even if you've been bad with money your whole life, now is a great time to start making changes. You may decide to downsize sooner rather than later if you're worried about finances. Reassess what's important. Watch the urge to spend, especially if you are newly single—sometimes the newly single are tempted to spend a lot of money on themselves in an attempt to stay young looking or start over fresh.

If your financial concerns are real, then addressing them is vital. This often begins with a specific plan for increasing your savings, getting rid of debt, and planning for the future. Consider meeting with a financial advisor who can help you come up with a long-term savings plan. These services are available through your local bank, or your bank can recommend someone in your area to work with.

Part of the reason we have trouble saving money is because we don't imagine who we're going to be or what's going to happen in the future. It's hard to get out of that just-now mindset. If you've never saved before, you're not too late; because we're living so much longer, we now have time on our side. Personal finance expert Alexis Neely recommends starting to save with a goal in mind, which she calls "backward budgeting." She asks her clients to imagine how much money they actually need in order to have the life they want. From there, they can create a savings plan that will actually meet their needs, even if they're just starting at midlife.

There's plenty of research showing that women in midlife are better at saving and investing than they may realize or give themselves credit for. It may just be that their financial abilities peak in midlife. *Today* show financial editor and author Jean Chatzky told me that women hit their stride in earnings during midlife. In fact, midlife women are responsible for more purchases than any other group of women, and single women in midlife are buying houses and cars on their own more now than ever before.

Chatzky recommends that women in midlife create their own nest egg, which is just as important as investing. She believes personal savings allow women to develop trust in themselves. Even saving a little bit of money is empowering and can eventually lead to investing. Women should know their credit score and work to improve it if necessary. Internet sites like AnnualCreditReport.com and CreditKarma.com can be tremendously useful resources. Lastly, she strongly advises everyone to create an emergency cushion. Having access to one to two thousand dollars for emergencies, in cash, is huge, especially when you don't need to add this debt to a credit card.

YOUR MIDLIFE BRAIN AT WORK

The unflattering stereotype of a midlife woman in the workplace is an intense menopausal mess: weak, unfriendly, forgetful, and fatigued.

Not such a nice portrait! This description seemed to match the universally accepted truth: the brain and body—and therefore productivity—deteriorate as we get older. This thinking assumes that a decline in mental prowess inevitably follows a decline in physical ability. However, the latest research and even our own scouts on the ground confirm this is not the case at all. According to findings from the now famous Seattle Longitudinal Study, both men and women are reaching new physical peaks during midlife, so it's quite possible we can be strong enough to continue to work effectively. What's more, we now know that few, if any, of us are at the height of our cognitive abilities in youth, and more important, the midlife brain is best suited for the workplace.

Research shows the midlife brain is also less likely to get overwhelmed during times of crisis and more capable of finessing social situations. In a study published in *Neurology* in 2007, researchers tested pilots aged forty to sixty-nine as they performed in flight simulators. Older pilots took longer to learn to use the simulators but did a better job than their younger colleagues at achieving their objective: avoiding collisions. The midlife brain is better, too, at abstract reasoning, logic, verbal skills, detecting patterns, making judgments, and reaching conclusions. As we get older we incorporate years of learning and behaviors and build on them, using this wisdom as a reference point for everything we do.

Midlife workers are ideally positioned to provide leadership and mentoring as well. One recent Harvard study found that our ability to read other people's emotions doesn't even take shape until we're in our forties, and that ability continues maturing until we are well into our sixties.

These are some of the reasons why our best age for working effectively is now. Within this good news we can see important shifts already taking place. In some industries, women in midlife are already running the show. For example, a 2014 article in the *Hollywood Reporter* listed the one hundred most powerful women in the entertainment industry, and nearly all of them were women in midlife.

So if we're up to the task of work, why do we get so much pushback in the workplace? We've learned to lean in, yet we don't believe in our value in the workplace. It's time to change that way of thinking and embrace the new midlife working women we want to become.

The Midlife Work Crises

At midlife, we know ourselves, or at least we are well on our way. So it's no surprise that it's quite common at midlife to become disenchanted with our job, or our profession, even if we've been enjoying it for some time. According to Gallup's 2013 *State of the American Workplace* report, only 30 percent of American workers are enthusiastic about and committed to their jobs—with those aged forty-nine to sixty-seven the least engaged of all. At midlife, many of us are looking for something different, even if we don't have to. We might be turned off or burned out, or need to make more money than our current position allows. But even more important, staying on the treadmill of work may make us search for a new purpose in life. While a paycheck may have been your original purpose, you could eventually find that you've lost the joy in your work.

Or you're considering going back to work after taking some time off, but you feel a little lost about how to start. Even though you finally have more time for yourself, you may need to return to work so you can help out financially. I have many friends in their forties whose kids are settled enough that they can consider going back into the workforce. They confide in me that they're fearful about even looking for a job. Some are a bit sad that they're ending one chapter of their lives, while others are looking forward to their reentry into the work world.

Feeling dissatisfied or restless with your career is normal during midlife, even if it's unsettling or scary. However, these feelings provide the perfect impetus to reevaluate your life. My patient Molly was on a fast-track position at a major Wall Street bank. She had wanted a serious career from the time she was young, and she enjoyed the travel her job required. But when she lost her job during the recent recession, she felt her first of many of what I call "midlife work crises." Even though she was highly employable, her heart wasn't in the game. Specifically, she wasn't excited about the way her job would influence the rest of her life. As she began interviewing for other positions, the usual drawbacks came up: a lot of travel, 24/7 responsibilities, the brilliant yet difficult bosses she would have to work for. She recognized that the job descriptions hadn't changed, but she had. At forty-four, she was ready to have a second child. What used to seem like perks were now impositions. She told me, "I want to enjoy my personal life. I want to spend time with my family. But we need the money, and I don't want to give up on my old dream now."

I told Molly that she didn't have to give up on her dream, but it might be time for her to take a proverbial right turn in her career. Then I told her about one of my midlife mentors, Judge Judy Sheindlin, who had recently released a free, downloadable ebook called *What Would Judy Say?*, which told her story. Her commonsense wisdom really resonated with me, but what I thought was most interesting was how she had transitioned into a second, impressive career at midlife.

Before Judy appeared on television, she was one of very few female judges. At fifty-two she was "discovered" because she was known for her professionalism as well as being someone who had a knack for relating to people through humor. In the book, she said her second career was carefully orchestrated. She took control of her own destiny and didn't let others define her. She said, "It wasn't luck, I was prepared, I was truly myself." Judge Judy makes a great point regarding the "having it all" conversation, which I think particularly resonates with women in midlife. She said, "You have to determine your own 'all'—and it's an individual matter." This was particularly good advice for Molly.

Judge Judy wrote, "I don't want to say anything's possible. I realize there are women out there who have to work; they can't give up their jobs because a lot is weighing on them. They don't have the freedom to do that. But even so, include something you like that you feel passion about. Make sure you have that private space for yourself to enjoy whatever it is you love doing. It is really important to have that. And then you never know what is going to happen; you never know what roads open up from that place." This is very much my philosophy as well.

Molly needed to reevaluate how to fit a new job in with the rest of the pieces in her life that she felt passionate about. I asked her to spend some time really figuring out what she wanted out of her career and what roles she wanted to take on outside the office. We also discussed redefining success. Judge Judy said that defining our success in terms of dollars is too narrow: at midlife we need to see ourselves as a success; however big or small our participation is at our job, we just need to feel we make a difference.

Molly took my advice to heart, and within a few months she found a job that met all her needs. She didn't have to leave the banking industry, but she could put away her travel bags, at least for a while. Her new job made it possible for her to leave the office at a reasonable hour every evening and ignore work until the next morning. It pays a little less than what she'd been making, but she's never been happier.

Engaging in negativistic, black-or-white, or all-or-nothing thinking can make navigating through the four most common work crises all the more frightening and challenging. The first step is to recognize which of the following four crises you are experiencing, so you can develop a plan to get out of crisis mode and into a career you'll love.

The Lost-Job Crisis

One midlife work crisis occurs when seemingly out of nowhere, or not, you're unemployed. If you lose something you value, it's natural to feel angry or sorry for yourself. Losing a job can carry one hell of a sting, because work can mean so much to us: money, prestige, a sense of purpose, a sense of community, a feeling of mastery. Let's face it: our identities are very much merged with what we do. I know mine is. It's a hard loss to recover from. Losing a job is just that: a loss, and one that must be grieved. This is true especially if you're confronting continued rejection in the job market.

I like to approach change with a different philosophy: *Whatever happens to me, happens for me.* When something occurs that you didn't plan for or didn't want to occur, you will learn from it, even if it doesn't feel like you can in the moment. Sometimes the sharp, unexpected turns of life end up being the best teachers and, ultimately, might just be in your best interest, too. It may not always be pleasant, but a difficult situation can sometimes push your life into a much better direction than you would have chosen otherwise.

The Getting-Back-in-the-Saddle Crisis

Reentering the workforce after a long or short break can feel intimidating for anyone. The first thing to remember is that you are not alone. According to a survey conducted by *Occupational Outlook Quarterly,* a large number of workers can expect to change their jobs up to ten times over the course of their careers. In fact, nonlinear career trajectories are becoming the rule rather than the exception. There are thousands of female workers out there just like you who have chosen career detours, opting out of full-time work either to raise children or to take care of aging family members. So take a deep breath and stay focused. You can get back into the swing of the working world; it just might take a little longer than you first imagined.

The Crisis of Confidence

My patient Jen experienced another type of work crisis, even though she was still employed. Jen was in her fifties when she first came to see me. She works with high school students to help them develop college admission essays, often traveling up to sixty miles in a day. She told me that she worried she was aging out of her job. Specifically, she was tired all the time and was concerned she might look too old for the teenagers she worked with to relate to. She was afraid they would view her, and her advice, as not hip, cool, or valid. This fear had become intermittently paralyzing, interfering with her ability to think proactively about her work and to expand her client list. It was also testing her already waning self-esteem, and she was no longer confident that she would be able to make her business work.

The only way for Jen to move past her fears was to confront them, explore them, then devise a plan of action. I explained that she had not only a youthful appearance but also a youthful personality. Her likability was predicated not on her appearance but on her lively, relatable approach to the kids she works with. We also identified other real concerns that were bubbling beneath her fears. Together, we talked through ways she could make her job less taxing on her time and her body. We explored her business adopting online video services, like FaceTime, Vidyo, and Skype, to help expand her clientele, cut her travel time, and allow her to make room for exercise to increase her energy level.

Jen embraced these new ideas and thanked me for helping her see options she had never considered. She began to realize there was something ageless about her career choice. She really liked being surrounded by teens and felt they kept her young. Why would she ever want to give that up? Luckily, she figured out a way to not only keep her job but also improve on the way she did it.

Other women worry about job security inside their office. Too often women in midlife either feel threatened by younger workers or have the attitude *I've arrived at this place of comfort and status. I shouldn't have to do anything else to secure my position,* then, to their surprise, they are let go, or they see other women their age with the same attitude being asked to leave. In either case, they are missing the point that we all need to constantly evolve within the workplace. Today's workplace is a competitive environment, and you don't get a pass just because you've reached a certain stage, or age, in your career. You should still be open to learning new skills. In many professions, you're only as good as your last success. People respond to you based on the energy you put out there. If you're sending out the energy that you're counting the days until your retirement, that's not so fabulous (unless you really are that close to retirement, then more power to you). But if you really want to be in the game, then you have to present yourself in a way that makes you visible, important, valuable, and relevant all the time.

As I mentioned before, fears can alert you to areas of your life that need attention. If fear is holding you back from pursuing what you want in your work life, start exploring what your fears point toward. Then you'll be able to bust through them and find valuable solutions.

The Hating-My-Job Crisis

If you carry around a negative attitude about your work, you are shutting down the possibility of actually learning something new. Any work road can lead you to where you want to go, even if it doesn't look like it will at first. When I started working at a psychiatric hospital—a job I really loved but knew wasn't going to be my final professional destination—I had a feeling this experience would be my long-sought-after launching pad into television. I recognized that everything I was doing at that hospital would serve me well in life and transfer to the TV world. I decided that as long as I was there, I was going to learn everything I could. The truth is, there was no direct pathway from my job at the hospital to TV, but my will to find the linking doors to my goal made it happen.

We can also work with our job instead of against it, especially while we are looking into other interests or career choices. My dear friend Lisa was a profitable artist in her twenties and thirties, but then she decided to take a break to raise her son and accepted a more traditional full-time job. Since she was married to a musician, her salary became very important to the family household income. Even though her full-time job put her in contact with very interesting and high-powered people, she hated the work because her artistic needs were not being met, and she resented having to give up precious time to be in an office.

After a year of deep depression, she decided she had had enough. Since I have known Lisa for a long time, I told her in a forceful but loving way that she was a great talent and there was no excuse for her not to pursue her artistic talents in a grander way. She agreed and she made a commitment to herself: the next year was going to be different. She wanted more out of her life and wasn't going to let fear stop her from fulfilling her dreams or goals anymore. She decided to live what she called "dangerously"—to use her time well and to say yes to her soul. We worked on figuring out how she could create alone time, away from the responsibilities of work and her family, in order to follow her passion. She began working on new projects in the evenings, and within a few months, word about her artwork spread. She was invited to participate in new art shows, where she sold some of her art.

She was so grateful that she was able to change up her life and get off the road of monotony to discover who she was beyond her roles as a mother and wife. While she still couldn't afford to work as a full-time artist, she was okay with that. In fact, once she became a part of her local artist community, she realized that the way she was living was more the rule than the exception, which made her feel better about her day job.

Yet after a while Lisa didn't want her work life to just feel lackluster. She actively and aggressively looked for another part-time job she would enjoy. When I asked her if she had any concerns about looking for a new job at this point in her life, she told me, "I absolutely did! I was worried employers would want someone younger and cheaper, but my friends all told me to keep looking, because when you interview, you never know what these meetings will lead to." This advice really paid off. She fell in love with one of the jobs she interviewed for, and she worked hard to secure the position. Her approach worked, because she was hired, and she is thrilled to be working for a company she feels good about.

Carl Jung and Erik Erikson believed middle age forced people toward their greatest achievements. So many writers, musicians, filmmakers, poets, and painters have talked about midlife as a time of artistic insight. But the bottom line is that it's okay if you can't live off your passion. You might have to keep your day job, too. But so what? Include what you love to do in your life and take the magical moments as they come.

TEEN TOOL: GET PASSIONATE ABOUT FIGURING OUT YOUR NEXT MOVE

If you're ready to embark on a job quest at midlife, you're in luck. This time, you're much better equipped to understand the working world and how you fit into it. Access the energy of youth and combine it with the wisdom and insights you've gained to forge your path. Women want to do work that gratifies their souls, and at midlife they have a unique opportunity to discover what this really means.

One of the greatest things about midlife is that many of us have been unconsciously cured of the people-pleaser disease. We used to live for others, do for others, and care deeply about what everyone thought of us. We followed the rules. Now it's time to take a cue from our adolescent selves, think outside the box with a little bit of moxie, and make up our own rules. It's never too late to follow our passions and turn them into a profession.

Look to adolescents as you consider pursuing a new vocation. Recall your days as a student, and take the time to learn the skills you need to get the job you want. Read up on your new interests. Increasing numbers of educational choices have sprung up in the past few years that are designed for midlifers who want to become more competitive or launch new careers, including online programs and opportunities at a variety of universities. Some women at midlife decide to go back to school, including the full four-year college route, but this is certainly not the only option.

Young adults today have grown up in the shadow of very stressful times. They no longer believe that corporate America is the finish line of career goals. Many have taken their economic needs into their own hands, launching their own ventures. They're looking at work from a much more entrepreneurial perspective than most of us did at their age, and they are at the forefront of a powerful trend of self-employment and small-business creation.

What if you created your own work life? Launched a business that speaks to both your heart and a market need? Midlife is the perfect time to embrace your inner passion and let it drive you to do your own thing.

However, if you want to start a new career around midlife, think through the financial ramifications. First, don't quit your day job. Some people get overly optimistic about their second career and then it doesn't turn out well, at least not at first. Test the waters, and get as much advice as possible from others who've been successful. Talk to friends or colleagues who are already in the business or field you're interested in pursuing. You may be surprised how many people are willing to help with your goals. Career counselors or coaches can also be good go-to people during this time; many of them have started their business as a new midlife career, so they would be perfectly poised to help with your transition. With the right plan and insight, you can successfully and safely move toward a new venture.

Young adults today are not satisfied with just one job. They are also filling their lives with creative outlets. They may be a lawyer and an actor, a retail salesperson and a writer. This is more of an artistic approach to living. Like adolescents, we no longer have to define ourselves by our careers. There is so much more to our lives than attaching our self-worth to our jobs. At midlife, you might be a great mother, a great wife, or an inspiring artist.

Listen to your inner adolescent energy and see what else defines your life, and pursue those interests as well. Of course, you want to do it in a smart way, not a reckless way, and make it a conscious choice.

MIDLIFE MENTOR

Kate White

Kate White is a *New York Times* bestselling author of ten works of fiction—six Bailey Weggins mysteries and four suspense novels. Before she began her career as a bestselling author, she spent fourteen years as the editor in chief of *Cosmopolitan*. She is married and the mother of two children, and she is also the author of several very popular career books, including *I Shouldn't Be Telling You This: How to Ask for the Money, Snag the Promotion, and Create the Career You Deserve* and *Why Good Girls Don't Get Ahead but Gutsy Girls Do*. In her spare time (ha!), she lectures to women in their fifties about their earning potential and their place in the workforce. She's one of my midlife mentors because she knew how to re-create herself at midlife, move toward her dreams, and build on her existing talent. She's pragmatic, creative, and knows how to manage it all, but she'd never describe herself this way because she's too humble.

Kate told me, "Women in their forties and fifties can become concerned, appropriately so, that they'll either be replaced by someone younger and/or by someone who can do their job for less. While there may be ageism in the workplace, a separate problem is what I call 'salaryism.' Women who are earning top dollar can be replaced by someone the company can pay less to. In some cases, women, as well as men, are fired not because of age but the size of their paycheck. This is why midlife women need to really ask themselves if they are bringing their best work attitude to the table."

In order to stay relevant in the workplace, Kate encourages women to remain aggressive at work. In today's business world, employees need to be willing to grow, think big, take on new projects and responsibilities, be flexible, and be open to new roles. But what is probably the most important is to never get sluggish or too comfortable in your job. Figure out what makes you indispensable and then make sure everyone around you knows it. Midlife women need to be asking themselves, *What am I bringing to the table? Am I still worth my salary?*

Kate's days at *Cosmo* reinforced for her the importance of dressing appropriately for work. She suggests women in midlife watch their wardrobe and make sure not to dress "old." She recommends we ask ourselves before we leave for work, *Do I look like someone at the top of her game?* She suggests getting feedback about your look from those who can be honest with you. She told me, "You want to always make the other person you're talking to realize you have something important and special to offer. In order to stay current, pay attention to what the next generation is wearing. For instance, in some industries, no one wears pantyhose anymore. You don't want to be the only woman in hose that look like you've just been caught in a rust storm."

Because the workplace can be aggressive and competitive, her best advice for this time of life is "Don't plan for fair!" She told me, "Every woman should have a plan B, whether it's a backup plan for a new job or some other financial backup. Ask yourself, 'What's another way for me to feel fulfilled and make an income?' Fields shift and can even disappear when they become obsolete. Ask yourself what are the business shifts happening in your industry and then find a way to get ahead of them. Use your intuition, which I call the 'gift of paranoia.' What is your paranoia telling you? Don't ignore the red flags and go into denial. Don't ignore the warning signs in your business."

The good news Kate sees, as I do, is that midlife women have the advantage over men the same age, because they already know how to juggle a few balls in the air at the same time. She suggests, "Educate yourself if you need to. Do volunteer work to familiarize yourself with other potential fields and options for yourself. Know this ahead of time and prepare for it. If you want to change jobs or want to pursue a dream job, you must plan ahead. Network with those you know. Speak to people in the field you're interested in to get ideas about the best way to move forward in this new direction. Make sure you're connected to all the people you've ever worked with through LinkedIn and other forms of social media. Have several reverse mentors in your life, young women in their twenties who can keep you abreast of what's new and on the horizon. Stay connected, because you never know when that next opportunity is going to come.

"At the same time, if you want to make a change of careers at midlife, have a clear plan. Don't mortgage your house. Be realistic and deliberate. You want to be looking ahead financially so that you have the right protections in place."

NOW GET BUSY

If you are in a period of transition in your career and looking for a job—whether by choice or not—remember that the working world has changed dramatically since you were fresh to the job market. Getting a job is a lot more complicated than looking through the want ads. Job seekers are not just using the Internet to search for jobs; they are creating their own websites to advertise their skills as loudly as possible. Roy Cohen is a career counselor and executive coach who advises that the biggest mistake midlife women make when they are interviewing for a job is apologizing for themselves and their résumé. He says, "An interview is a performance where you are presenting your unique set of skills to an audience. At midlife, your age is actually a solution for a set of problems, because you have the passion, enthusiasm, and experience to be proactive and offer value immediately. Offer examples from the recent past of how you have been effective. Always focus on what they need."

In discussing ageism, Cohen sees it both ways. "Remember there is always discrimination. Sometimes someone could be considered too young, too inexperienced, or too expensive. And sometimes your maturity helps. I had a client, a woman of sixty-two, who was hired because the rest of the staff was young, and so the employers wanted someone who was older, who was mature and could be a mentor. Her age helped her get the job."

Another big advantage at midlife is your connections. By this time, you've gotten to know a lot of people who might have ideas, advice, or leads. Work your network, and always keep your ears, eyes, and mind open for possibilities. Seek out connections in all aspects of your life, because they tend to lead you to other connections—which can lead to all sorts of possibilities. If you haven't joined some sort of social media, now's the time. LinkedIn has become one of the most powerful tools midlifers use for networking and working their professional connections.

If you've advertised your skills boldly and worked your networks effectively, and you still have significant trouble finding a job, it might be time to assess what else might be getting in the way of your finding the right job for you. I knew a woman who worked in public relations who wanted to break into print and electronic media as a writer and on-air personality, but she wasn't having much luck. Eventually she blamed her age for her lack of success. "Maybe I'm too old," she told me, and she asked if I had any contacts I could share with her. As it so happened, I did, and I gladly gave them to her. But she never called them. Her problem wasn't her age; it was her lack of follow-through. If you're having difficulty getting what you want, whether it's a job or an opportunity to go in a different direction, take a hard, objective look at the way you are going about it.

It's important first to figure out the job you want and to make sure you're going for something realistic. Harvard researchers Strenger and Ruttenberg suggest, and I agree, that the key to midlife career change is to stay open to the range of possibilities your experience has actually qualified you for—and remain realistic about what your experience can achieve. Becoming an opera singer might be a realistic goal if you have a glass-shattering singing voice, but for most of us, that ambition probably goes too far. I've always loved the idea of being an international rock star, but since I can't sing *at all* I know I have to settle for just dressing like one, on the weekends, when I'm with my friends.

Just as you evaluate your needs in terms of your relationships, evaluate your needs when it comes to finding a new job or even a new career. Getting a clear sense of what you're capable of, what you want, and what you're willing to do to get it become the first steps toward taking stock of yourself and your values pertaining to work. Ask yourself the following:

What did I dream of doing or being when I was a teen?

What brings me joy?

What's my top priority now?

What am I simply not willing to do or put up with at this stage of my life?

What do I want my lifestyle to be in five years?

How much money do I need to live on?

How much time, energy, and money am I willing to commit to a career goal?

How much would I be willing to give up to do the work I love?

What career could give me a sense of purpose?

If your goals are realistic, then take a good look at what you are doing to get them. When you want something, you have to become an opportunity magnet. Put yourself and your desires out there. Midlife is the time to fully explore your path. Don't stop until you feel like you've reached your potential. What's most important is to never give up on yourself. Trust that you know what's best for you and what you're meant to do.

NINE

A SPIRITUAL
OPPORTUNITY

There have been moments in my life, both positive and painful, that appeared to be driven by fate. These include some of the people I've met and situations I've experienced; they all seem to have influenced the direction of my life. Some moments of crisis ended up being fortuitous. I remember one so vividly: I had just graduated from college and moved to Philadelphia with some of my friends. I didn't have a job and was feeling pretty overwhelmed, yet at the same time I felt hopeful. I had some vague ideas about what my next move should be, and I was waiting for my life to unfold.

After a few months of waitressing, I landed a job as a counselor in North Philadelphia. At the time, it was considered a pretty dangerous part of the city, but I took the job without much thought because I was so excited to finally get that first job in what I hoped would be my career.

My boss was a tough woman who clearly didn't like me, and as much as I tried to learn, do my job well, and present myself professionally, I got fired. I was devastated. It was the first time I had failed at anything really big, and I thought my career was over and I would never be able to do what I had hoped and dreamed of doing. Then I remembered a book that had been given to me in college, *The Power of Positive Thinking*, by Norman Vincent Peale. The basic message of the book is to figure out how to turn a negative situation into a positive one. I remember saying to myself, *What can I do to turn this loss around?*

Focusing on this instruction changed my life. I remember using this phrase as my own little mantra and visualizing the images of a minus sign and a plus sign floating around in my head. I'll never know if I benefited from divine intervention, my creative problem-solving strategies, or a little bit of both, but I did figure out how to be the professional I wanted to be. I got a new job as a counselor fairly soon after getting fired, and this time it felt like a gift. I had a wonderful, supportive boss and the freedom to learn and grow. That experience made me realize I needed more training, so I applied and got accepted to graduate school at the University of Pennsylvania. Going there was intellectually stimulating and enlightening, and has led me to become the therapist I am today.

Was it fate that the first job didn't work out? I like to think so. I learned from this experience that my dark moments may not always feel good or make sense at the time, but if I can make a commitment to use these moments as opportunities for growth, I can get through anything, especially the tough times at midlife.

Some of our challenges are the external ones we've discussed throughout the book: a loss, changes in our relationships, or another's illness. One of the most significant changes during midlife is internal and involves the increasing need to belong, find renewal, and take stock of our lives. Women often describe midlife as bestselling author Joan Borysenko put it: "a time of mental housecleaning." The process involves a conscious relinquishing of old, unhealthy relationships and beliefs, then reconnecting with ourselves and trying to understand how we connect to others or new values. As we've seen in the previous chapters, relationships both at home and at work get reexamined, and interestingly, so does our spiritual foundation. This renewal of spiritual and religious interest is important for helping women in midlife experience a sense of purpose and well-being, now and going forward. In fact, many women choose to explore spiritual growth during midlife.

WHY SPIRITUALITY NOW?

If we look at midlife in the context of human development, we can see why women our age are attracted to spirituality. Dr. Carl Jung observed midlife as a time when we transform ourselves from an "energetic, biologically focused person into a more spiritual and philosophical one." Once the spiritual quest begins, Jung believed, it opens the door to a lifelong journey into self-discovery, improved mental health, increased happiness, and an overall sense of life satisfaction.

Whenever life feels somewhat tumultuous, we need to find a way to navigate it. For women, midlife is when we become most capable of managing the ambiguities and polarities of life. We come to terms with the fact that the world doesn't always make sense and usually can't be controlled. Our worldview shifts, giving us the opportunity to become more aware, enlightened, and mature. As we continue to discover and reinvent who we are throughout midlife, spirituality can be an important framework to help us know ourselves better while building relationships with other people in our world.

Midlife offers you the possibility to grow emotionally, but you have to recognize and come to terms with the more negative aspects of your personality first. It is very natural and developmentally appropriate to focus on the self at midlife, which you've been doing throughout the book. You've explored many different facets about yourself in terms of your relationships, personality, and more. But there is also value to putting a cap on this type of self-scrutinizing, because intense nitpicking can leave you depressed. As I've said before, we all have a natural tendency to fixate on what's wrong instead of what's right about our lives. When our quiet time is spent reviewing regrets, pains, insults, and disappointments, we inadvertently and sometimes unknowingly become more self-centered. And while we each deserve to be the star of our own life, we are not the center of the universe, nor are we meant to be. Having an all-about-me type of approach to life can leave us feeling psychically void or emotionally empty, viewing life as without meaning or feeling disconnected from others and the world around us. This kind of emptiness, in its most extreme form, can leave us feeling dissociated, numb, or like a shell of our former self, instead of a whole and complete person.

Ironically, self-centered people are often overly sensitive and easily offended. Their underlying grandiosity influences how they expect to be treated. When these expectations go unmet, they feel wounded or offended. Or they might act in ways that are harmful to themselves and other people in a misguided attempt to achieve happiness. This can take the form of addictive or impulsive behaviors, which may feel good in the moment but only create problematic consequences. And since a self-centered person's endless desires are impossible to satisfy, their ongoing dissatisfaction creates a wall between them and others. If someone is only interpreting the world in terms of him- or herself, it makes it hard for that person to empathize with others and consider alternate points of view.

A self-centered view can also interfere with our ability to reach our highest potential. Staying stuck in the all-about-me mode leaves us with a one-sided and inaccurate vision of the world. This limited view doesn't just rob us of our happiness; it also separates us and stops us from experiencing our personal power and potential. To evolve emotionally we must be able to rise above what happens to us, so we can break free from our feelings of ill treatment and elevate ourselves to a place where we can love more, be more, and give more, which is exactly what the spiritual quest is about. Our task during midlife is to overcome our egocentric view of the world and move from an *I* perspective to a *we* perspective. Susie Meister, a doctorate in religious studies, told me, "While my instinct is often to focus on myself at midlife, the more attention I pay to others and the ways all living beings interact and intersect, the happier and more fulfilled I am."

THE DIFFERENCE BETWEEN SPIRITUALITY AND RELIGION

First, let's parse out the difference between spirituality and religion, which I believe are two separate yet connected entities. Religion of any sort is the interpretation or the institutionalization of spirituality. Beliefs and practices guided by faith address concerns and behaviors regarding life in this world and what exists beyond. Religion usually promotes a particular creed, has a defined code of ethics, and creates community and a sense of feeling a part of something bigger than oneself. At its best, religion reminds us that we are worthy, we have purpose, and life has value and meaning. All the major world religions—Christianity, Judaism, Islam— share these tenets.

Within each religion are rules for healthy living. If you look at the laws and rules of various religions, they offer insight into how to think well about yourself, how to handle dark times, how to be good to the people around you, and how to make other people's lives better and happier. They show a distinct path as to how to clear your conscience and become your best self. Followers absorb these healthy notions through specific teachings.

Spirituality, on the other hand, is much larger than religion and, at the same time, much more personal. It is the individual journey of finding meaning, purpose, and direction for your life as you search for a greater sense of connectedness to yourself and others. Borysenko describes spirituality as "earthy, relational, mystical, intuitive, and compassionate."

Spirituality is found in every religion, yet at the same time, it requires no specific religious context. While many people seek their spiritual needs through a more organized religion, the enlightenment that comes from having a spiritual point of view doesn't require the same rules or boundaries that any particular religion does, and because of this, even atheists and agnostics can find their own spiritual perspective. In fact, a lot of people consider themselves to be spiritual but don't identify with any religion.

Several years ago, I researched a number of definitions of spirituality in order to create a universal definition for my patients. To me, spirituality is a personal expression and set of practices that inform our lives in order for us to make meaning out of the world.

There are two forms of spirituality: the first is the inner or personal, the quest for connecting with a higher power. This type of spirituality is about getting in touch with our inner voice and figuring out our greater purpose. I once met a woman who was one hundred years old, and she was glam. I asked her what her secret was, and she told me, "I live each day actively and passionately." Even though her motivations weren't religious, I could see the inner spirituality in her creed: she was enjoying the miracles of living every day to its fullest potential.

The second form is the altruistic *we* of spirituality, the same feeling found in a religious congregation, *I'm part of something bigger than myself.* This feeling might be entirely removed from religion, such as when you get involved in a charity or connect yourself with a cause you feel passionate about. My friends who are animal rights activists feel spiritual about their work. As they raise awareness about animals, it contributes to a greater good.

THE BENEFITS OF SPIRITUALITY AT MIDLIFE

Spirituality has recently become a focal point in psychology because various studies have shown the tangible benefits of adopting a spiritual approach. Some studies refer to the convergence of spirituality and midlife as "religious maturity," and researchers make clear that differences in overall religious maturity are more important for psychological well-being than any particular religious affiliation, practice, or belief. Mature religion refers to an evolved, inquiring faith that relates the individual to a higher power, provides a unifying philosophy of life, and inspires wholesome living and social responsibility. Other studies describe adopting spirituality as a component of "spiritual wellness." Many believe that a spiritual dimension is essential for helping us integrate other aspects of wellness.

Researchers have identified four components of spiritual wellness:

Meaning and purpose—searching for or participating in activities or relationships that increase our sense of hopefulness and internal motivation

Inner resources—relying on our inner strength or intuition to find peace with what is and to move forward in life with a greater sense of resiliency

Transcendence—rising above our personal interests to meet the needs of others as well as the world around us

Positive interconnectedness—connecting to ourselves, other people, and nature while considering the idea of a higher power

A spiritual perspective elevates our mind, body, and spirit, and scientific studies clearly show an impressive link exists between adopting a spiritual approach and achieving overall happiness in terms of life satisfaction, lower depression, reduced anxiety, and lower psychological distress. This may be because spirituality helps us to feel less alone and offers us an escape from the rut of self-pity, anxiety, and despair by opening our eyes to the beauty and connectedness of the universe. A spiritual perspective at midlife helps us focus on what's really important in terms of feeling more connected to the world in a meaningful and purposeful way. The more we have a sense of purpose, the less lonely and isolated we feel. Feeling part of something bigger than ourselves can also help us share our experiences— both the problems and the joys—with those around us, which in turn helps us feel more connected and supported.

The transcendence of spirituality forces us to look at our life from a different vantage point. Susie Meister, Ph.D., believes that having a spiritual perspective provides an avenue for looking at life from outside our typical point of view. By working within the framework of our own narrow point of view, we limit our understanding, life, and potential. For example, the ego part of our personality represents the *I* identity, how we each see ourselves. Yet the ego represents only a small component of who we are, because it excludes our unconscious, the primitive part of our personality or the Freudian id that wants to be satisfied. The ego, or *I* point of view, can be materialistic, and spiritualism helps us to see how being connected to others is always more important than the things we own.

Spirituality also lifts us out of the self and reminds us that, with faith or positive connectedness, anything is possible. If we embrace a spiritual perspective, we will be elevated to see the bigger picture of life from afar instead of the detailed imperfections. At midlife, we begin to recognize that there are many different ways to look at ourselves, our options, and our circumstances. As we begin to embrace a more spiritual perspective, we develop a deeper understanding of ourselves as well as become more open to new experiences and relationships, both of which can offer different perspectives than the ones we currently hold.

Embracing a spiritual perspective helps us adjust to difficult life events and feel satisfied with life in general. It also provides a therapeutic lens through which to look at our life. Plus, it builds our resiliency. When each day offers the opportunity to transcend the ordinary and enter the extraordinary, it underscores the valuable idea that we don't always have to know how everything turns out in order for things to turn out well. Sometimes we need to be open to incredible and synchronistic possibilities. In this way, having a spiritual approach becomes self-protective in terms of our psyche and how we experience both perspective and acceptance. Part of what can drive us crazy is chasing the things we don't have, making it hard to just sit where we are and say, *What do I already have that I can feel good about?*

Spirituality has helped many of my midlife patients get to a place where they can try to feel as good as they can in the moment, even when they are facing personal challenges. Sometimes you need to feel the whole range of emotions; there's something healthy and cathartic about allowing yourself to indulge and even luxuriate in them. But if you get stuck in this bad place, then it can be toxic for you. However, if you can use faith to say to yourself *I believe this bad situation is not going to be endless and there is more for me,* it gives you a way to shift your emotional state from discomfort to relief.

My client Donna discovered her own style of spirituality during midlife, and it really changed her perspective. She came to me after suffering from a series of professional setbacks. She had been a successful entrepreneur and had driven very flashy cars and spent lots of money. But when the stock market crashed in 2008, she had to sell the company, leaving her floundering financially, lost, and depressed. I recommended that she read *When God Winks,* by SQuire Rushnell, a book highlighting how nothing happens by chance. Rushnell believes, as I do, that each moment can contain synchronistic signs from the universe to notice, explore, and make the most out of in our lives.

From this spiritual perspective, Donna was able to reevaluate and feel more uplifted about her life and what was important to her. This new mindset led her to feel more centered and resilient; we were able to reinterpret her financial setback as an opportunity, which then gave her the energy to start moving forward. Her new spiritual mindset also taught her that she decides how she wants to get through life. I helped her understand that when we believe there is meaning to life, we automatically feel less bitter, hateful, and even depressed. It helped her put the past behind her so she could focus on making the most out of the present, which then leads to making better choices in the future.

Emmy Award–winning journalist Deborah Norville believes spirituality offers women in midlife the sense that there is a point to our lives and our existence. She told me, "Happy people do have this sense about themselves. People who are unhappy feel adrift. They have not discovered their purpose yet."

Psychologist Martin Seligman used science to explore what is necessary for a happy life. He found that the most satisfied people were those who discovered and used a combination of kindness, self-control, and perseverance. Seligman determined that a happy, fulfilled life can be defined by three practices, which are all linked to spiritual pursuits:

The pleasant life—pursuing positive emotions about the present, past, and future (which correlates to the spiritual component *meaning and purpose*)

The good life—using your unique strength to gain gratification through enjoyable activities (which correlates to *inner resources*)

The meaningful life—using your signature strength to be of service to something larger than yourself (which correlates to both *transcendence* and *positive interconnectedness*)

THE POWER OF ALTRUISM

Some of the positive by-products of spirituality are the altruistic attitudes and behaviors it seems to encourage. Susie Meister, Ph.D., shared that when one looks across religions to find themes, many faiths embrace some form of the Golden Rule, or a sense of being good to others and limiting self-interest. This component of faith speaks to the wisdom that is found in equality, kindness, love, and goodness to others. I believe that people who view themselves as spiritual feel, think, and value things in a way that emphasizes the importance of others' interests and needs. Ironically, when we think of others, it benefits us. Altruism teaches us to develop an "other"-oriented value system and goals, which leads us to accept that we matter to others.

According to psychologist Abraham Maslow, the father of positive psychology, the true purpose of life is not necessarily to make ourselves perfect but to rise above ourselves by connecting with others. Multiple studies have shown how volunteering can lead to a better quality of life. It develops in us a willingness to help both the unknown and known people in our lives, to have a citizen-of-the-world mentality, and to identify ourselves beyond a specific ethnic or national identity.

Altruism takes on a special importance during midlife because we can now use the insights and wisdom we've gained through our experiences in a new and creative way. Taking this step out of our own world can help us live in a deeper, more productive, meaningful, and caring way.

Here are some ways to nurture and cultivate your altruistic side:

Just reading or thinking about words like "community" and "relationship" can make you feel more altruistic. Even the most subtle reminders can help put you back on the right track. Tack a piece of paper to the fridge with the word "community" printed on it and watch how it changes your perspective. Or create or collect motivational sayings or words that speak to, or inspire you to become more of, the type of person you want to be.

Share honest, uplifting thoughts with the people around you. This creates a ripple effect of happy vibes.

Reframe your thoughts about the people in the world who need help as individuals who are like you rather than lifeless statistics. The similarity can be as small as "We all need to eat." This increases your emotional connection to them, which encourages your desire to help.

Find a charitable organization that speaks to your midlife mindset and become a volunteer.

Commit yourself to at least thirty acts of kindness within a month. During this time, you can train yourself to engage in small, or not so small, acts of kindness.

Find altruistic mentors, either in your community or in history, who motivate you and after whom you can model your inner altruism. Just reading about altruistic acts of kindness can encourage you to feel and act more generously. It also elevates your sincere and uplifting feelings.

Ask yourself how you can be a better example of thoughtfulness and selflessness for others, especially the people in your life. Lead by example.

AT MIDLIFE, WE HAVE SO MUCH TO BE GRATEFUL FOR

We've already discussed how gratitude can be a tool to banish regrets. Gratitude, or the ability to show thankfulness, is also a benefit of spirituality, because when you're in a state of gratitude you see life with a more positive and appreciative outlook. Being grateful also makes you pay attention to the present moment so you can experience feelings of love, compassion, and closeness to a greater universal power.

Deborah Norville wrote in her book *Thank You Power: Making the Science of Gratitude Work for You* that it's important to practice gratitude when everything is not right in your world, and then to look for what is right. She told me, "Gratitude is a tool that's only now being appreciated for the strength that it has. I write down three things I'm grateful for every day, even if it's on my smartphone. They even have apps for it. Search for 'gratitude journal' and you'll be amazed at what you find."

Dr. Robert Emmons at University of California, Davis, studies the impact of gratitude and being thankful. He found that people who kept gratitude journals exercised more regularly, had fewer physical symptoms, felt better and more optimistic about their lives, and were more likely to offer emotional support to others. The participants in his study also reported being more alert, enthusiastic, determined, and attentive. Gratitude is so effective because it counterbalances our negativity bias, through which the "bad stuff" in our life gets more of our attention than the good. The brain's fundamental organizing principle is to avoid threat and maximize rewards, and because of this, we are programmed to recognize and experience both. However, we can't feel rewards and threats unless we focus attention on them. So when we focus on feeling thankful, we release the brain chemicals that have a positive effect on mood and emotional well-being—the same chemicals released when we are naturally happy and focused. Not surprisingly, Norville found when researching her book that having an attitude of thankfulness is linked to being smarter and better at problem solving. These are two important qualities to cultivate during midlife, when we are making so many important decisions about our life and our future.

BECOMING A MORE SPIRITUAL WOMAN

While spirituality might be intimidating, particularly to those who were not raised in a tradition or who have been long separated from one, there's no wrong way to engage in it. Whether you find spiritual fulfillment through volunteering, attending religious services, working with children, or even cooking, you can find your own path.

Deborah Norville's advice for someone who's not particularly religious but wants to tap into their spirituality is to find a way to get in touch with nature. She told me, "Nature makes you feel something that is accessible to everyone. We all can see a sunrise and a gorgeous sunset. Take a moment to notice the beauty around you. Get out and breathe in some fresh air. Do something that reconnects you with nature. Stop and look at the flowers. Lose yourself in the moment. Go into a pet store. Look at a baby. There are miracles everywhere."

Rabbi Vicki Axe told me that while spirituality can be found in solitude, women in midlife seem to thrive in community. I think it's because it fulfills their desire to have strong relationships and to feel connected with other, like-minded people. It also provides a sense of belonging and a sense of security. "Without the community, spirituality can be less powerful and profound," Rabbi Axe explained. "It's more profound to share the sacred moments with other people. It's not only for the worship but is for so many other things. In our congregation, anytime that we are together in any combination of the membership, there's just a cohesiveness and sense of belonging. It creates a sense of intimacy. The community, the music, the social action and interaction—all is a conduit for worship."

Groups of any faith, or women getting together to explore some aspect of spirituality, whether it's a sisterhood group, social action group, or Bible study, have been found to provide relationships and social support. The whole idea behind these kinds of groups is to feel supported and challenged by the members as well as to have a unique experience. These groups can end up feeling like family, and they promote feelings of being valued and loved. Give yourself the opportunity to try a group on for size to see if it's a good fit before making any long-term commitments. It's important to feel comfortable and safe with any group you choose to participate in. Ask around, and don't settle for anything less than what works for you.

Women in midlife can also tap into spirituality through creative pursuits. Through our creativity we allow ourselves to imagine without judgment, to transform the ordinary, to use our bodies, emotions, and desires, and to find different ways of being. Through the creative process we can give meaning and voice to our truth, values, and ideas. We honor and learn to surrender to a process greater than ourselves. Stimulating our artistic creativity helps us to discover new ways of being in the world.

Psychologist Rollo May brilliantly described creativity as "the process of bringing something new into being." Carl Jung believed that the images we create both express a deep human experience and provide key information about our authentic selves. He also believed that the images symbolically give us clues about who we are and the life we have yet to live, and in doing so, they help us to access our spirituality.

Being in the moment of creating produces a meditative space where you can just lose yourself. When you view creativity as a practice of self-discovery rather than get caught up in what the end product should look like, you can approach it in a less inhibited way. Like your spiritual life, engaging in creativity is always more about the journey and the process.

It doesn't matter how you choose to express yourself creatively in order to get in touch with your sacredness. It doesn't matter if it's drawing, choreographing a dance, taking photographs, scrapbooking, gardening, or cooking. If you like to sing, you might connect with spiritual music. It can quiet your mind so you can listen to yourself. The power of music registers time, space, and the communal experience, and it reinforces the idea of spiritual community.

Free your imagination and try to connect with a higher wisdom that guides you. You can even use your dreams as inspiration. Nurture spirituality through your creativity by reading poetry that speaks to you, or spend some time writing without holding back. Deborah Norville believes her handicrafts are part of her spiritual expression. She told me, "I think it's important for everyone to be crafty, to take raw materials and turn them into something meaningful. Your source of meaning can't be how beautiful you are, because beauty fades, or how popular you are, because that's not lasting either. It has to be something deeper than that. Maybe it's making a meal everyone will love. Maybe it's fabric that you sew together to make a beautiful outfit. I have balls of yarn in my office. I know I can make a hat where every stitch is made with love. I can give it to my child so they can think of me when I'm away working. But I think it is important for it to be something tangible."

The processes of creativity can increase your resilience in the face of daily stressors, making this an appropriate option for midlife women. Others believe, as I do, that applying creativity to individual therapy can be transformational. I often use creativity exercises as one approach to help my patients effect healing, acquire insight, and maintain a greater sense of well-being.

TEEN TOOL: SNAP AND POST

Theologian Jeremy Begbie said the desire to make and appreciate art is universal, which may be why so many teens post their photos on social media. Art can certainly be an important pathway to discovery. It encourages us to be spontaneous, playful, and curious, and to see what lies beneath the surface of our inner life. Art helps us look at life from a deeper and more intuitive perspective.

This exercise is about nurturing your inner photographer, and it can help reveal that creativity always lies within you. Any time you want to explore creativity, just take out your camera or your smartphone and snap away.

Take photos of whatever speaks to you.

From those photos, choose up to twenty images you like the most, and create your own gallery. Underneath each photo, write your analysis of what you think the image means or represents about you, your life, your dreams. Are there any themes or recurring thoughts that come up? What have you learned about yourself that you didn't know before? Is there a spiritual theme or message this project has crystallized for you?

Now post your photos and see how your friends and family respond. What action steps does your art bring up for others?

MIDLIFE MENTOR

Kathie Lee Gifford

Kathie Lee Gifford is one of my midlife mentors because she has enjoyed such a diverse career as a television host, actress, singer, playwright, songwriter, and author. Aside from her current role as co-anchor with Hoda Kotb on the fourth hour of the *Today* show, Kathie Lee writes a weekly article for the *NY Daily News* (with Hoda), holds a weekly interview-based podcast, and devotes her time to the Association to Benefit Children. At sixty, she is amazingly relevant and looks fabulous.

One of the many reasons why so many women, particularly in midlife, connect with her is because of her openness about how religious and spiritually centered she is. She told me what she thinks about midlife: "Instead of getting older gracefully, why don't we say getting older gratefully, because each day is a gift." Love that!

During my interview with her, I asked if she has always been a spiritual person. She told me, "I've always had a sense that God was a presence. At twelve or thirteen years old, I saw a movie called *The Restless Ones*. In the movie, there was a little girl who was at a crossroads in her life. She could go a self-destructive path filled with drugs or believe and trust in God and that he has a purpose for her life. She chose God. It was around that time that I had my first experience of God talking to me and saying 'I love you.' I heard it in my spirit. I experienced this as an invitation to trust God. More than religion, I have a relationship with the Creator.

"Being spiritual helps me to be more forgiving, be more generous, and be more thoughtful. To pray for the people who hate me, which eliminates the need to be vindictive. You can't feel love and hate at the same time. Every morning I wake up at 4:00 A.M. to pray for an hour. This is the time for me to have intense conversations with God. I sit with my dogs and pray to be more like my dogs, who are grateful, enjoy simplicity, and are loving. We don't make enough time for this in our lives. We have trouble being still. This is not only my time to speak to God but to listen, too. It's also a time to hear my own voice."

When I asked her why spirituality is important for women to embrace during midlife, she said, "By midlife, we've given everything a chance. Some goals have been met, some not met. By the time you get to midlife, you've experienced disappointment. Spirituality gives us the ability to do better, to be less petty. I know I won't stay in the dark place. But more than anything, spirituality offers this joy in your life that nothing else can satisfy. There is a void people try to fill up with things that ultimately don't make them happy. This is a God-filled void. Spiritual people fill up this void.

"When I first entered midlife I found that my spirituality has helped me to have a deeper understanding of life. I'm more understanding. I'm instantly more aware and have the strength and humility to say 'I'm sorry.' Now I make more of an effort to learn. We have a tendency to be lazy. If you want to be more spiritual, you have to work at it.

"I spend time investing in my spirituality and relationship with God. I partner with the Lord as a way to discover the tools in life. If you want to tap into your spirituality, avoid the trappings of religion—this can be too limiting. The great thing about spirituality and developing a relationship with God is that it's free and accessible to everyone."

Kathie Lee also talked about some of the people she has met because of her spirituality and how her spirituality helps her feel more connected to others. She told me, "I really believe the Lord puts people in my path or on my mind. One homeless woman was on my mind and I prayed for her. It gives me a sense of humility, a purpose. Nothing is random. God places people in our path."

A SEARCH FOR MEANING

During midlife, there's a desire to understand the meaning of our setbacks and frustrations so we can feel hopeful about ourselves and our lives. In our attempt to find meaning, we rely on either spirituality or faith in the form of the adage "Everything happens for a reason." One reason we take this attitude is that, culturally, we have no other dialogue that provides a way to get to this level of wisdom.

I've reported on some pretty grueling crimes and incidents as a psychological commentator on television. So while I'm inclined to believe everything happens for a reason, I also realize bad things happen to good people, and life isn't always fair. So while I don't know for sure if everything happens for a reason, one thing I do know is that our search for meaning offers a much healthier way to live. Our attitude can help us to look at the more painful events in our lives as empowering opportunities to mature, become stronger, and make important breakthroughs that can influence us in midlife and beyond.

I believe life is a combination of free will and destiny. Painful things have happened and are going to continue to happen in our lives; there's no way around it. But every single one of these events is part of a bigger puzzle that often is very hard to understand fully while we're experiencing it. The eighteenth-century Jewish mystic Kabbalist the Baal Shem Tov defined this idea as "specific divine providence." Nothing happens by accident and everything we experience is coming to us for some reason. Kabbalists believe that if we can understand these situations with an increased awareness and take responsibility where possible, we can both heal our wounds and connect to our deepest spirituality.

Aristotle believed there was a reason for everything that happened on life's journey and this reason was to help us to become stronger and higher as our mightiest selves. There is something to be said for seeing these moments as signs meant to take us to a better, more elevated, and evolved place.

In Eastern religions, this same idea is referred to as "karma," which is connected to the notion that we're all here on this planet to correct ourselves. "Karma" means "action," "effect," or "fate," and it refers to the principle of causality in which our actions have consequences. Good intent and good deeds contribute to good karma and happiness, while bad intent and bad deeds contribute to bad karma and suffering. Judaism has a different take on it, known as "tikkun," which means "fixing" or "repairing." Kabbalists believe we each have a tikkun, or a "repair," to make to our soul and this is in fact the reason for our birth. They believe we come into this world in an imperfect way so we can work on ourselves. Some even believe that our soul knows what it's getting into, even if we don't consciously know what's in store for us. Our soul makes this arrangement ahead of time so we can correct ourselves the way our soul needs to be corrected. It's a really interesting idea: the events in our lives are happening for us, so we can grow the way we need to grow.

The reason for certain life events might not always be obvious. Sometimes they may even feel traumatic. The goal is to understand how to get through trauma in a way that makes you a better, wiser person. The goal is always to make all life events work to your advantage. There are a lot of different choices you make along the way that certainly influence how your life looks.

Deborah Norville told me that she also believes everything happens for a reason: "But I also believe it's up to us to find that reason and purpose. These events can be like 'Snap out of it' moments in our lives. Maybe they are there to force us to move. These events shake us up a bit, forcing us to look at things differently. They force us to take a step back and evaluate where we are in life and what's not right, so we can create something better."

TEN

DISCOVERING NEW PURPOSE AND MEANING

A t midlife, the conversations with my friends have taken on a slightly different tone than when we were younger. During our twenties our discussions were often filled with lofty ideas about our future and the stuff we'd have. We shared our goals, hopes, and dreams with more than the occasional bit of romantic gossip. Many of us have met some, if not most, of our goals. As a result, I once assumed whenever my same friends would get together it would be a happiness fest, yet the opposite has been true.

Today, the talk about goals and dreams continues. We still want more out of life or think there is more for us to experience. Or we've rethought some of those earlier goals and figured out which ones we really wanted and which ones we could walk away from. What's most interesting is that our goals have changed. They no longer include a pragmatic checklist of acquisitions: home, car, husband. Now they include understanding how we fit into the bigger picture. My now goal-oriented, ambitious friends and I are searching for purpose and meaning.

Busy women like us can easily get sidetracked with our obligations, but if life is just filled with requirements, it doesn't answer the calling of the soul. At midlife, we're looking for what we need in order to feel happy, inspired, grateful, and at peace with ourselves. These answers come with finding your true self and determining your purpose.

CHANGE HAPPENS: WHY NOT EMBRACE IT NOW?

At any point in your life you can want something and really strive to get it. But as you go through midlife, you may find that what you wanted earlier—in terms of a job, a relationship, or yourself—has changed or shifted. Many women find themselves thinking *I'm really not happy, I want to do something else now, This career is no longer fulfilling my needs,* or *I better get my act together.*

By the time we reach midlife, our purpose has been influenced by all sorts of events. We might have been searching for approval from our parents and bosses, or we had a general need to fit the mold of what society or our peers expected. It's likely that at some point we tried to present a picture of ourselves to the world that didn't match our internal desires. Or we've simply outgrown our former life, even if that life served us well for years.

Sometimes change is thrust upon us. This can happen when we have a new life experience or some kind of trauma forces us to see the world through different eyes and subsequently changes our priorities. Traumas make us pause and take a timeout from our daily lives. If we use these pauses in healthy ways, they can get us to think about the bigger picture. In a successful midlife, we are ideally using life's pauses to add value, meaning, and direction to our lives.

Regardless of the reason, these shifts in what we want and need are not only perfectly normal but, at midlife, developmentally predictable. The good news is that women—and men, for that matter—really don't see these shifts as part of a larger midlife crisis anymore. As you've already learned, we've come to terms with the fact that we are always growing and changing, and therefore our purpose in life isn't fixed, or as fixed as we once thought.

I firmly believe finding one's purpose is the true elixir of youth. The path toward finding your purpose is, by definition, creative, and with this exploration, you'll once again feel the youthful energy of trying something new. Using your passions to illuminate your path requires courage and investigation, both of which can be exhilarating. Best of all, once you've found your purpose, it brings a sense of calmness: you can be less anxious about the future because you're fulfilling your purpose *now*. There is also a sense of connectedness to other women in midlife who are following the same path, and you'll be less bored because your life is no longer routinized. When you are operating within your purpose, there's always something new to do, something new to learn, which makes your journey fun and pleasurable.

Uncovering your purpose gives you permission to take back your choices. There's no longer an idealization of other people over yourself. Your inner thoughts no longer sound like *My family knows what's better for me. Society knows what's better for me. My friends know better than I do.* Now your wisdom is coming through like a healthy rebellion, saying, *Other people do not necessarily know any more than I do. I know what works for me. I know my soul. I really feel pulled in this direction and I need to follow it.* This quest can begin when you can say, *Hey, what am I doing this for?*

This experience is similar, in some ways, to adolescence. A teenager's task is to become more independent, so they pull away from their parents and start listening to their own voice. In midlife, we are separating ourselves emotionally from family and societal or cultural pressures that have kept us feeling suffocated or are ill-fitting for us. Midlife is the time when we finally have the resources to honor our feelings over these external pressures, and with that new freedom, we can explore who we are meant to be.

DEFINING YOUR PURPOSE AT MIDLIFE

Defining your purpose is knowing who you are and what you want to do, which leads you to be honest and content, and to make life choices that truly suit you and serve your interests. It involves using your talent and skills to impact others as well as yourself. This is why your purpose would not be to go on a diet and lose weight, but it might be to help your family live a healthier lifestyle.

When you choose a purpose, make sure you understand the difference between a real purpose and a wish or fantasy. I always tell my patients that I'd love to be an international rock star, but this is definitely not my purpose in life. I can't sing. I've never taken a class and I never will. I'm not doing anything to move myself toward this fantasy goal; it's just not happening. I'm not going to be upset if it never happens, which is a good thing because it's never going to happen. (Please, you should never hear me sing! I do have empathy!)

The difference between a purpose and a wish is that your purpose is propelled by a deep need to use your unique gifts in a way that makes a difference. If you believe you will not be happy without including a particular passion of yours in your life in some way, then you've found your purpose. For example, many women at midlife experience an urge to do good in the world. Doing good can mean a lot of things, like devoting more time to your family, volunteering for a charity, or working on a cause you really care about. It can mean simply committing to meaningful projects at work, knowing that you're contributing in your own special way, or seeing aspects of your life in a new way and discovering your purpose where you never saw it before.

Finding your purpose is not necessarily an overhaul to your entire life, but it's recognizing all the different facets of your personality and giving them an opportunity for expression. For example, if you've always wanted to be more active and physically fit, but your job is entirely sedentary, you have to figure out how to make the necessary changes to incorporate this new purpose into your life. Sometimes adding just one other element to your life is enough to make you feel like you are being true to yourself. You don't have to earn money from your purpose; it can be a component of your day, an aspect of who you are. My colleague television host Joy Behar, for example, worked in an office until midlife, but she had always wanted to be a comedienne. For a year she started going to open mic nights at comedy clubs, and she didn't even tell her husband because she didn't know how he would feel. Eventually, she was able to make a change in careers and found herself doing what she knew she would love.

By now, you may have started to formulate some new ideas on how you want to reshape your life in terms of your relationships, your job, your health, your finances. Changes in any of these categories can also help you find your purpose. It's time to start putting these ideas into action and, by doing so, begin the next adventure.

Please take your pursuit seriously. If you love the idea of being an artist, consider yourself an artist. Midlife allows you to not look further than yourself for validation. You don't need validation to come from the outside world, but you do need to validate yourself. So hire yourself, rebrand yourself, promote yourself, become your own publicist. Then if you want to look for further validation from the outside world, great. That's something you can certainly do. But you have to own it yourself first.

There are lots of different ways to legitimize yourself. Let's say you're awesome at making gorgeously decorated, tasty cupcakes, and you want to spend more of your time as a baker. Once you start owning this idea, make a business card. It's cheap to do. Print CUPCAKE MAKER and then hand it out to your friends and family. Dedicate part of your day, your week, your month, to doing what you want to do. Start defining yourself as this person, and before you know it, everyone will know you as "Sara Lee, the gal who bakes."

If you are completely unsure of your purpose, don't stress about it. Explore the lives of your role models as well as your daydreams and fantasies. Do they provide information about what you want to do? Your daydreams and fantasies can give you amazing access and a front-row seat to your secret desires without considering the limitations of reality—this is why they are so important to explore. Daydreaming allows you to test out different roles and try different lifestyles on for size. While your daydreams may not always point you in the right direction, they are great at capturing the true spirit of who you want to be.

THE SECRETS TO A MEANINGFUL LIFE

A meaningful life is the result of achieving your purpose or value. When we live a life filled with meaning, it helps us find the underlying reasons for why we choose one path over another. It lets us spot opportunities to express ourselves in a way that gives us a sense of satisfaction and a personal sense of self-worth. Some of the essential features of living a meaningful life are expressing ourselves authentically, taking on challenging situations, and pushing ourselves to achieve more than we ever thought possible.

A search for meaning is a core component of spiritual wellness, which we discussed in the previous chapter. Viktor Frankl, whose book *Man's Search for Meaning* is considered one of the ten most influential books in America, wrote, "Meaning comes to us when we accept full responsibility for how we will respond to life and how we will give ourselves to the world." To me there is no better expression for the connection between pursuing purpose and meaning and living a spiritual, compassionate life.

A meaningful life is different from a happy life, although of course I want you to have both. And you are far less likely to be unhappy about other aspects of midlife—like disappointments or decisions you regret, or changes in appearance or relationships—if you are connected to something meaningful. The research consistently shows that when we incorporate purpose and meaning into our lives, our overall sense of life satisfaction and well-being increases. Our resiliency and self-esteem also increase, and our feelings of depression decrease, even more so than when we pursue a goal of happiness. In fact, the pursuit of happiness without having a sense of meaning results in living a selfish and shallow life. Perhaps Viktor Frankl said it best when he said, "The more one forgets himself by giving himself to a cause to serve or another person to love, the more human he is." I would add, the more fulfilled you'll be as well.

According to Roy Baumeister, Ph.D., of Florida State University, meaning is not connected with whether one is healthy, has enough money, or feels comfortable in life, while happiness is. He identified four other differences between a happy life and a meaningful one:

> Happiness involves being focused on the present, whereas meaningfulness involves thinking more about the past, present, and future. Happiness can be fleeting, while meaningfulness has a lasting power. This may be why purpose and meaning so clearly go together.

> Meaningfulness is derived from giving to other people; happiness comes from what they give to you.

> Meaningful lives involve challenges that can be pleasant, but are sometimes not. Engaging in challenging or difficult situations that are beyond oneself promotes meaningfulness, but not happiness.

> Self-expression is important to meaning but not happiness. Doing things to express oneself [again, your purpose] is linked to a meaningful life, but not a happy one.

TEEN TOOL: START A NEW CHAPTER

I hope the lessons and encouragement I've shared with you will allow you to see all the promise and potential of midlife. This can help you in your quest to find more purpose and meaning in your life. Like teens, you have so much time ahead of you; don't waste one more moment feeling stuck or feeling that you have no options. If there is one single message that I want you to take away, it is that midlife is not the end of anything; it's really the beginning of a whole new phase you can look forward to.

To that end, let's write an entirely new script about your midlife. Think of all the topics we covered, and describe yourself and the life you have in those terms. Is this the life you want? Remember, be kind to yourself as well as objective; support your decisions with love, compassion, and understanding. Include the answers to the following questions:

> *What have I learned about myself and my life that I didn't know before?*
>
> *What talents did I discover about myself?*
>
> *What are the best things about being me?*
>
> *What do I need the most to make my midlife complete?*
>
> *What areas of my life do I think need a bit of tweaking in order to make my midlife feel more rewarding?*
>
> *Is there anything I can eliminate from my life that is not serving my best interests?*
>
> *What advice do I have for myself?*

MIDLIFE MENTOR

Suzanne Somers

Everything about Suzanne Somers is youthful and energetic. Her many career transitions have taught us that there is more to her than meets the eye. She is an accomplished actress, author, and businesswoman. She candidly told me, "The foundation of what I project is very simple. I eat only organic food. I exercise moderately. I have been on a full complement of bioidentical hormones and custom supplementation for twenty years. I am passionate about my work, which for the past twenty-five years includes twenty-five books on health and family, my TV marketing business, eleven years of network TV, and starring in my own show nightly in Las Vegas. And most important, my family: three kids, six grandkids, and my husband, Alan, who has been my life and business partner for forty-eight years. We are together 24/7 and have not spent one night apart in over thirty-five years. We are beautifully interdependent."

I was impressed how passionate she was about both her work and her family. Her positive attitude has certainly helped her become open to change and reinvention. When I asked if being an actress somehow contributed to her creative energy and assisted with forever being relevant in a youthful, ageless way, she quickly replied by connecting her youthful energy to what she is doing now rather than what she did in the past. She told me, "I have not acted for decades. I don't think acting has anything to do with personal energy or agelessness."

I asked her if she ever worried about aging or becoming irrelevant or invisible. She told me, "I have never worried about aging. I love my age, and in fact, I sell my age. By example, I want women to embrace midlife and not worry about what's down the road. Worry is a prayer that you don't want."

Suzanne has had many careers and continues to infuse meaning and passion into everything she does. She told me, "I have reinvented myself many times and will continue to do so. When I was fired from *Three's Company* for asking to be paid commensurate with the men, I decided to never work for anyone ever again. It was a great decision. I spent the 1980s in Las Vegas and became Entertainer of the Year. I authored twenty-five books, fourteen of which are *New York Times* bestsellers. I starred on *Step by Step* for seven years. My company has created hundreds of products that we license or market. I have lectured extensively in the United States, Canada, and Western Europe to women who have read my books, about how to achieve peak health without drugs and how to replace the biochemicals we lose from our bodies in the aging process, to minimize the possibility of those dreaded diseases: cancer, stroke, heart disease, and Alzheimer's. I am not bragging. I am simply telling you how I choreograph my life to achieve my personal and business goals."

She then told me that the best thing about midlife for her was the love she now has in her life. "I have more than most and am very grateful. Growing up, I lived in a house of horrors. My father was a crazed and abusive alcoholic, and my mother, sister, brothers, and I slept in a closet with a lock on the inside to avoid his nightly rampages and the possibility of being physically attacked. Lots of therapy and lots of love have allowed me to leave all that behind as a distant memory and really appreciate the life I have. There is no secret to happiness in life. It's what you decide you want and then go after. With me, I first visualize what I want in my relationships or in business and then make it happen. Unfortunately, most people wait for life to happen to them. I believe one has to insist on life happening for them the way they want it."

Suzanne doesn't seem to fear aging because she lives entirely in the present and doesn't worry about the future. She told me, "Fear and anxiety about aging is living in the future. I live in the present. I am acutely aware of every moment of my present, and it's peaceful."

REALLY, LIFE JUST KEEPS GETTING BETTER

When MIDUS researchers asked women over sixty-five what age they would most like to return to, most of them bypassed their teens, their twenties, and their thirties, and they said their forties. There is truth in the U-shaped curve: while midlife can pose the most challenges, once you get through those challenges, it's smooth sailing. So if you started this book feeling in a dark place, the good news is, you're well on your way to happiness. Midlife and the challenges it contains might be your prep work, in a way, for getting to a better place.

By now you know that rebelling against the ageist myths, rewriting your stories to better conform with your reality, and borrowing the energy, optimism, and rebelliousness of youth can set you free to enjoy a range of intoxicating possibilities. You have an unprecedented chance to live the life you truly want. You're in the driver's seat now. Go out and enjoy the ride.

ACKNOWLEDGMENTS

One reason why I love writing books is that it's never been a solo process. I have been so fortunate to meet and work with the most interesting, intelligent, and magnificent people. I want to first thank my longtime literary agent, Andrew Stuart, for his loyalty and support. Your extraordinary knowledge of the written word and your finger on the pulse of what people want to read gave me the confidence to start this journey. Thank you for your ongoing encouragement.

A big thank you to Nancy Hancock and to HarperOne for believing in me, investing in me, and ultimately green-lighting this book. My amazing editor, Genoveva Llosa, came into the project with enthusiasm. I feel so very lucky to have worked with her and her assistant, Hannah Rivera and, in so doing, benefited from their brilliant and insightful ideas and recommendations. You added so much joy to this process while being an absolute pleasure to work with.

Thank you to Pam Liflander! Your writing talent, editing, organizational skills, and unwavering support during the entire writing process have been absolutely invaluable. I am beyond grateful fate brought us together. I not only got to work with a great writer-editor, but I also made a great friend in the process.

I also would like to thank my beautiful and supportive friends. Barbara Carol, you are not only wonderful—luckily for me—but also a librarian extraordinaire. My research process would not have been as complete, or as in depth, without your willingness to go above and beyond for me. I adore you! Dr. Wendy Walsh for sharing her time and relationship research with me. My literary salon was one of the highlights of writing this book. Christine Chidoub, Stacy Schneider, Elizabeth Bradley, Didi Fenlon, Karen Niro, Denise Sharp, Judy Brill, Barbara Carol, Elise Margolis, Sheryl Berk, Erica Skolnick, Sue Orchant, and Pam Price, you inspired me by sharing your feelings about midlife so openly and honestly. The way you each live your midlife has served as a major inspiration for this book. I also want to send a special shout-out to Donny Deutsch; Yvonne Over; my sisters, Ramy Sharp and Lori Rosenbaum; and my sisters-in-law, Denise Sharp and Joan Ryder Ludwig, for sharing their special perspectives about midlife with me. And a special thank you to the restaurant team at the Hi-Life Restaurant and Lounge in NYC, especially to Earl Geer, our coordinator, for graciously hosting our salon and making it such a success. The staff was beyond lovely and professional.

Many, many thanks to my television agent, Mark Turner. You are always there for me, supportively moving me forward so I can achieve my many career goals. I really appreciate your willingness to connect me with some of your other fantastic clients for this project, so I could learn from their insights into midlife.

I want to especially thank my mother, Helene Shalotsky, for serving as my personal midlife mentor. Your perspective about aging, in addition to the ageless and timeless way you carry yourself, has always inspired and helped me to feel good about getting older and bolder. I'm also grateful for your honest feedback about the manuscript. I know your tough-love feedback has always helped to make me the best that I could be.

And last but certainly not least, I want to thank my amazing husband, David, and my children, Jason and Jaimie. I could not have completed this book without your unwavering love and support. I love you "to the moon and back!" Thank you for always being there for me and, most of all, for believing in me. I am who I am and able to do what I do every day because of you.

RECOMMENDED READING

Apter, Terri. *Secret Paths: Women in the New Midlife.* New York: W. W. Norton, 1995.

Braverman, Eric R. *Younger (Thinner) You Diet.* Emmaus, PA: Rodale, 2009.

Carmona, Richard. *Canyon Ranch 30 Days to a Better Brain.* New York: Atria Books/Simon & Schuster, 2014.

Christakis, Nicholas and James Fowler. *Connected: The Surprising Power of Our Social Networks and How They Shape Our Lives.* New York: Little, Brown, 2009.

Cohen, Patricia. *In Our Prime: The Invention of Middle Age.* New York: Scribner, 2012.

Diller, Vivian and Jill Muir-Sukenick. *Face It: What Women* Really *Feel as Their Looks Change and What to Do About It.* Carlsbad, CA: Hay House, 2010.

Fadal, Tamsen. *The New Single: Finding, Fixing, and Falling Back in Love with Yourself After a Breakup or Divorce.* New York: St. Martin's, 2015.

Frankl, Viktor. *Man's Search for Meaning.* Boston: Beacon Press, 2006.

Levine, Suzanne Braun. *The Woman's Guide to Second Adulthood: Inventing the Rest of Our Lives.* London: Bloomsbury, 2005.

Ludwig, Robi and Matt Birkbeck. *Till Death Do Us Part: Love, Marriage, and the Mind of the Killer Spouse.* New York: Atria Books, 2006.

Maine, Margo and Joe Kelly. *The Body Myth: Adult Women and the Pressure to Be Perfect.* Hoboken, NJ: John Wiley, 2005.

Matson, Michelle. *Rich Chick: The Nine Must-Have Accessories Every Girl Needs to Create Financial Confidence, Independence and Freedom—the Smart Way.* ebook, 2009.

Newman, Mildred, Bernard Berkowitz, and Jean Owen. *How to Be Your Own Best Friend: A Conversation with Two Psychoanalysts.* New York: Random House, 1973.

Norville, Deborah. *Thank You Power: Making the Science of Gratitude Work for You.* Nashville: Thomas Nelson, 2007.

Peale, Norman Vincent. *The Power of Positive Thinking.* New York: Prentice-Hall, 1952.

Pine, Karen. *Mind What You Wear: The Psychology of Fashion.* ebook, 2014.

Rodman, Abby. *Should You Marry Him?: A No-Nonsense, Therapist-Tested Guide to Not Screwing Up the Biggest Decision of Your Life*. Bloomington, IN: Balboa Press, 2013.

Roese, Neal J. *If Only: How to Turn Regret into Opportunity*. New York: Broadway Books/Random House, 2005.

Rudder, Christian. *Dataclysm: Who We Are When We Think No One's Looking*. New York: Crown, 2006.

Rushnell, SQuire. *When God Winks: How the Power of Coincidence Guides Your Life*. New York: Atria Books, 2002.

Scheindlin, Judy. *What Would Judy Say?* ebook, 2013.

Schwartz, Barry. *The Paradox of Choice: Why More Is Less*. New York: Ecco, 2004.

Sheehy, Gail. *Daring: My Passages: A Memoir*. New York: William Morrow, 2014.

Sheehy, Gail. *Passages: Predictable Crises of Adult Life*. New York: Dutton, 1976.

Shellenbarger, Sue. *The Breaking Point: How Female Midlife Crisis Is Transforming Today's Women*. New York: Henry Holt, 2005.

Siegel, Daniel J. *Brainstorm: The Power and Purpose of the Teenage Brain*. New York: Jeremy P. Tarcher/Penguin, 2013.

Smiler, Andrew P. *Challenging Casanova: Beyond the Stereotype of the Promiscuous Young Male*. San Francisco: Jossey-Bass, 2013.

Somers, Suzanne. *Ageless: The Naked Truth About Bioidentical Hormones*. New York: Crown, 2006.

Vaillant, George E. *Triumphs of Experience: The Men of the Harvard Grant Study*. Cambridge, MA: Belknap Press/Harvard Univ. Press, 2012.

Von Fürstenberg, Diane. *The Woman I Wanted to Be*. London: Simon & Schuster, 2014.

Wallerstein, Judith S. and Sandra Blakeslee. *The Good Marriage: How and Why Love Lasts*. Boston, Houghton Mifflin, 1995.

Ware, Bronnie. *The Top Five Regrets of the Dying: A Life Transformed by the Dearly Departing*. Carlsbad, CA: Hay House, 2012.

White, Kate. *I Shouldn't Be Telling You This: How to Ask for the Money, Snag the Promotion, and Create the Career You Deserve*. New York: HarperBusiness, 2013.

White, Kate. *Why Good Girls Don't Get Ahead—but Gutsy Girls Do: Nine Secrets Every Career Woman Must Know*. New York: Warner Books, 1995.

Whitehurst, Tess. *Magical Fashionista: Dress for the Life You Want*. Woodbury, MN: Llewellyn Publications, 2013.

Winch, Guy. *Emotional First Aid: Practical Strategies for Treating Failure, Rejection, Guilt, and Other Everyday Psychological Injuries*. New York: Hudson Street Press, 2013.

Wolf, Naomi. *The Beauty Myth: How Images of Beauty Are Used Against Women*. New York: William Morrow, 1991.

NOTES

....

Chapter 1: It's Time for a New Midlife

3–4. *Perceptions of age are sometimes more convincing than reality.*
Becca R. Levy et al., "Subliminal Strengthening: Improving Older
Individuals' Physical Function over Time with an Implicit-Age-Stereotype
Intervention," *Psychological Science* 25, no. 12 (December 2014): 2127–35,
doi:10.1177/0956797614551970.

6–7. *Even fixed personality traits can evolve over time.*
Sanjay Srivastava et al., "Development of Personality in Early and Middle
Adulthood: Set like Plaster or Persistent Change?" *Journal of Personality and
Social Psychology* 84, no. 5 (May 2003): 1041–53.

9–10. *The age at which we consider ourselves middle-aged keeps creeping up.*
Louise Eccles, "When Does Middle Age Really Begin? On Your 53rd
Birthday: Rising Life Expectancy Means It No Longer Hits When You're 41,"
DailyMail.com, August 27, 2013, http://www.dailymail.co.uk/news
/article-2402732/Middle-age-begins-53-says-new-survey.html.

10. *The inaugural year of middle age was on average pegged at forty-four.*
Carol A. Darling, Catherine Coccia, and Natalie Senatore, "Women in
Midlife: Stress, Health, and Life Satisfaction," *Stress & Health* 28, no. 1
(February 2012): 31–40, doi:10.1002/smi.1398.

11–12. *Among Americans aged fifty and older who currently have jobs, 82 percent
expect to work in some form during their post-sixty "retirement years."*
Jennifer Benz et al., "Working Longer: Older Americans' Attitudes on Work
and Retirement," Associated Press-NORC Center for Public Affairs Research,
March 7, 2014, http://www.apnorc.org/projects/Pages/working-longer-older-
americans-attitudes-on-work-and-retirement.aspx.

13. *Women over fifty feel more confident in their bikinis than women at any other age.*
Steve Robson, "Getting Better with Age: Women Feel Most Bikini Confident Once They Reach Their 50s," DailyMail.com, June 26, 2013, http://www.dailymail.co.uk/femail/article-2349289/Getting-better-age-Women-feel-bikini-confident-reach-50s.html.

13. *Women in Terri Apter's survey felt they looked far better at forty and fifty than they had expected.*
Terri Apter, *Secret Paths: Women in the New Midlife* (New York: W. W. Norton, 1995).

13. *Scientists are beginning to understand the ways by which aging increases the risk of disease.*
Laura Carstensen, "Why We Live Longer—and Can Still Live Better," Next Avenue, Twin Cities Public Television, October 18, 2012, http://www.nextavenue.org/why-we-live-longer--and-can-still-live-better/.

13–14. *At midlife we not only maintain many of the cognitive abilities of youth but also acquire some new ones.*
K. Warner Schaie, *Intellectual Development in Adulthood: The Seattle Longitudinal Study* (New York: Cambridge Univ. Press, 1996).

14. *Laura Carstensen developed a life-span theory of motivation she calls the Socioemotional Selectivity Theory.*
Laura Carstensen, "Motivation for Social Contact Across the Life Span: A Theory of Socioemotional Selectivity," *Nebraska Symposium on Motivation* 40 (1992): 209–54.

14. *Feeling older reliably predicts lower psychological well-being among those with negative attitudes toward aging.*
Steven E. Mock and Richard P. Eibach, "Aging Attitudes Moderate the Effect of Subjective Age on Psychological Well-Being: Evidence from a 10-Year Longitudinal Study," *Psychology and Aging* 26, no. 4 (December 2011): 979–86, doi:10.1037/a0023877.

Chapter 2: Adopt the "Best Practices" of Youth

20. *"Imagine the day you turn 45 as the infancy of another life."*
Gail Sheehy, "Yes, Life Really Does Begin at 40: Why Should Middle Age Seem like the End of the Road? What If It Is Really Just the Beginning? Starting Today, and Continuing Next Week, Award-Winning Writer Gail Sheehy Encourages You to Look Forward to the Most Important Time of Your Life," *Daily Mail (London),* May 4, 1996, accessed July 17, 2015, HighBeam Research, http://www.highbeam.com/doc/1G1-111414661.html.

26. *Brené Brown offered advice during a 2010 TED Talk that focused on vulnerability.*
Brené Brown, "The Power of Vulnerability," TEDxHouston video, June 2010, transcript posted December 2010, http://www.ted.com/talks/brene_brown _on_vulnerability/transcript?language=en#t-173830.

28. *People who consider themselves younger are overall happier.*
Margie E. Lachman, "Development in Midlife," *Annual Review of Psychology* 55, no. 1 (February 2004): 305–31.

29–30. *The behavior of rebellious, rule-breaking teens was the greatest predictor of kids growing up to earn more than their peers.*
M. Spengler et al., "Student Characteristics and Behaviors at Age 12 Predict Occupational Success 40 Years Later Over and Above Childhood IQ and Parental Socioeconomic Status," *Developmental Psychology* 51, no. 9 (September 2015): 1329–40, doi:10.1037/dev0000025.

Chapter 3: Fighting Regrets with Resilience

34. *Midlife is typical of any experience we're in the middle of.*
Margie E. Lachman and Jacquelyn B. James, eds., *Multiple Paths of Midlife Development* (Chicago: Univ. Chicago Press, 1997).

38. *Many people suppress their feelings in order to keep the peace with others.*
Bronnie Ware, *The Top Five Regrets of the Dying: A Life Transformed by the Dearly Departing* (Carlsbad, CA: Hay House, 2012).

42. *Through counterfactual reflection, the upsides to reality are identified, a belief in fate emerges, and ultimately more meaning is derived from life events.*
Laura J. Kray et al., "From What *Might* Have Been to What *Must* Have Been: Counterfactual Thinking Creates Meaning," *Journal of Personality and Social Psychology* 98, no. 1 (January 2010): 106–18, doi:10.1037/a0017905.

45. *People who let opportunities pass them by or chose the virtuous road instead of the iconoclastic one had more regrets in their lives over time.*
Ran Kivetz and Anat Keinan, "Repenting Hyperopia: An Analysis of Self-Control Regrets," *Journal of Consumer Research* 33, no. 2 (September 2006): 273–82, doi:10.1086/506308.

46. *The ability to navigate adversity in a manner that protects well-being can also protect against the negative impact of disability in later life.*
Lydia K. Manning, Dawn C. Carr, and Ben L. Kail, "Do Higher Levels of Resilience Buffer the Deleterious Impact of Chronic Illness on Disability in Later Life?" *The Gerontologist* (July 25, 2014): 1–12, doi:10.1093/geront/gnu068.

47. *Downward social comparison allows us to look at what we have through a new, appreciative, less entitled lens.*
Isabelle Bauer, Carsten Wrosch, and Joelle Jobin, "I'm Better Off than Most Other People: The Role of Social Comparisons for Coping with Regret in Young Adulthood and Old Age," *Psychology and Aging* 23, no. 4 (December 2008): 800–11, doi:10.1037/a0014180.

52. *The Grant Study was one of the longest-running longitudinal studies of human development.*
George E. Vaillant, *Triumphs of Experience: The Men of the Harvard Grant Study* (Cambridge, MA: Belknap Press, 2012).

Chapter 4: A Midlife Without Anxiety or Stress

54. *The stress we experience has a greater impact on our emotions during midlife than at any other age.*
David M. Almeida and Melanie C. Horn, "Is Daily Life More Stressful During Middle Adulthood?" in *How Healthy Are We?: A National Study of Well-Being at Midlife,* eds. Orville G. Brim, Carol D. Ryff, and Ronald C. Kessler (Chicago: Univ. of Chicago Press, 2004), 425–51.

55–56. *Women provide more emotional support to others at midlife than at any other period.*
Kelly E. Cichy, Karen L. Fingerman, and Eva S. Lefkowitz, "Age Differences in Types of Interpersonal Tensions," *International Journal of Aging and Human Development* 64, no. 2 (March 2007): 171–93, doi:10.2190/8578-7980 -301V-8771.

56. *Levels of happiness over the life cycle present themselves as a U-shaped curve.*
David G. Blanchflower and Andrew J. Oswald, "Is Well-Being U-Shaped over the Life Cycle?" *Social Science and Medicine* 66, no. 8 (April 2008): 1733–49, doi:10.1016/j.socscimed.2008.01.030.

58. *Without a grounded connection, these dreams are nothing more than idle fantasies.*
Carlo Strenger and Arie Ruttenberg, "The Existential Necessity of Midlife Change," *Harvard Business Review* 86, no. 2 (February 2008): 82–90, 137.

60. *"Anxiety is freedom's actuality as the possibility of possibility."*
Søren Kierkegaard, *The Concept of Anxiety: A Simple Psychologically Orienting Deliberation on the Dogmatic Issue of Hereditary Sin, vol. 8,* ed. and trans., Reidar Thomte, contributor, Albert Anderson (Princeton, NJ: Princeton Univ. Press, 1980).

63. *"For anyone who is over 50."*

Benedict Carey, "The Older Mind May Just Be a Fuller Mind," *The New Old Age* (blog), *New York Times,* January 27, 2014, http://newoldage.blogs .nytimes.com/2014/01/27/the-older-mind-may-just-be-a-fuller-mind/.

63. *The reason behind these mood changes is an enzyme triggered by stress.*
Michael A. van der Kooij et al., "Role for MMP–9 in Stress-Induced Downregulation of Nectin–3 in Hippocampal CA1 and Associated Behavioural Alterations," *Nature Communications* 5, article 4995 (September 2014), doi:10.1038/ncomms5995.

65. *Developing a higher level of vocabulary can protect against cognitive impairment.*
Cristina Lojo-Seoane, David Facal, and Onésimo Juncos-Rabadán, "Does Intellectual Activity Prevent Cognitive Impairment? Relationships Between Cognitive Reserve and Mild Cognitive Impairment" [in Spanish], *Revista Española de Geriatría y Gerontología* 47, no. 6 (November–December 2012): 270–78, doi:10.1016/j.regg.2012.02.006.

66. *Researchers compared blood levels of reproductive hormones in women with perimenopausal depression to the hormones of women who weren't depressed and found no differences.*
M. A. Will and J. F. Randolph, "The Influence of Reproductive Hormones on Brain Function in the Menopausal Transition," *Minerva Ginecologica* 61, no. 6 (December 2009): 469–81.

69. *Long-term stress suffered by women can ultimately lead to some form of physical complaint.*
Dominique Hange et al., "Perceived Mental Stress in Women Associated with Psychosomatic Symptoms, But Not Mortality: Observations from the Population Study of Women in Gothenburg, Sweden," *International Journal of General Medicine* no. 6 (April 24, 2013): 307–15, doi:10.2147/IJGM.S42201.

69. *Stress doesn't just increase your risk of dementia.*
Joan L. Shaver et al., "Stress Exposure, Psychological Distress, and Physiological Stress Activation in Midlife Women with Insomnia," *Psychosomatic Medicine* 64, no. 5 (September–October 2002): 793–802.

71. *During stressful situations women produce the brain chemical oxytocin.*
Wesley G. Moons, Baldwin M. Way, and Shelley E. Taylor, "Oxytocin and Vasopressin Receptor Polymorphisms Interact with Circulating Neuropeptides to Predict Human Emotional Reactions to Stress," *Emotion* 14, no. 3 (June 2014): 562–72, doi:10.1037/a0035503.

74. *Formalized meditation practice has allowed Buddhist monks to develop a profound ability to reduce their sense of pain.*

Antoine Lutz et al., "Long-Term Meditators Self-Induce High-Amplitude Gamma Synchrony During Mental Practice," *Proceedings of the National Academy of Sciences* 101, no. 46 (November 2004): 16369–73, doi:10.1073/pnas.0407401101.

74. *Successful meditators are able to control their stress levels better than non-meditators.*
Antoine Lutz et al., "Regulation of the Neural Circuitry of Emotion by Compassion Meditation: Effects of Meditative Expertise," *PLoS ONE* 3, no. 3 (March 2008): e1897, doi:10.1371/journal.pone.0001897.

83. *People in their forties and fifties have learned how to take more responsibility for their actions and the consequences of these actions.*
Deborah Gilbert, "'Midlife Crisis' Better Described as 'Midlife Turning Points,'" *The University Record,* September 21, 1992, http://ur.umich.edu/9293/Sep21_92/26.htm.

Chapter 5: Feeling Stronger Every Day

88. *Women report more health problems than men during midlife.*
Paul D. Cleary, Lawrence B. Zaborski, and John Z. Ayanian, "Sex Differences in Health over the Course of Midlife," in *How Healthy Are We?: A National Study of Well-Being at Midlife,* eds. Orville G. Brim, Carol D. Ryff, and Ronald C. Kessler (Chicago: Univ. of Chicago Press, 2004), 37–63.

90–91. *Science will be able to provide the context necessary for treatments based on the personalized information in our genes and blood type.*
Ron Zimmerman, "Genetic Code Unlocking Future of Medicine, Craig Venter Says," *Medscape Medical News,* March 10, 2014, from the Future of Genomic Medicine (FoGM) VII conference, La Jolla, CA, March 6–7, 2014, http://www.medscape.com/viewarticle/821729.

94. *Once you've gone a full year without having a period, then you've entered menopause.*
Nancy E. Avis et al., "Duration of Menopausal Vasomotor Symptoms over the Menopause Transition," *JAMA Internal Medicine* 175, no. 4 (April 2015): 531–39, doi:10.1001/jamainternmed.2014.8063.

99. *These lifestyle changes alone can often reverse the progression of severe coronary heart disease, type 2 diabetes, and some forms of cancer.*
Jenny Koertge et al., "Improvement in Medical Risk Factors and Quality of Life in Women and Men with Coronary Artery Disease in the Multicenter Lifestyle Demonstration Project," *American Journal of Cardiology* 91, no. 11 (June 2003): 1316–22.

99. *Cameron Diaz was quoted in a recent* Vogue *article.*
Alex Kuczynski "The Ageless Body: Who Has It and How to Get It," *Vogue,*
July 31, 2014.

100. *As age increases, so do the waist-to-hip ratio and the percentage of women who are overweight in midlife.*
Jamila Bookwala and Jenny Boyar, "Gender, Excessive Body Weight, and Psychological Well-Being in Adulthood," *Psychology of Women Quarterly* 32, no. 2 (June 2008): 188–95, doi:10.1111/j.1471-6402.2008.00423.x.

102. *A high-protein, low-carbohydrate, healthy-fat diet has been clinically proven to be the best prescription.*
Richard Carmona, *Canyon Ranch 30 Days to a Better Brain* (New York: Atria Books, 2014).

104. *When healthy subjects consumed a small amount of red chili pepper flakes or chili powder before each meal, it decreased their caloric intake by as much as 16 percent.*
Pilou L. H. R. Janssens et al., "Acute Effects of Capsaicin on Energy Expenditure and Fat Oxidation in Negative Energy Balance," *PLoS ONE* 8, no. 7 (July 2013): e67786, doi:10.1371/journal.pone.0067786.

105. *Vitamin D is known to elevate your mood, improve bone health, and cause weight loss.*
Michael Zemel, "Calcium Modulation of Adiposity," *Obesity Research* 11, no. 3 (March 2003): 375–76, doi:10.1038/oby.2003.50.

107. *Twins who shared the same sports and other physical activities as youngsters but developed different exercise habits as adults had quite different bodies and brains.*
Mirva Rottensteiner et al., "Physical Activity, Fitness, Glucose Homeostasis, and Brain Morphology in Twins," *Medicine and Science in Sports and Exercise* 47, no. 3 (July 2014): 509–18, doi:10.1249/MSS.0000000000000437.

107. *Cardiovascular—aerobic—exercise is best for maintaining brain health.*
Charles H. Hillman et al., "Physical Activity and Cognitive Function in a Cross-Section of Younger and Older Community-Dwelling Individuals," *Health Psychology* 25, no. 6 (November 2006): 678–87.

107–8. *The ideal exercise prescription for people in midlife to increase their life span is to work out moderately for 450 minutes per week.*
Hannah Arem et al., "Leisure Time Physical Activity and Mortality: A Detailed Pooled Analysis of the Dose-Response Relationship" *JAMA Internal Medicine* 175, no. 6 (June 2015): 959–67, doi:10.1001/jamainternmed.2015.0533.

107. *The ideal exercise intensity includes at least 20 to 30 minutes of vigorous activity.*
Klaus Gebel et al., "Effect of Moderate to Vigorous Physical Activity on
All-Cause Mortality in Middle-Aged and Older Australians," *JAMA Internal
Medicine* 175, no. 6 (June 2015): 970–77, doi:10.1001
/jamainternmed.2015.0541.

108. *Resistance training in particular can boost self-esteem, improve mood, reduce
anxiety levels, and increase the ability to handle stress.*
Moé Kishida and Steriani Elavsky, "Daily Physical Activity Enhances Resilient
Resources for Symptom Management in Middle-Aged Women," *Health
Psychology* 34, no. 7 (July 2015): 756–64, doi:10.1037/hea0000190.

118. *How much we eat, our personal taste, and our emotional state are all influenced
by the community we associate with.*
Michael Sagner et al., "Lifestyle Medicine Potential for Reversing a World of
Chronic Disease Epidemics: From Cell to Community," *International Journal of
Clinical Practice* 68, no. 11 (November 2014): 1289–92, doi:10.1111
/ijcp.12509.

118–19. *The influence of friendship over health, and especially over obesity, remained
even when two friends ended up living hundreds of miles apart.*
Nicholas A. Christakis and James H. Fowler, "The Spread of Obesity in a Large
Social Network over 32 Years," *New England Journal of Medicine* 357, no. 4
(July 2007): 370–79.

Chapter 6: Beauty Can Be a Beast

128. *The women who perceived themselves as looking younger after their hair had been
styled experienced a drop in blood pressure.*
Laura M. Hsu, Jaewoo Chung, and Ellen J. Langer, "The Influence of Age-
Related Cues on Health and Longevity," *Perspectives on Psychological Science* 5,
no. 6 (November 2010): 632–48, doi:10.1177/1745691610388762.

129. *Anxiety about attractiveness is higher among women who are younger.*
Anne E. Barrett and Cheryl Robbins, "The Multiple Sources of
Women's Aging Anxiety and Their Relationship with Psychological
Distress," *Journal of Aging and Health* 20, no. 1 (February 2008): 32–65,
doi:10.1177/0898264307309932.

130. *Worrying actually makes you less active.*
Markus J. Rantala et al., "Facial Attractiveness Is Related to Women's Cortisol
and Body Fat, but Not with Immune Responsiveness," *Biology Letters* 9, no. 4
(May 2013): 20130255, doi:10.1098/rsbl.2013.0255.

130. *If we look at our reflection in a mirror for up to ten minutes, we can become increasingly anxious and depressed about our looks.*
Katja Windheim, David Veale, and Martin Anson, "Mirror Gazing in Body Dysmorphic Disorder and Healthy Controls: Effects of Duration of Gazing," *Behaviour Research and Therapy* 49, no. 9 (September 2011): 555–64, doi:10.1016/j.brat.2011.05.003.

131. *Women who develop anorexia or bulimia in midlife may have experienced long-term struggles with body image, had an eating disorder during the adolescent years, or developed an eating disorder after a critical illness.*
"Profiling Midlife Eating Disorders," *Eating Disorders Review* 17, no. 6 (November 2006): 4

134. *The lifestyle choices you make show up in your skin.*
Bahman Guyuron et al., "Factors Contributing to the Facial Aging of Identical Twins," *Plastic and Reconstructive Surgery* 123, no. 4 (April 2009): 1321–31, doi:10.1097/PRS.0b013e31819c4d42.

135. *While we know the mind influences the body, the body can also have a strong influence on the mind.*
Sian Beilock, *How the Body Knows Its Mind: The Surprising Power of the Physical Environment to Influence How You Think and Feel* (New York: Atria Books, 2015).

136. *Those who used sunscreen every day had noticeably more resilient and smoother skin than those who didn't.*
Maria C. B. Hughes et al., "Sunscreen and Prevention of Skin Aging: A Randomized Trial," *Annals of Internal Medicine* 158, no. 11 (June 2013): 781–90, doi:10.7326/0003-4819-158-11-201306040-00002.

136. *Salicin, a compound produced from willow bark, may regulate functional "youth gene clusters."*
Remona Gopaul, Helen E. Knaggs, and Janet F. Lephart, "Salicin Regulates the Expression of Functional 'Youth Gene Clusters' to Reflect a More Youthful Gene Expression Profile," *International Journal of Cosmetic Science* 33, no. 5 (October 2011): 416–20, doi:10.1111/j.1468-2494.2011.00645.x.

Chapter 7: Finding Love

148. *Couples now have far higher expectations from the institution of marriage.*
Tara Parker-Pope, *For Better: The Science of a Good Marriage* (New York: Dutton, 2010).

149. *Risk for divorce drops significantly when couples wait to wed until after the age of twenty-five.*

Scott M. Stanley et al., "Premarital Education, Marital Quality, and Marital Stability: Findings from a Large, Random Household Survey," *Journal of Family Psychology* 20, no. 1 (March 2006): 117–26, doi:10.1037/0893 -3200.20.1.117.

157. *Having strong social connections of any sort is one of the secrets of healthy aging.*
Ilene C. Siegler et al., "Consistency and Timing of Marital Transitions and Survival During Midlife: The Role of Personality and Health Risk Behaviors," *Annals of Behavioral Medicine* 45, no. 3 (June 2013): 338–47, doi:10.1007 /s12160-012-9457-3.

158. *Those who consider their spouse or partner to be their best friend get twice as much life satisfaction from marriage.*
John F. Helliwell and Shawn Grover, "How's Life at Home? New Evidence on Marriage and the Set Point for Happiness" (Working Paper no. 20794, National Bureau of Economic Research, Cambridge, MA, December 2014), http://www.nber.org/papers/w20794.

159. *Nearly six in ten adults over the age of forty-five believe that sexual activity is critical to a good relationship.*
Linda L. Fisher et al., *Sex, Romance, and Relationships: AARP Survey of Midlife and Older Adults,* publication D19234 (Washington, D.C.: American Association of Retired Persons, 2010).

160. *Gratitude and being appreciative increase relationship satisfaction.*
Sara B. Algoe and Jonathan Haidt, "Witnessing Excellence in Action: The 'Other-Praising' Emotions of Elevation, Gratitude, and Admiration," *Journal of Positive Psychology* 4, no. 2 (March 2009): 105–27, doi:10.1080/17439760802650519.

160. *Gratitude improves our personal happiness, our overall health, and our sexiness factor.*
Alex M. Wood, Jeffrey J. Froh, and Adam W. A. Geraghty, "Gratitude and Well-Being: A Review and Theoretical Integration," *Clinical Psychology Review* 30, no. 7 (November 2010): 890–905, doi:10.1016/j.cpr.2010.03.005.

161. *Writing true emotions can help in terms of professing feelings.*
James W. Pennebaker, "Writing About Emotional Experiences as a Therapeutic Process," *Psychological Science* 8, no. 3 (May 1997): 162–66, doi:10.1111 /j.1467-9280.1997.tb00403.x.

164. *A husband is more willing to stay in an unhappy marriage.*
Aline G. Sayer et al., "Analyzing Couples and Families: Multilevel Methods," in *Sourcebook of Family Theory and Research,* eds. Vern L. Bengtson et al. (Thousand Oaks, CA: SAGE Publications, 2005), 289–315, doi:http:// dx.doi.org/10.4135/9781412990172.n12.

164–65. *Life satisfaction does not necessarily increase after a divorce.*
Daniel N. Hawkins and Alan Booth, "Unhappily Ever After: Effects of Long-Term, Low-Quality Marriages on Well-Being," *Social Forces* 84, no. 1 (September 2005): 451–71, doi:10.1353/sof.2005.0103.

174. *Only 29 percent of divorced adults say they want to remarry.*
Wendy Wang and Kim Parker, "Record Share of Americans Have Never Married: As Values, Economics, and Gender Patterns Change," Social and Demographic Trends project, Pew Research Center, September 24, 2014, http://www.pewsocialtrends.org/2014/09/24/record-share-of-americans -have-never-married/.

Chapter 8: Making a Living, Making a Life

179. *The average midlife woman today has as many years of productivity ahead of her as she has behind her.*
Carlo Strenger and Arie Ruttenberg, "The Existential Necessity of Midlife Change," *Harvard Business Review* 86, no. 2 (February 2008): 82–90, 137.

179–80. *Four in ten households with children under eighteen include a mother who is either the sole or primary breadwinner for the family.*
Kim Parker and Wendy Wang, "Modern Parenthood: Roles of Moms and Dads Converge as They Balance Work and Family," Social and Demographic Trends project, Pew Research Center, March 14, 2013, http://www .pewsocialtrends.org/2013/03/14/modern-parenthood-roles-of-moms-and -dads-converge-as-they-balance-work-and-family/.

180. *Women who fall short of their career goals suffer from lower levels of psychological well-being.*
Deborah Carr, "The Fulfillment of Career Dreams at Midlife: Does It Matter for Women's Mental Health?" *Journal of Health and Social Behavior* 38, no. 4 (December 1997): 331–44.

180. *Researchers studying both men and women in midlife find their judgment surrounding financial matters has reached an all-time high.*
Sumit Agarwal et al., "The Age of Reason: Financial Decisions over the Life Cycle and Implications for Regulation," in *Brookings Papers on Economic Activity, Fall 2009* (Washington, D.C.: Brookings Institution Press, 2009), 51–117.

180–81. *Women experience more work-related tension than men.*
American Psychological Association, "APA Survey Finds U.S. Employers Unresponsive to Employee Needs," press release, March 5, 2013, http://www .apa.org/news/press/releases/2013/03/employee-needs.aspx.

182. *Forty-nine percent of all women fear ending up broke and homeless.*
Jan Bruce, "The One Thing Women Should Stop Worrying About,"
Entrepreneurs, *Forbes,* April 1, 2014, http://www.forbes.com/sites
/janbruce/2014/04/01/bag-lady-syndrome-how-to-stop-fearing-the-worst/.

184. *Personal finance expert Alexis Neely recommends starting to save with a goal in
mind, which she calls "backward budgeting."*
Alexis Neely, "Backwards Budgeting: How Doing It Backwards Leads
to Everything You Want," *DailyWorth,* October 22, 2014, https://www.
dailyworth.com/posts/3042-backwards-budgeting?utm
_source=Sailthru&utm_medium=email&utm_term=DailyWorth&utm
_campaign=DW_tues_hedonly-liveintent.

184. *Women in midlife are better at saving and investing than they may realize.*
Gregory R. Samanez-Larkin, "Financial Decision Making and the Aging
Brain," *APS Observer* 26, no. 5 (June 2013): 30–33, http://www.ncbi.nlm.nih
.gov/pmc/articles/PMC3740974/.

185. *The midlife brain is less likely to get overwhelmed during times of crisis.*
Joy L. Taylor et al., "Pilot Age and Expertise Predict Flight Simulator
Performance: A 3-Year Longitudinal Study," *Neurology* 68, no. 9 (February
2007): 648–54, doi:10.1212/01.wnl.0000255943.10045.c0.

185. *Our ability to read other people's emotions doesn't even take shape until we're in
our forties.*
Joshua K. Hartshorne and Laura T. Germine, "When Does Cognitive
Functioning Peak? The Asynchronous Rise and Fall of Different Cognitive
Abilities Across the Life Span," *Psychological Science* 26, no. 4 (April 2015):
433–43, doi:10.1177/0956797614567339.

185. *Nearly all of the one hundred most powerful women in the entertainment
industry are in midlife.*
"The Hollywood Reporter's 2014 Women in Entertainment Power 100,"
Hollywood Reporter, December 4, 2014, http://www.hollywoodreporter.com
/list/hollywood-reporters-2014-women-entertainment-754104.

187. *Judge Judy wrote, "I don't want to say anything's possible."*
Judy Sheindlin, *What Would Judy Say?: Be the Hero of Your Own Story* (Arena
Publishing, 2014).

189. *A large number of workers can expect to change their jobs up to ten times over the
course of their careers.*
Michelle Vessel, "Secrets to Re-Entering the Workforce After a Break,"
HCareers.com, June 4, 2015, http://www.hcareers.com/us/resourcecenter
/tabid/306/articleid/566/default.aspx.

197. *Roy Cohen is a career counselor and executive coach who advises that the biggest mistake midlife women make when they are interviewing for a job is apologizing for themselves and their résumé.*
Roy Cohen, *The Wall Street Professional's Survival Guide: Success Secrets of a Career Coach* (Upper Saddle River, NJ: Pearson Education, 2010).

Chapter 9: A Spiritual Opportunity

201. *One of the most significant changes during midlife involves the increasing need to belong, find renewal, and take stock of our lives.*
Alice G. Sargent and Nancy K. Schlossberg, "Managing Adult Transitions," *Training and Development Journal* 42, no. 12 (December 1988): 58–60.

201. *Women often describe midlife as bestselling author Joan Borysenko put it: "a time of mental housecleaning."*
Joan Borysenko, *A Woman's Journey to God: Finding the Feminine Path* (New York: Riverhead, 1999).

202. *Dr. Carl Jung observed midlife as a time when we transform ourselves from an "energetic, biologically focused person into a more spiritual and philosophical one."*
Carl Jung, editor, *Modern Man in Search of a Soul* (New York: Harcourt: 1933).

204. *Borysenko describes spirituality as "earthy, relational, mystical, intuitive, and compassionate."*
Joan Borysenko, *A Woman's Journey to God: Finding the Feminine Path* (New York: Riverhead, 1999).

205–6. *A spiritual dimension is essential for helping us integrate other aspects of wellness.*
Charlene E. Westgate, "Spiritual Wellness and Depression," *Journal of Counseling and Development* 75, no. 1 (September–October 1996): 26–35.

206. *Researchers have identified four components of spiritual wellness.*
Judy W. Howden, "Development and Psychometric Characteristics of the Spirituality Assessment Scale" (doctoral dissertation, Texas Woman's University, 1992), Dissertation Abstracts International 54(1-B): 166.

206. *An impressive link exists between adopting a spiritual approach and achieving overall happiness.*
Leo E. Missinne, "Death and Spiritual Concerns of Older Adults," *Generations* 14, no. 4 (September 1990): 45–47.

210. *Volunteering can lead to a better quality of life.*

Vassilis Saroglou, "Religion, Spirituality, and Altruism," chap. 24 in *APA Handbook of Psychology, Religion, and Spirituality, Vol. 1: Context, Theory, and Research* (Washington, D.C.: American Psychological Association, 2013), 439–57.

211. *Dr. Robert Emmons studies the impact of gratitude and being thankful.*
Robert A. Emmons and Robin Stern, "Gratitude as a Psychotherapeutic Intervention," *Journal of Clinical Psychology* 69, no. 8 (August 2013): 846–55, doi:10.1002/jclp.22020.

213. *Groups of any faith, or women getting together to explore some aspect of spirituality, have been found to provide relationships and social support.*
Elisabeth J. Geertsma and Anne L. Cummings, "Midlife Transition and Women's Spirituality Groups: A Preliminary Investigation," *Counseling and Values* 49, no. 1 (October 2004): 27–36, doi:10.1002/j.2161-007X.2004.tb00250.x.

213. *Psychologist Rollo May brilliantly described creativity as "the process of bringing something new into being."*
Rollo May, *The Courage to Create* (New York: Norton, 1795).

214. *The processes of creativity can increase your resilience in the face of daily stressors.*
Pamela Schmidt, "A Brush with Resilience: Creative Experiences Among Older Artists," *The Gerontologist* 48, Special Issue III (October 2008): 626.

214. *Applying creativity to individual therapy can be transformational.*
Mary B. Carlsen, "Meaning-Making and Creative Aging," chap. 7 in *Constructivism in Psychotherapy* (Washington, D.C.: American Psychological Association, 1995): 127–53.

217. *"Everything happens for a reason."*
Konika Banerjee and Paul Bloom, "Why Did This Happen to Me? Religious Believers' and Non-Believers' Teleological Reasoning About Life Events," *Cognition* 133, no. 1 (October 2014): 277–303, doi:10.1016/j.cognition.2014.06.017.

Chapter 10: Discovering New Purpose and Meaning

226. *Roy Baumeister, Ph.D., identified four differences between a happy life and a meaningful one.*
Roy F. Baumeister et al., "Some Key Differences Between a Happy Life and a Meaningful Life," *Journal of Positive Psychology* 8, no. 6 (August 2013): 505–16, doi:10.1080/17439760.2013.830764.